CUL DE SAC

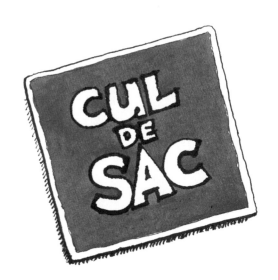

CUL DE SAC

Richard Thompson

Andrews McMeel
Publishing, LLC

Kansas City

08 09 10 11 12 TWP 10 9 8 7 6 5 4 3 2 1

ISBN-13: 978-0-7407-7651-9
ISBN-10: 0-7407-7651-7

Library of Congress Control Number: 2008926290

www.andrewsmcmeel.com

─── **ATTENTION: SCHOOLS AND BUSINESSES** ───

Andrews McMeel books are available at quantity discounts with bulk purchase for educational, business, or sales promotional use. For information, please write to: Special Sales Department, Andrews McMeel Publishing, LLC, 1130 Walnut Street, Kansas City, Missouri 64106.

To Amy, Emma & Charlotte,
with love.

Foreword

I thought the best newspaper comic strips were long gone, and I've never been happier to be wrong. Richard Thompson's *Cul de Sac* has it all—intelligence, gentle humor, a delightful way with words, and, most surprising of all, wonderful, wonderful drawings.

Cul de Sac's whimsical take on the world and playful sense of language somehow gets funnier the more times you read it. Four-year-old Alice and her Blisshaven Preschool classmates will ring true to any parent. Doing projects in a cloud of glue and glitter, the little kids manage to reinterpret an otherwise incomprehensible world via their meandering, nonstop chatter. But I think my favorite character is Alice's older brother, Petey. A haunted, controlling milquetoast, he's surely one of the most neurotic kids to appear in comics. These children and their struggles are presented affectionately, and one of the things I like best about *Cul de Sac* is its natural warmth. *Cul de Sac* avoids both mawkishness and cynicism and instead finds genuine charm in its loopy appreciation of small events. Very few strips can hit this subtle note.

I also like the nightmarish suburb that the Otterloop ("outer loop") family inhabits: the identical houses crammed in endless rows, the relentless highway traffic strangling the soulless development, the ugly shopping malls, the oppressive parking garages, and sticky-floored restaurants. Like most of us, the family negotiates this modern awfulness as a simple matter of course; the critique appears only in the drawings, where the strip suddenly works on another level.

And oh, those gorgeous drawings! With a mix of rambling looseness, blotchy crudeness, and sheer cartoony grace, Thompson's expressive pen line is the equal of any of cartooning's Old Masters. Thompson has a very sharp eye and a command of technique we almost never see anymore. He reminds us that comics can be more than illustrated gag writing, and that good drawings can bring a comic strip's world to life in countless ways that words cannot. The artwork in *Cul de Sac* bowls me over. It's a pleasure to study long after the strips are read.

The first fifty pages of this book are taken from the earlier incarnation of *Cul de Sac* that appeared in the *Washington Post Magazine*. Here we discover that Thompson has a natural flair for watercolor painting too. At this point, however, I'm not even surprised.

I hope you enjoy *Cul de Sac* as much as I do. I think you're in for a real treat.

Bill Watterson, 2008

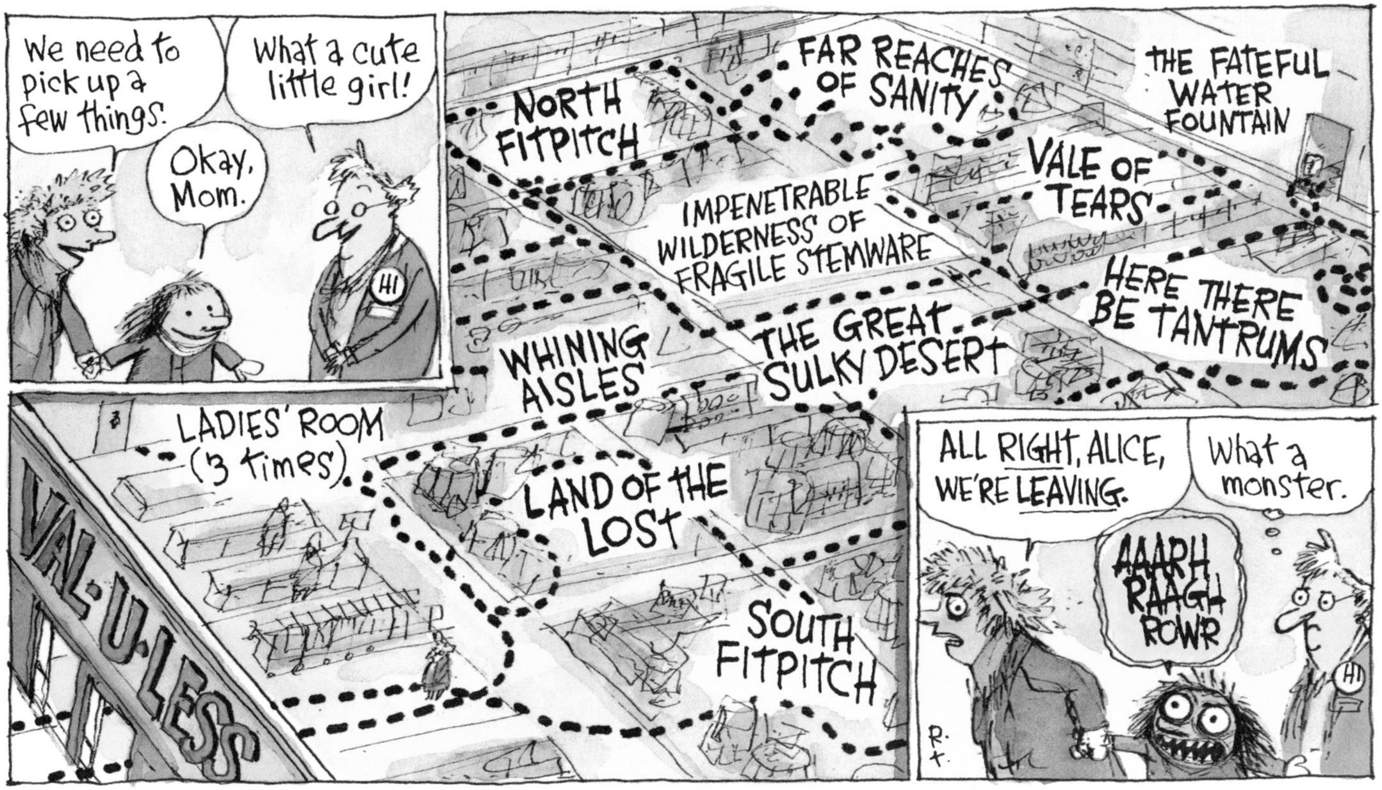
We need to pick up a few things.
What a cute little girl!
Okay, Mom.
HI
NORTH FITPITCH
FAR REACHES OF SANITY
THE FATEFUL WATER FOUNTAIN
VALE OF TEARS
IMPENETRABLE WILDERNESS OF FRAGILE STEMWARE
HERE THERE BE TANTRUMS
WHINING AISLES
THE GREAT SULKY DESERT
LADIES' ROOM (3 times)
LAND OF THE LOST
SOUTH FITPITCH
VAL-U-LESS
ALL RIGHT, ALICE, WE'RE LEAVING.
What a monster.
AAARH RAAGH ROWR
HI

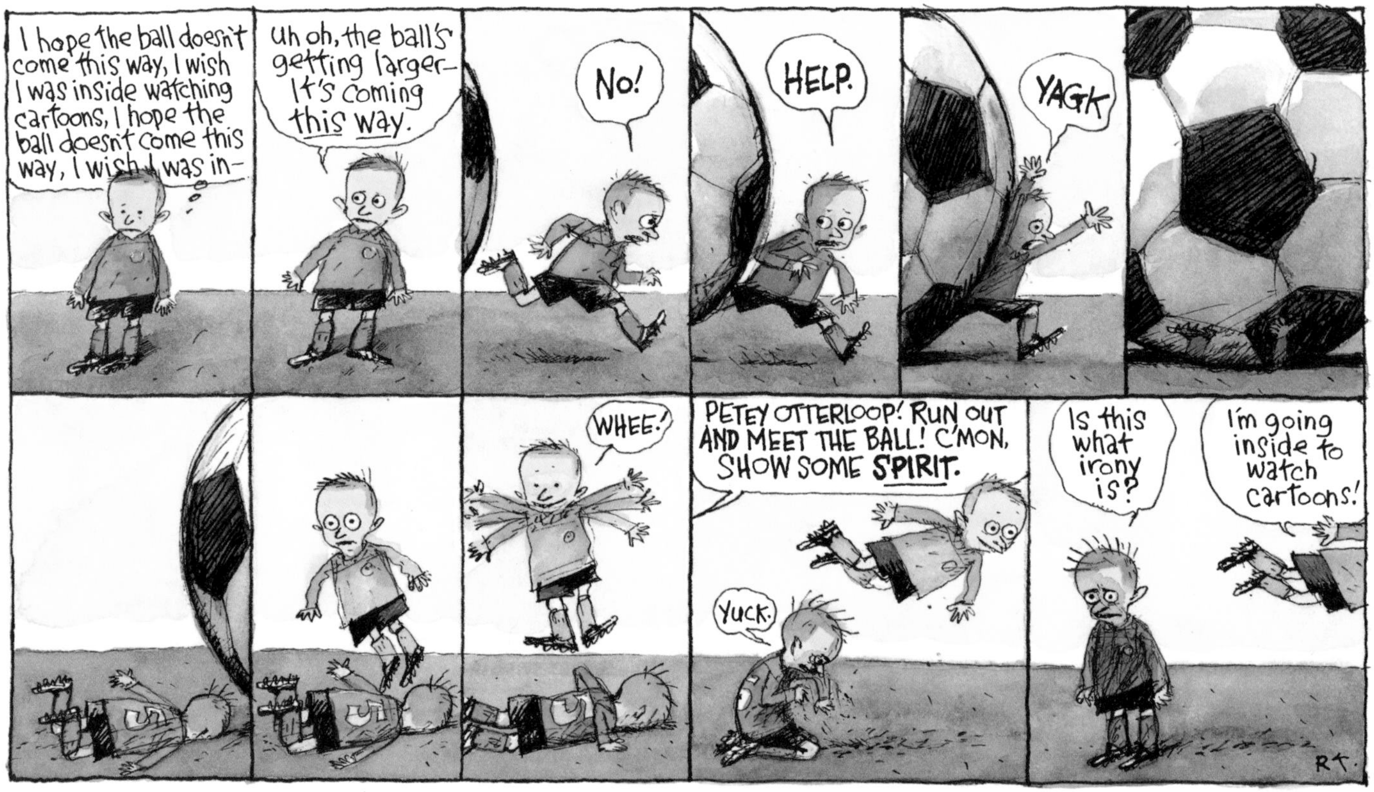
I hope the ball doesn't come this way, I wish I was inside watching cartoons, I hope the ball doesn't come this way, I wish I was in-
uh oh, the ball's getting larger- It's coming this way.
No!
HELP.
YAGK
WHEE.
PETEY OTTERLOOP! RUN OUT AND MEET THE BALL! C'MON, SHOW SOME SPIRIT.
YUCK.
Is this what irony is?
I'm going inside to watch cartoons!
RT.

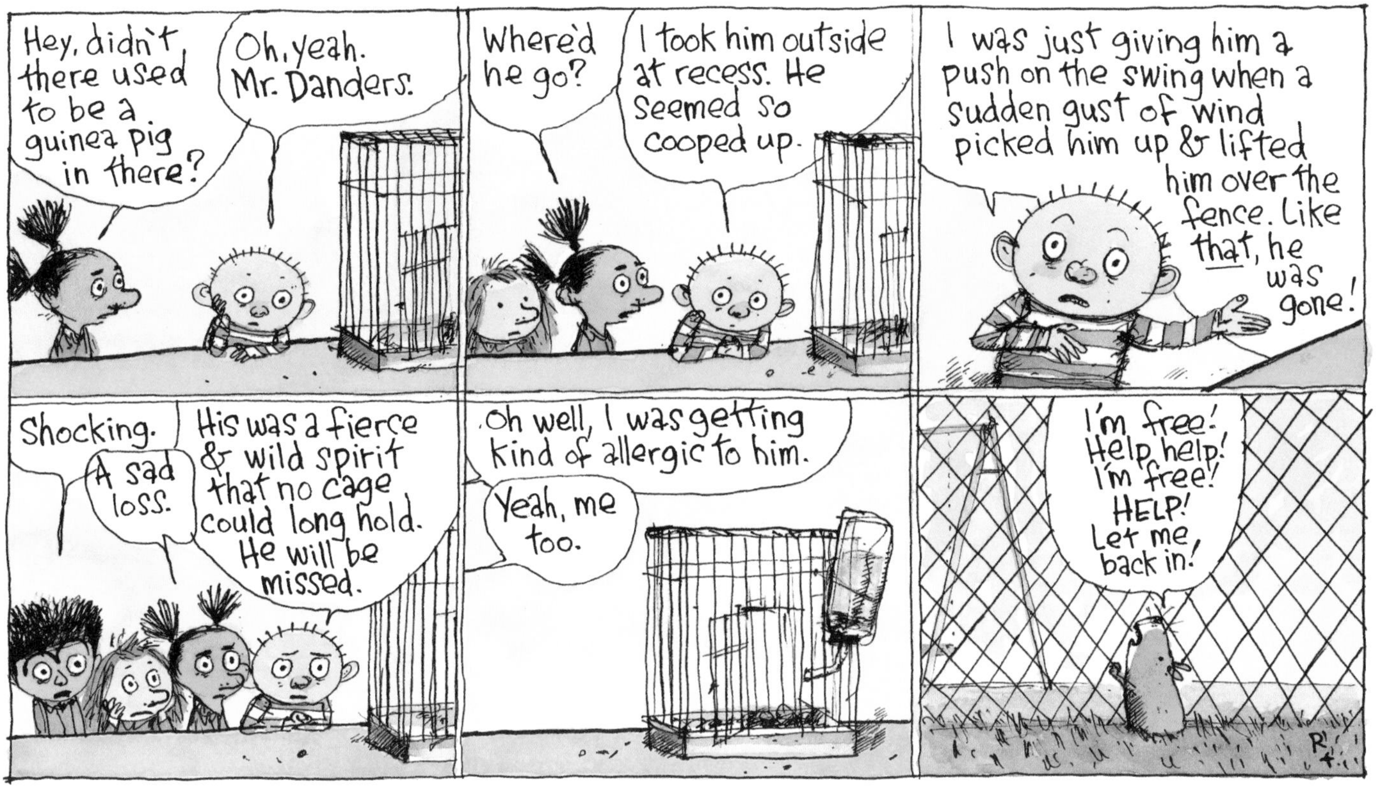
Hey, didn't there used to be a guinea pig in there?
Oh, yeah. Mr. Danders.
Where'd he go?
I took him outside at recess. He seemed so cooped up.
I was just giving him a push on the swing when a sudden gust of wind picked him up & lifted him over the fence. Like that, he was gone!
Shocking.
A sad loss.
His was a fierce & wild spirit that no cage could long hold. He will be missed.
Oh well, I was getting kind of allergic to him.
Yeah, me too.
I'm free! Help help! I'm free! HELP! Let me back in!

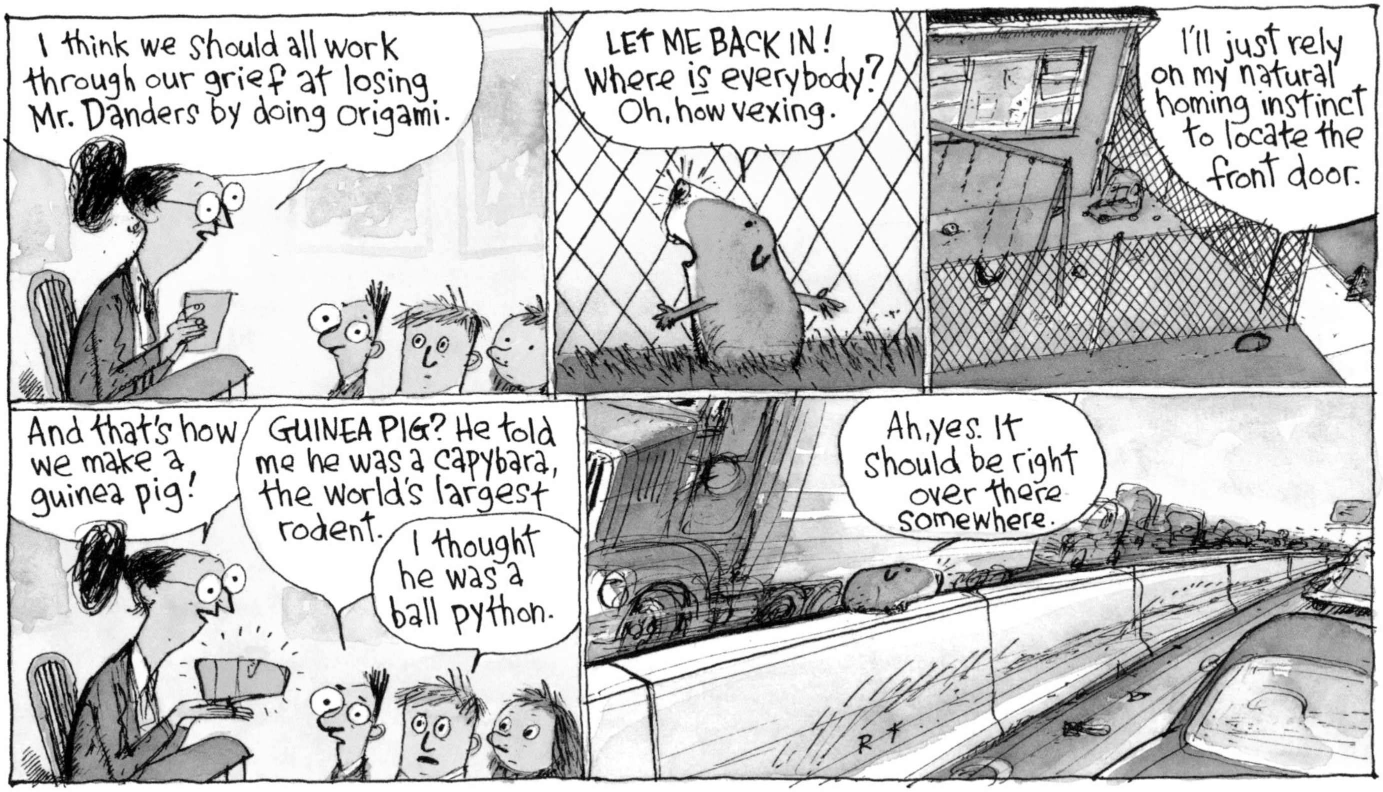
I think we should all work through our grief at losing Mr. Danders by doing origami.
LET ME BACK IN! Where is everybody? Oh, how vexing.
I'll just rely on my natural homing instinct to locate the front door.
And that's how we make a guinea pig!
GUINEA PIG? He told me he was a capybara, the world's largest rodent.
I thought he was a ball python.
Ah, yes. It should be right over there somewhere.
RT

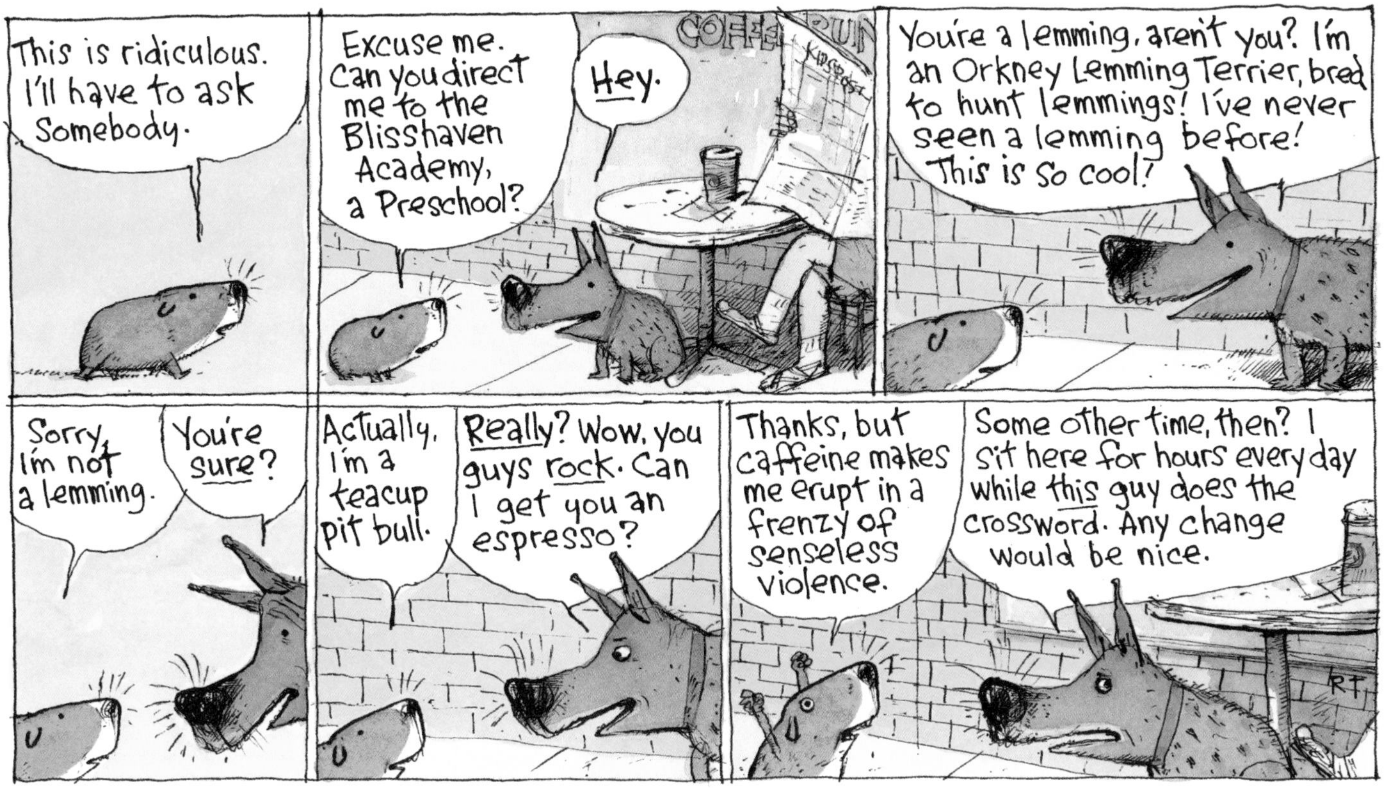
This is ridiculous. I'll have to ask Somebody.
Excuse me. Can you direct me to the Blisshaven Academy, a Preschool?
Hey.
You're a lemming, aren't you? I'm an Orkney Lemming Terrier, bred to hunt lemmings! I've never seen a lemming before! This is so cool!
Sorry, I'm not a lemming.
You're sure?
Actually, I'm a teacup pit bull.
Really? Wow, you guys rock. Can I get you an espresso?
Thanks, but caffeine makes me erupt in a frenzy of senseless violence.
Some other time, then? I sit here for hours every day while this guy does the crossword. Any change would be nice.
RT

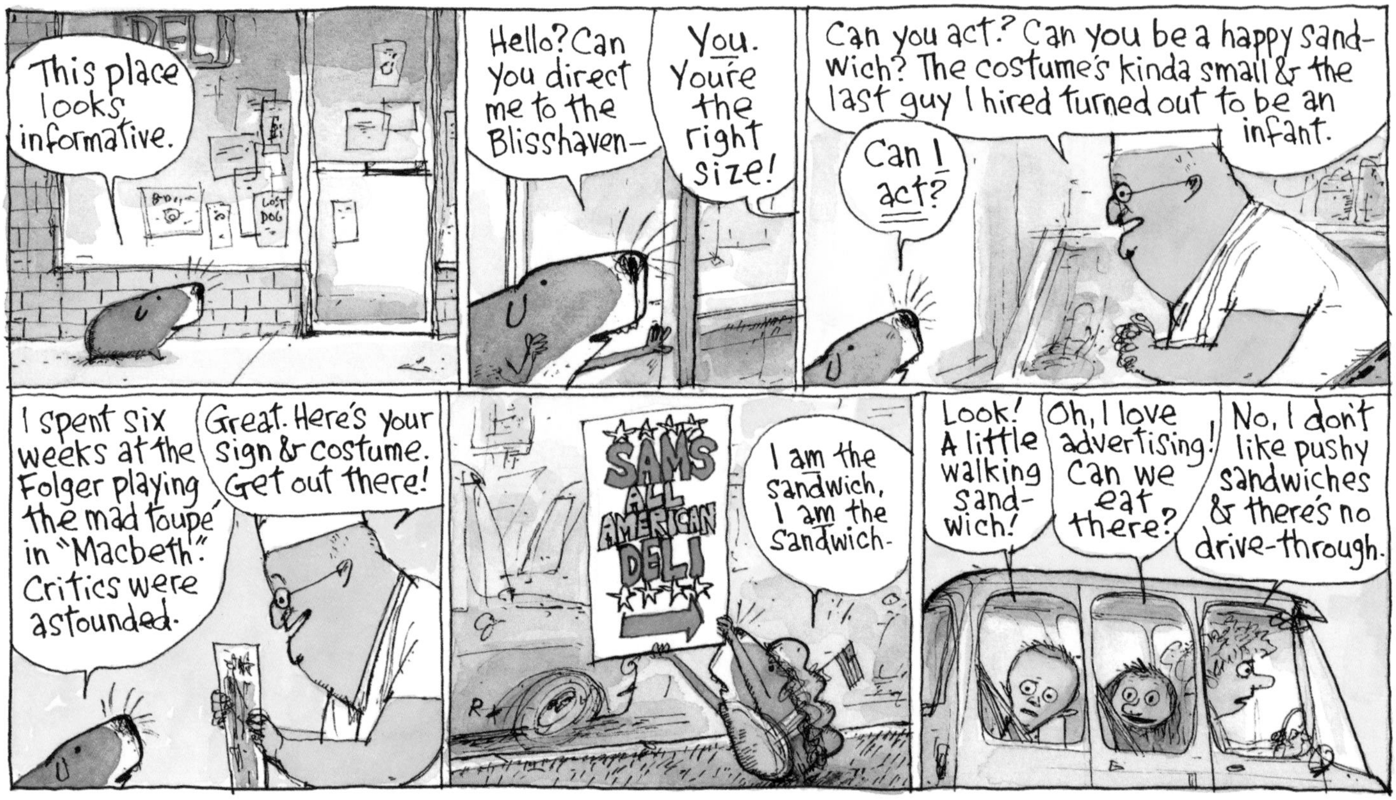
DELI
This place looks informative.
LOST DOG
Hello? Can you direct me to the Blisshaven–
You. You're the right size!
Can you act? Can you be a happy sandwich? The costume's kinda small & the last guy I hired turned out to be an infant.
Can I act?
I spent six weeks at the Folger playing the mad toupé in "Macbeth". Critics were astounded.
Great. Here's your sign & costume. Get out there!
SAMS ALL AMERICAN DELI
I am the sandwich, I am the sandwich-
Look! A little walking sandwich!
Oh, I love advertising! Can we eat there?
No, I don't like pushy sandwiches & there's no drive-through.

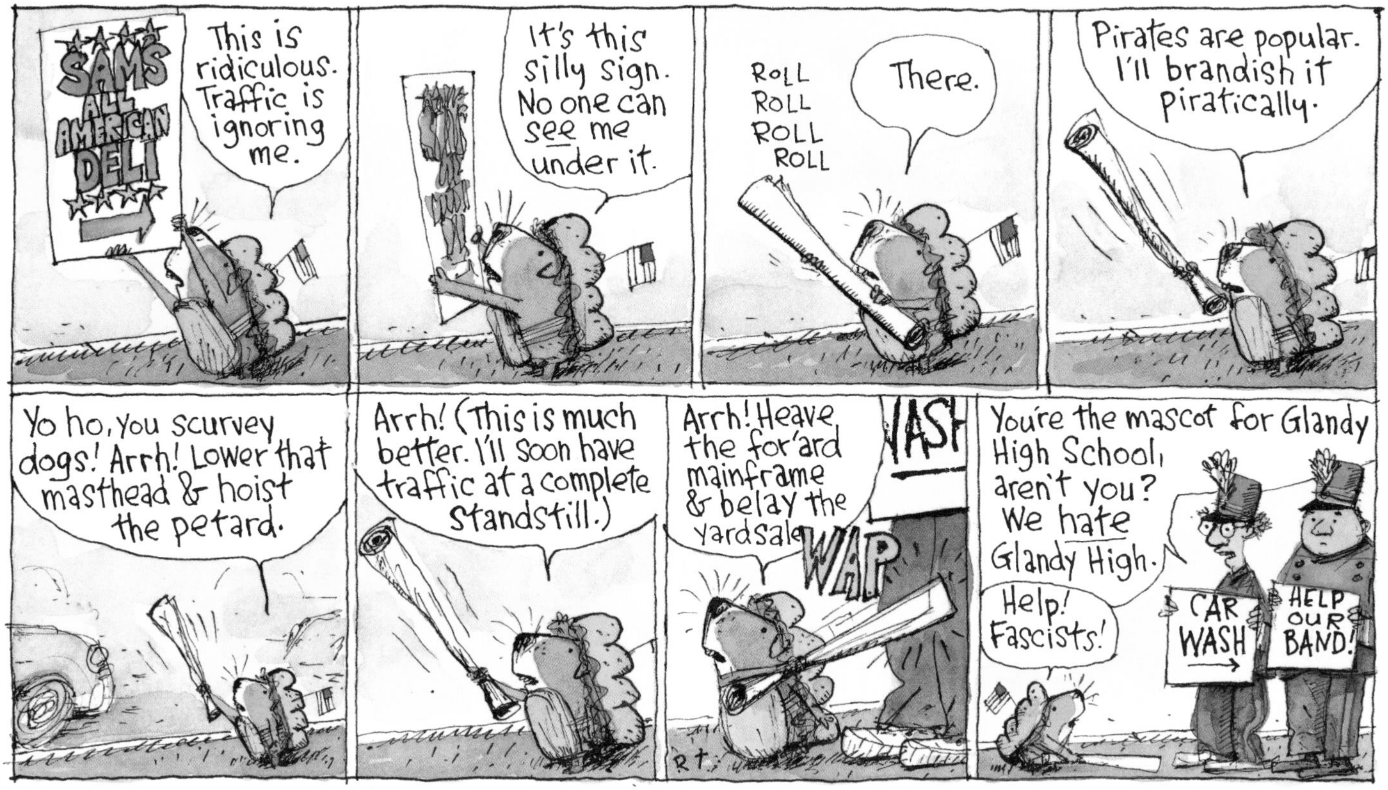
SAMS ALL AMERICAN DELI
This is ridiculous. Traffic is ignoring me.
It's this silly sign. No one can see me under it.
ROLL ROLL ROLL ROLL
There.
Pirates are popular. I'll brandish it piratically.
Yo ho, you scurvey dogs! Arrh! Lower that masthead & hoist the petard.
Arrh! (This is much better. I'll soon have traffic at a complete standstill.)
Arrh! Heave the for'ard mainframe & belay the yardsale
WAP
WASH
You're the mascot for Glandy High School, aren't you? We hate Glandy High.
Help! Fascists!
CAR WASH
HELP OUR BAND!

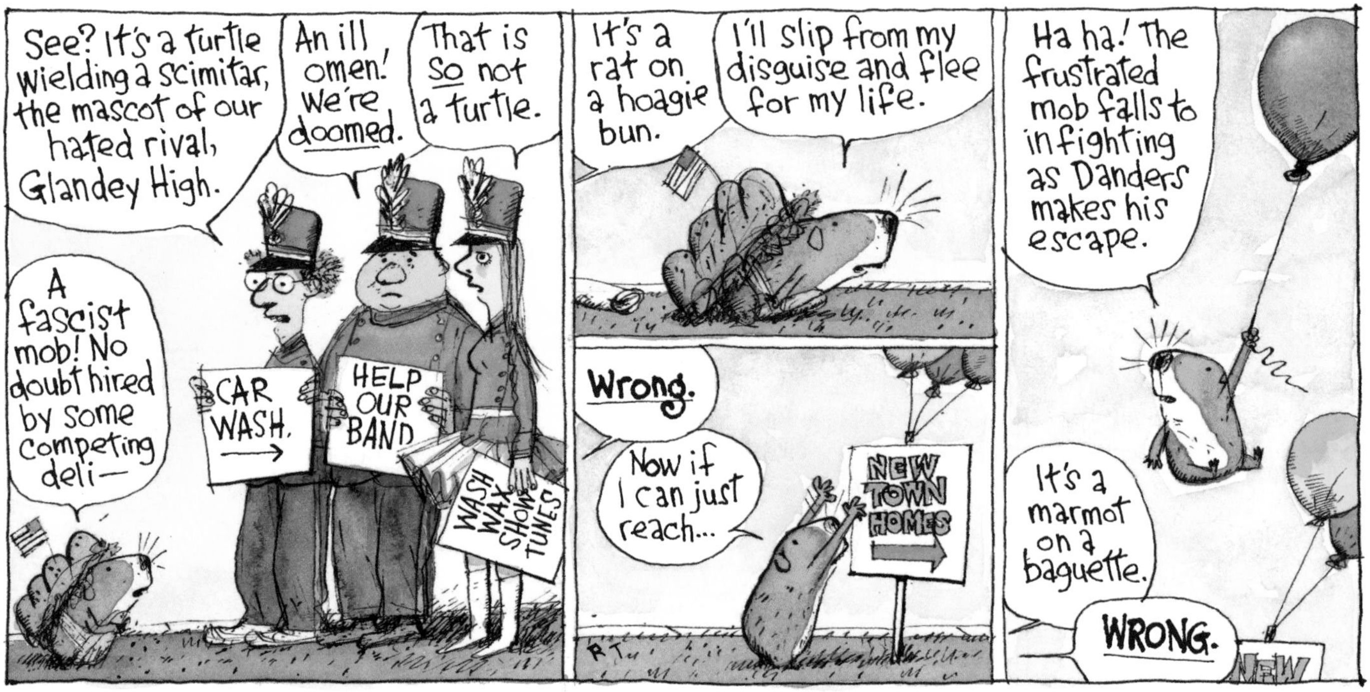
See? It's a turtle wielding a scimitar, the mascot of our hated rival, Glandey High.
An ill omen! We're doomed.
That is so not a turtle.
A fascist mob! No doubt hired by some competing deli—
CAR WASH.
HELP OUR BAND
WASH WAX SHOW TUNES
It's a rat on a hoagie bun.
I'll slip from my disguise and flee for my life.
Wrong.
Now if I can just reach...
NEW TOWN HOMES
Ha ha! The frustrated mob falls to infighting as Danders makes his escape.
It's a marmot on a baguette.
WRONG.
NEW

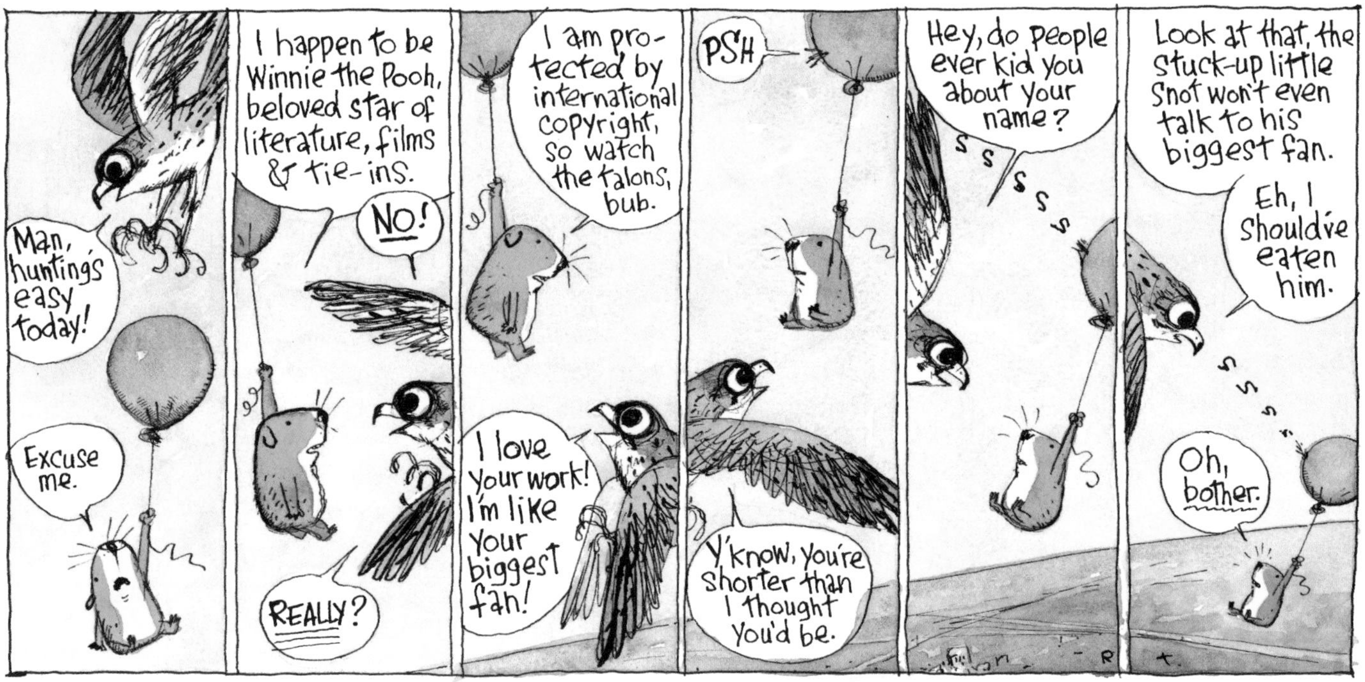
Man, hunting's easy today!
Excuse me.
I happen to be Winnie the Pooh, beloved star of literature, films & tie-ins.
NO!
REALLY?
I am protected by international copyright, so watch the talons, bub.
I love your work! I'm like your biggest fan!
PSH
Y'know, you're shorter than I thought you'd be.
Hey, do people ever kid you about your name?
Look at that, the stuck-up little snot won't even talk to his biggest fan.
Eh, I should've eaten him.
Oh, bother.

MAYDAY! MAYDAY! Is this the end of Danders?
Mama, your baby's comin' home.
YAGH
Z
OOF.
A BAT! A BAT'S IN MY HAIR!
It's not a bat. It's that guinea pig!
Plus, you don't have any hair.
Put him back in his cage. He might be rabid.
Sorry, guinea pig. We put a hermit crab in there while you were gone.
WHAT?
OUT, squatter! Go back to whatever cheesy Ocean City novelty store spawned you!
Okay, okay!
All right, children, the excitement's over, back to class. Now, which of these is a triangle?
The round one!
Ah, home.
ZZZZZ

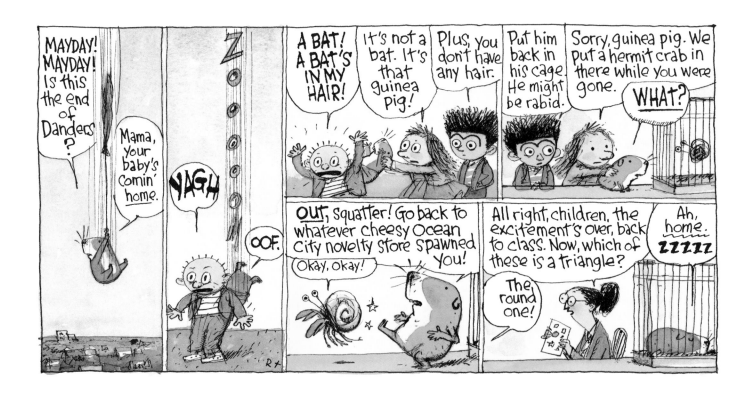

You know what I don't get?
What?
Where does the old dirt go?
They take it away in dump trucks, but my brother has a theory that dirt remembers where it was, no matter where they take it.
Sometimes it rises & re-forms into a big ball.
Houses, farms, even cows reappear on it.
Then it goes in search of its place of origin.
And haunts it like a phantom moon.
How about dinosaurs? Do they ever show up instead of the cows?
Stop being silly.
You know what? I'm never going near my sandbox again.
R.T.

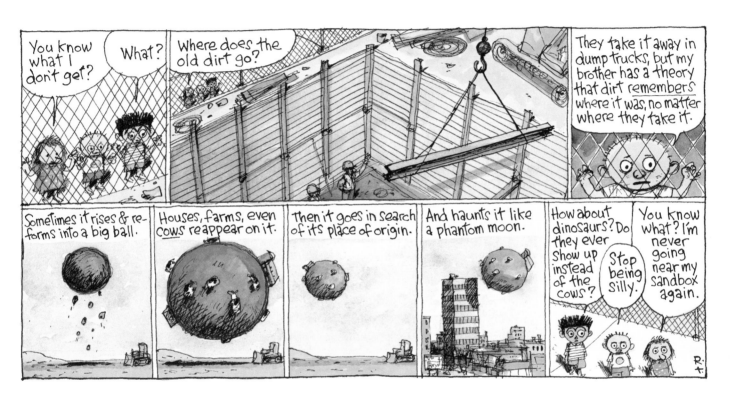

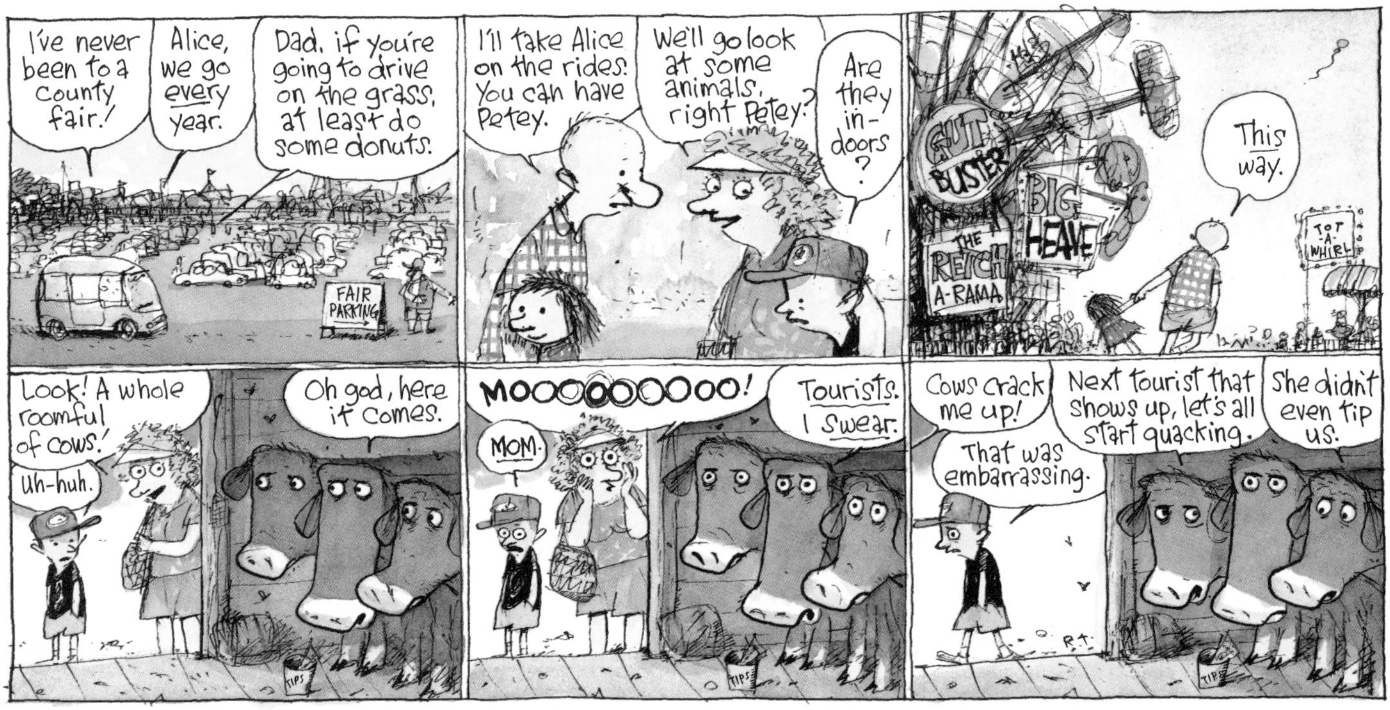
I've never been to a county fair!
Alice, we go every year.
Dad, if you're going to drive on the grass, at least do some donuts.
FAIR PARKING
I'll take Alice on the rides. You can have Petey.
We'll go look at some animals, right Petey?
Are they in-doors?
GUT BUSTER
BIG HEAVE
THE REICH A-RAMA
TOT-A-WHIRL
This way.
Look! A whole roomful of cows!
Uh-huh.
Oh god, here it comes.
TIPS
MOOOOOOOOOO!
MOM.
Tourists. I swear.
Cows crack me up!
That was embarrassing.
Next tourist that shows up, let's all start quacking.
She didn't even tip us.

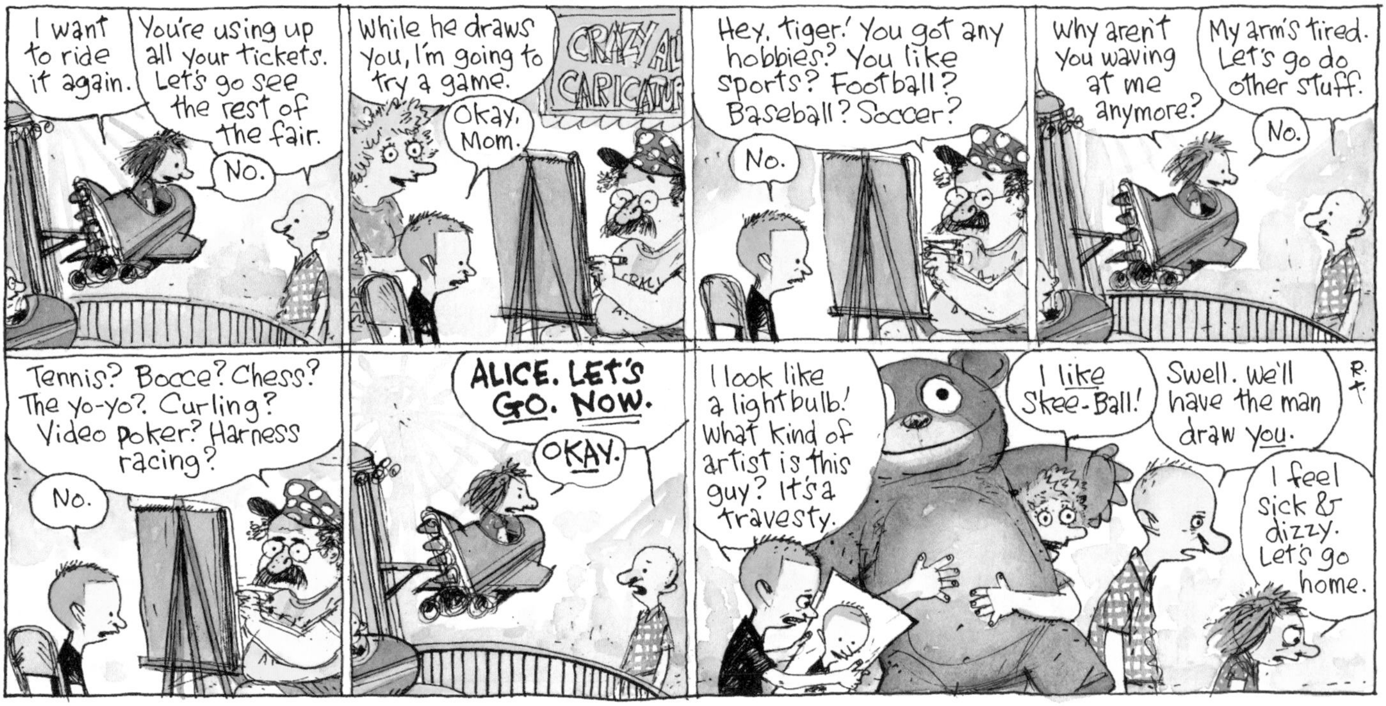
I want to ride it again.
You're using up all your tickets. Let's go see the rest of the fair.
No.
While he draws you, I'm going to try a game.
CRAZY AL
CARICATURES
Okay, Mom.
Hey, tiger! You got any hobbies? You like sports? Football? Baseball? Soccer?
No.
Why aren't you waving at me anymore?
My arm's tired. Let's go do other stuff.
No.
Tennis? Bocce? Chess? The yo-yo? Curling? Video poker? Harness racing?
No.
ALICE. LET'S GO. NOW.
OKAY.
I look like a lightbulb! What kind of artist is this guy? It's a travesty.
I like Skee-Ball!
Swell. We'll have the man draw you.
I feel sick & dizzy. Let's go home.
R.T.

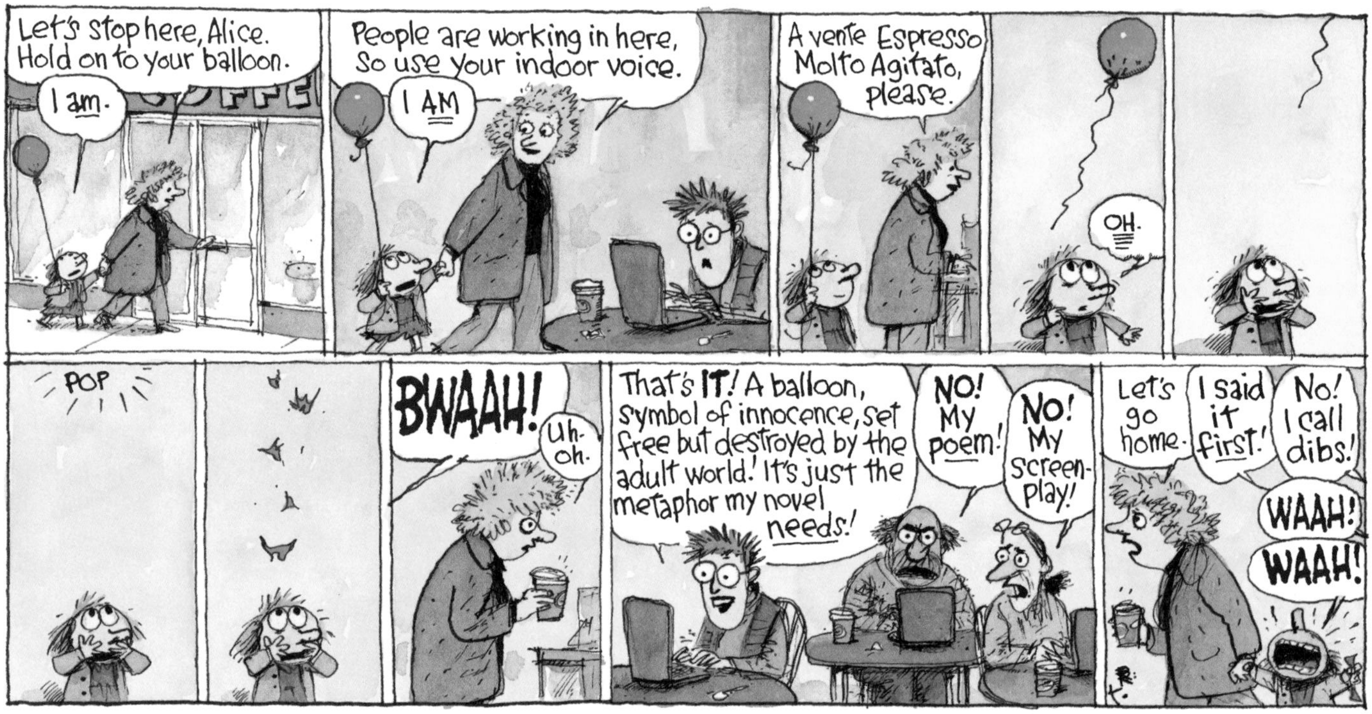
Let's stop here, Alice. Hold on to your balloon.
I am.
People are working in here, So use your indoor voice.
I AM
A vente Espresso Molto Agitato, please.
OH.
POP
BWAAH!
Uh-oh.
That's IT! A balloon, symbol of innocence, set free but destroyed by the adult world! It's just the metaphor my novel needs!
NO! My poem!
NO! My screen-play!
Let's go home.
I said it first!
No! I call dibs!
WAAH!
WAAH!

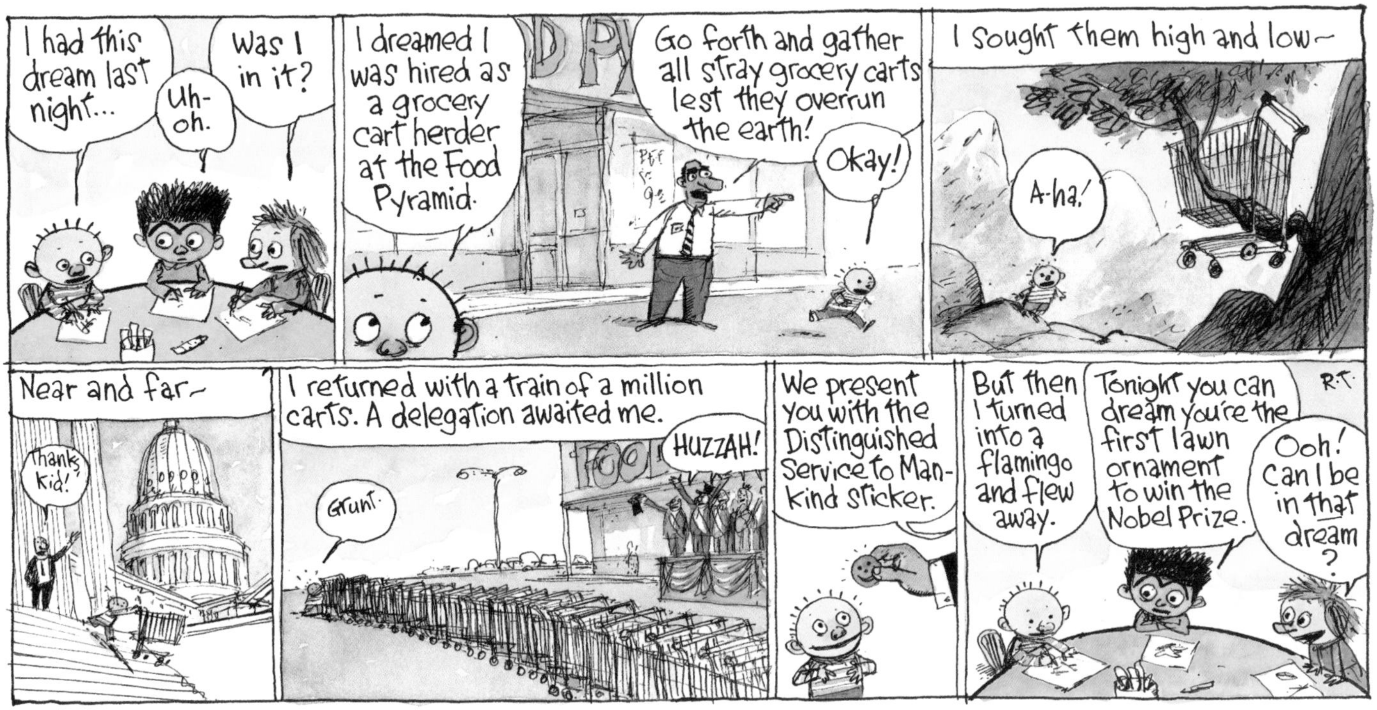
I had this dream last night...
Uh-oh.
Was I in it?
I dreamed I was hired as a grocery cart herder at the Food Pyramid.
Go forth and gather all stray grocery carts lest they overrun the earth!
Okay!
I sought them high and low~
A-ha!
Near and far~
Thanks kid!
I returned with a train of a million carts. A delegation awaited me.
Grunt.
HUZZAH!
We present you with the Distinguished Service to Mankind sticker.
But then I turned into a flamingo and flew away.
Tonight you can dream you're the first lawn ornament to win the Nobel Prize.
Ooh! Can I be in that dream?
R.T.

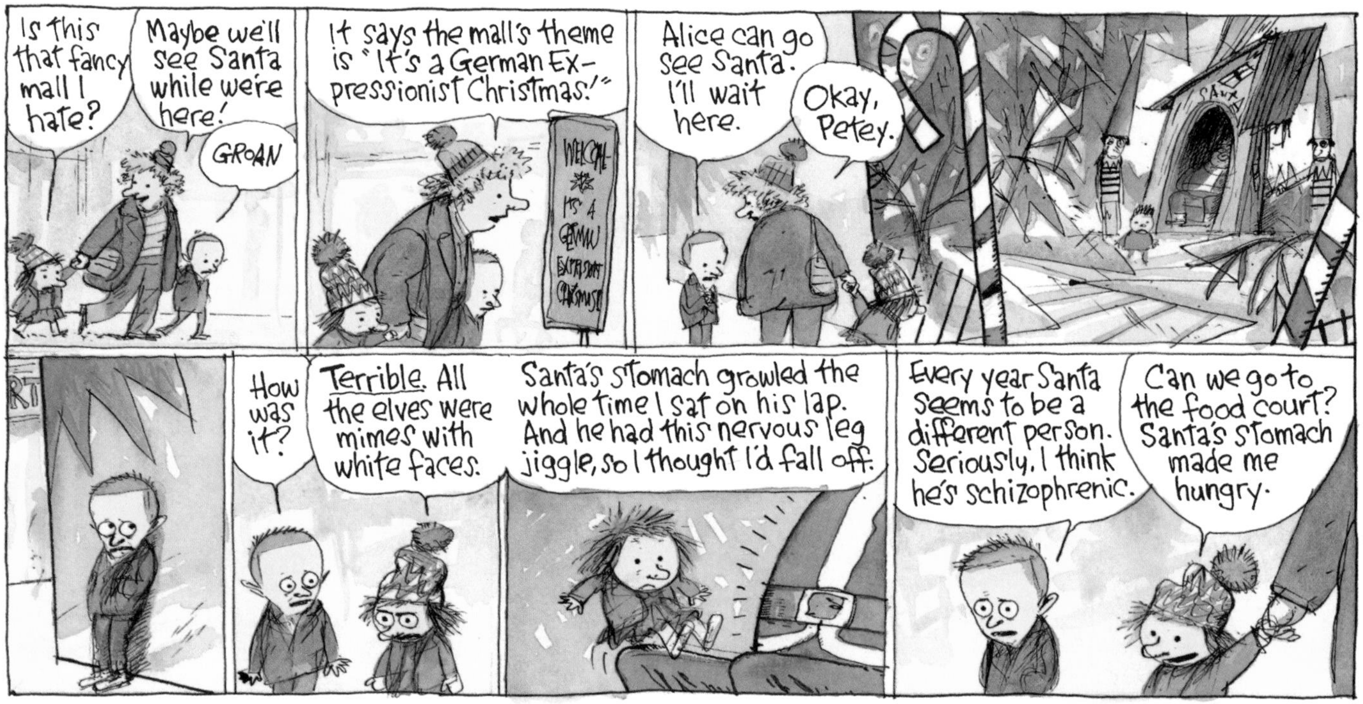
Is this that fancy mall I hate?
Maybe we'll see Santa while we're here!
GROAN
It says the mall's theme is "It's a German Expressionist Christmas!"
Alice can go see Santa. I'll wait here.
Okay, Petey.
How was it?
Terrible. All the elves were mimes with white faces.
Santa's stomach growled the whole time I sat on his lap. And he had this nervous leg jiggle, so I thought I'd fall off.
Every year Santa seems to be a different person. Seriously, I think he's schizophrenic.
Can we go to the food court? Santa's stomach made me hungry.

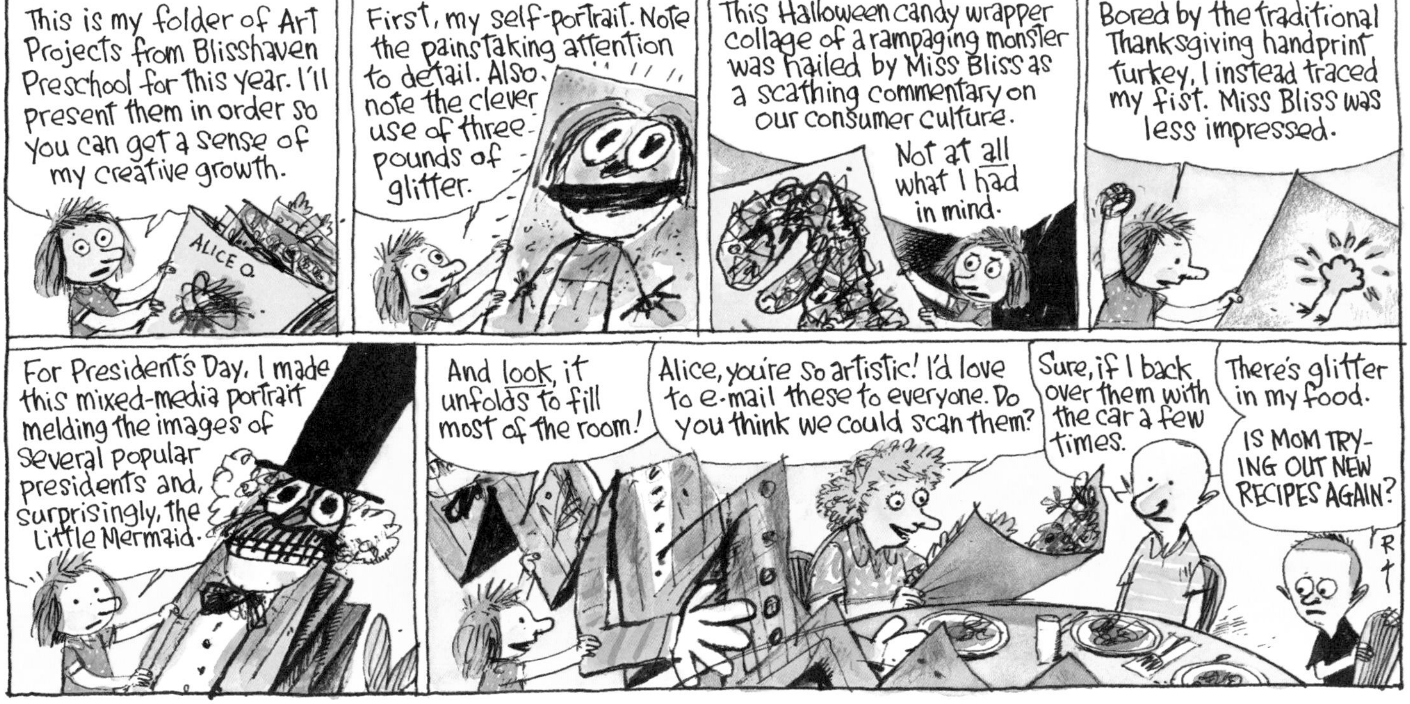
This is my folder of Art Projects from Blisshaven Preschool for this year. I'll present them in order so you can get a sense of my creative growth.
ALICE O.
First, my self-portrait. Note the painstaking attention to detail. Also, note the clever use of three pounds of glitter.
This Halloween candy wrapper collage of a rampaging monster was hailed by Miss Bliss as a scathing commentary on our consumer culture.
Not at all what I had in mind.
Bored by the traditional Thanksgiving handprint turkey, I instead traced my fist. Miss Bliss was less impressed.
For President's Day, I made this mixed-media portrait melding the images of several popular presidents and, surprisingly, the Little Mermaid.
And look, it unfolds to fill most of the room!
Alice, you're so artistic! I'd love to e-mail these to everyone. Do you think we could scan them?
Sure, if I back over them with the car a few times.
There's glitter in my food.
IS MOM TRYING OUT NEW RECIPES AGAIN?
RT

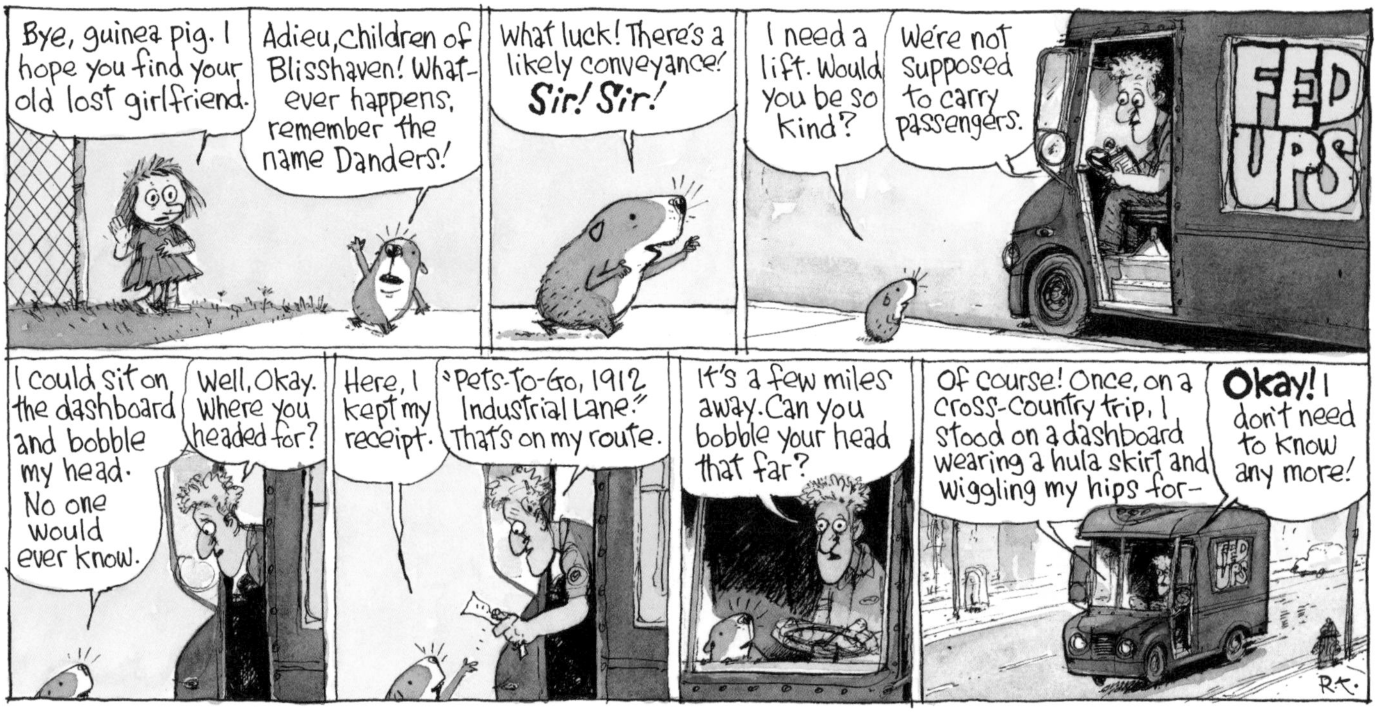
Bye, guinea pig. I hope you find your old lost girlfriend.
Adieu, children of Blisshaven! Whatever happens, remember the name Danders!
What luck! There's a likely conveyance! Sir! Sir!
I need a lift. Would you be so kind?
We're not supposed to carry passengers.
FED UPS
I could sit on the dashboard and bobble my head. No one would ever know.
Well, Okay. Where you headed for?
Here, I kept my receipt.
"Pets-To-Go, 1912 Industrial Lane." That's on my route.
It's a few miles away. Can you bobble your head that far?
Of course! Once, on a cross-country trip, I stood on a dashboard wearing a hula skirt and wiggling my hips for—
Okay! I don't need to know any more!
FED UPS
R.A.

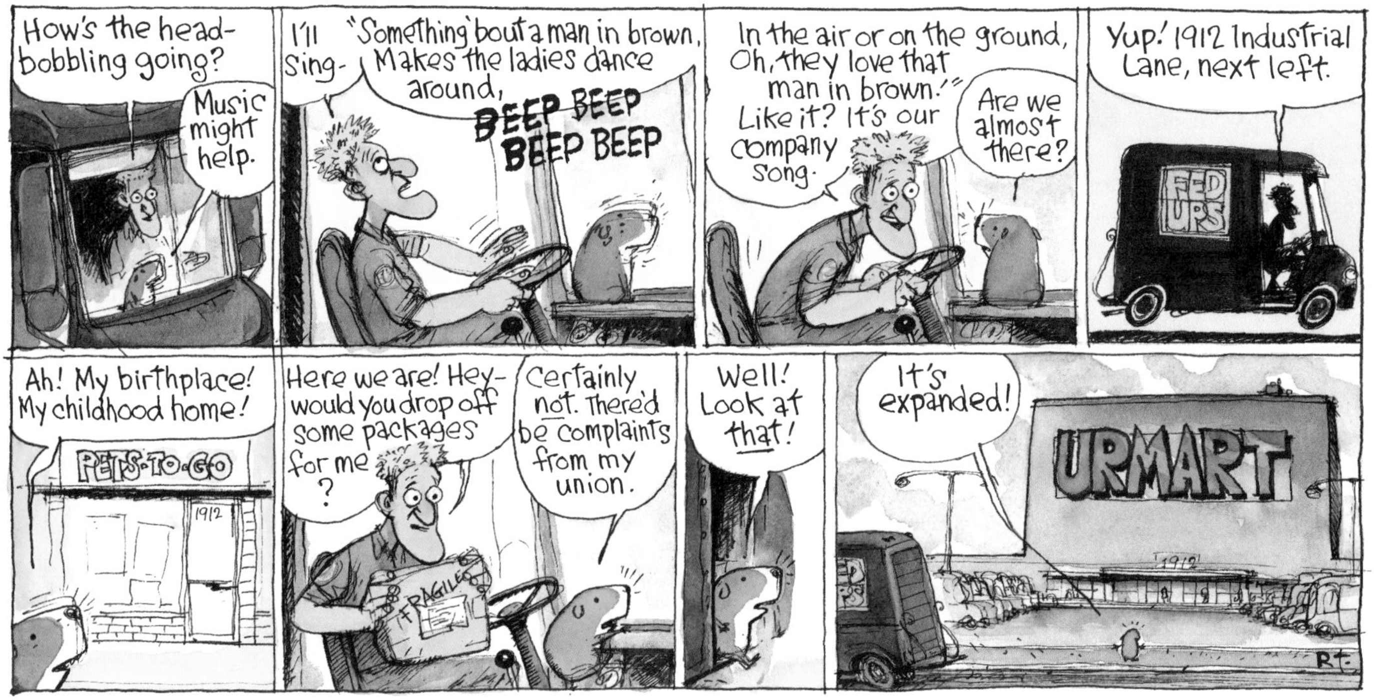
How's the head-bobbling going?
Music might help.
I'll sing-
"Something 'bout a man in brown, Makes the ladies dance around,
BEEP BEEP BEEP BEEP
In the air or on the ground, Oh, they love that man in brown."
Like it? It's our company song.
Are we almost there?
Yup! 1912 Industrial Lane, next left.
FED UPS
Ah! My birthplace! My childhood home!
PETS-TO-GO
1912
Here we are! Hey- would you drop off some packages for me?
FRAGILE
Certainly not. There'd be complaints from my union.
Well! Look at that!
It's expanded!
URMART
1912

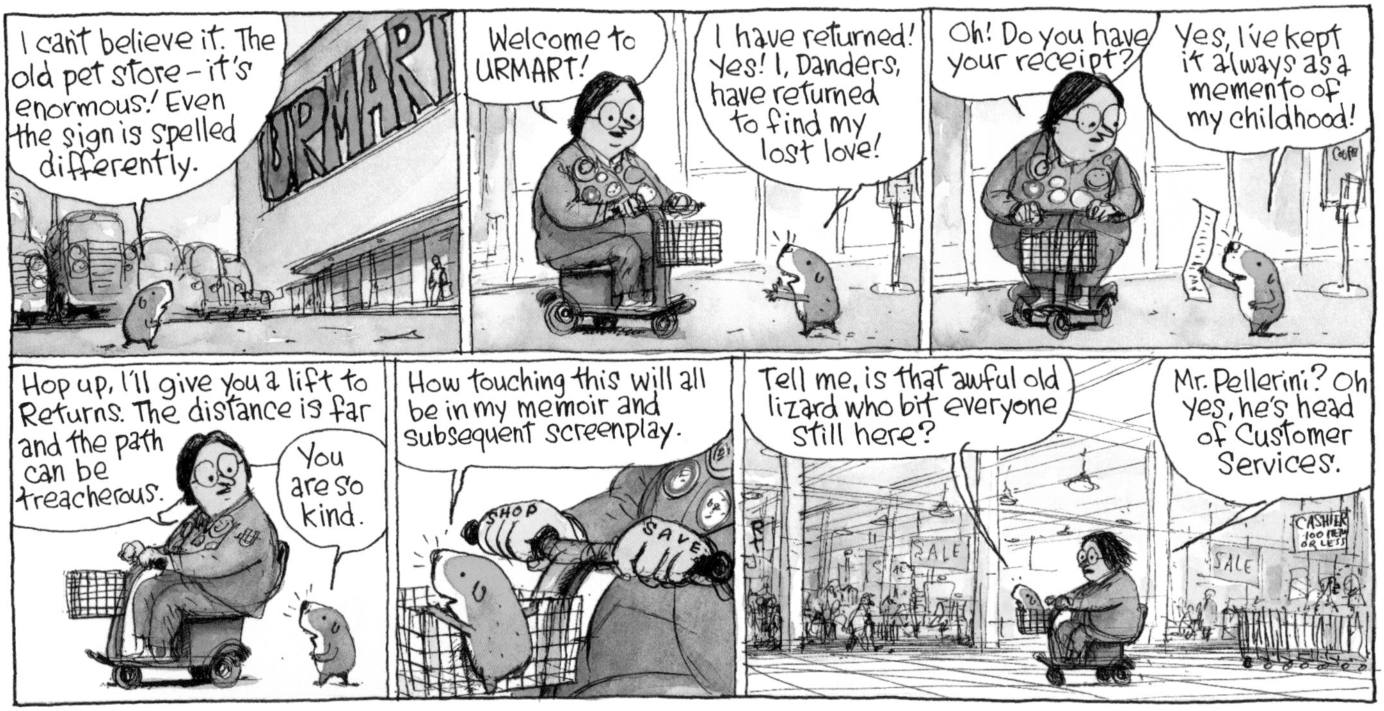
I can't believe it. The old pet store – it's enormous! Even the sign is spelled differently.
URMART
Welcome to URMART!
I have returned! Yes! I, Danders, have returned to find my lost love!
Oh! Do you have your receipt?
Yes, I've kept it always as a memento of my childhood!
Hop up, I'll give you a lift to Returns. The distance is far and the path can be treacherous.
You are so kind.
How touching this will all be in my memoir and subsequent screenplay.
SHOP
SAVE
Tell me, is that awful old lizard who bit everyone still here?
Mr. Pellerini? Oh yes, he's head of Customer Services.
SALE
SALE
CASHIER

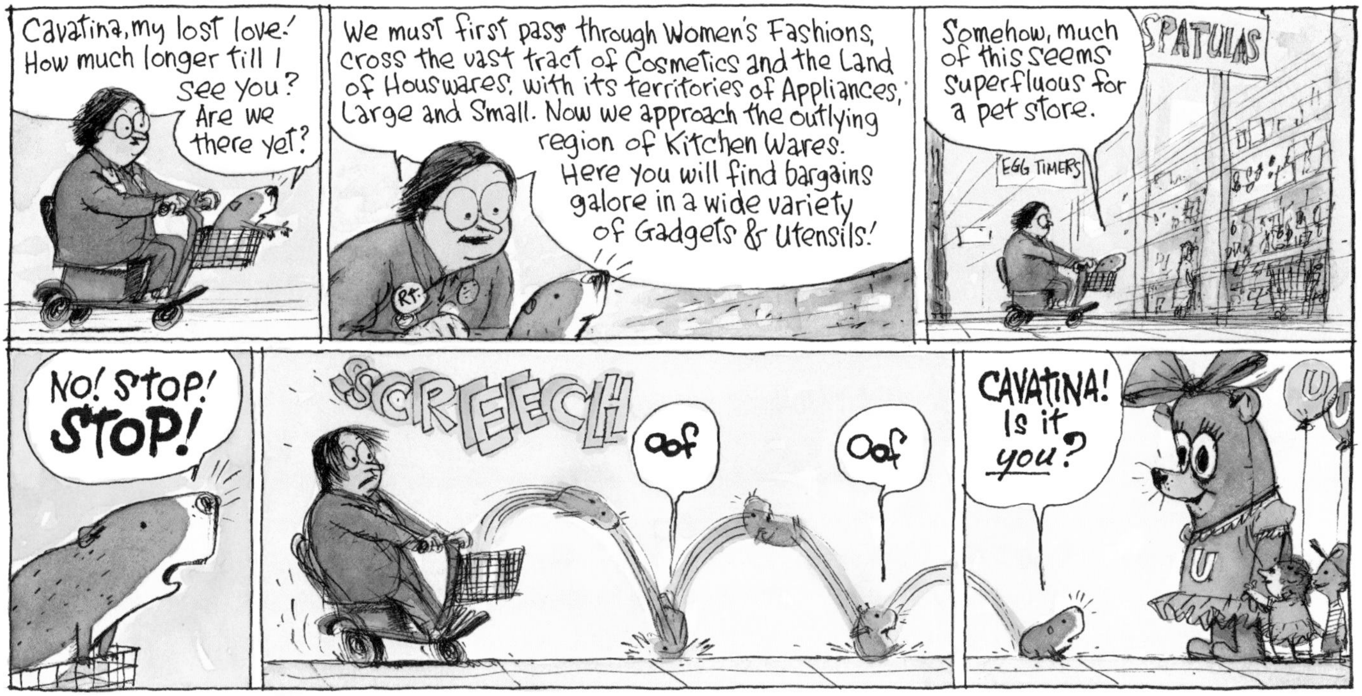
Cavatina, my lost love! How much longer till I see you? Are we there yet?
We must first pass through Women's Fashions, cross the vast tract of Cosmetics and the Land of Houswares, with its territories of Appliances, Large and Small. Now we approach the outlying region of Kitchen Wares. Here you will find bargains galore in a wide variety of Gadgets & Utensils!
Somehow, much of this seems superfluous for a pet store.
SPATULAS
EGG TIMERS
NO! STOP! STOP!
SCREEECH
oof
Oof
CAVATINA! Is it you?

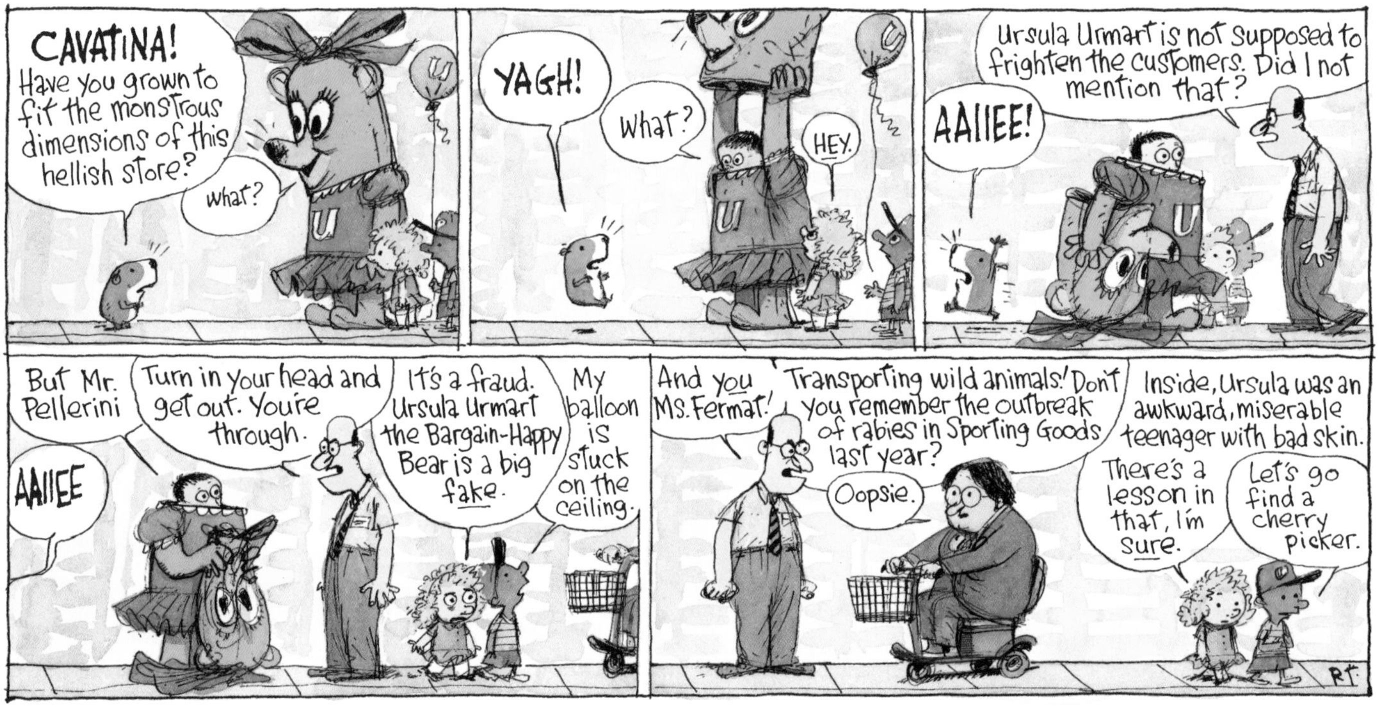
CAVATINA! Have you grown to fit the monstrous dimensions of this hellish store?
what?
YAGH!
What?
HEY.
Ursula Urmart is not supposed to frighten the customers. Did I not mention that?
AAIIEE!
But Mr. Pellerini
Turn in your head and get out. You're through.
AAIIEE
It's a fraud. Ursula Urmart the Bargain-Happy Bear is a big fake.
My balloon is stuck on the ceiling.
And you Ms. Fermat!
Transporting wild animals! Don't you remember the outbreak of rabies in Sporting Goods last year?
Oopsie.
Inside, Ursula was an awkward, miserable teenager with bad skin.
There's a lesson in that, I'm sure.
Let's go find a cherry picker.
RT.

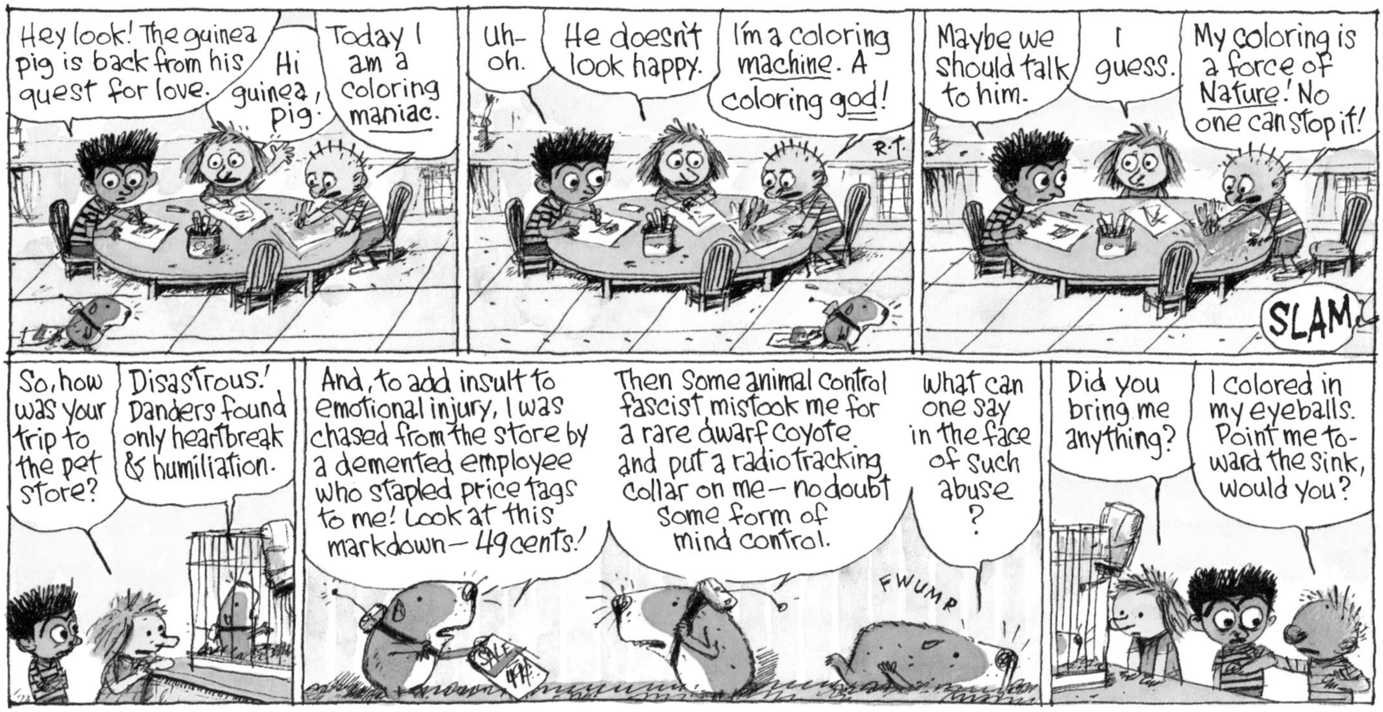
Hey look! The guinea pig is back from his quest for love.
Hi guinea, pig.
Today I am a coloring maniac.
Uh-oh.
He doesn't look happy.
I'm a coloring machine. A coloring god!
R.T.
Maybe we should talk to him.
I guess.
My coloring is a force of Nature! No one can stop it!
SLAM
So, how was your trip to the pet store?
Disastrous! Danders found only heartbreak & humiliation.
And, to add insult to emotional injury, I was chased from the store by a demented employee who stapled price tags to me! Look at this markdown—49 cents!
SALE 49¢
Then some animal control fascist mistook me for a rare dwarf coyote and put a radio tracking collar on me—no doubt some form of mind control.
What can one say in the face of such abuse?
FWUMP
Did you bring me anything?
I colored in my eyeballs. Point me toward the sink, would you?

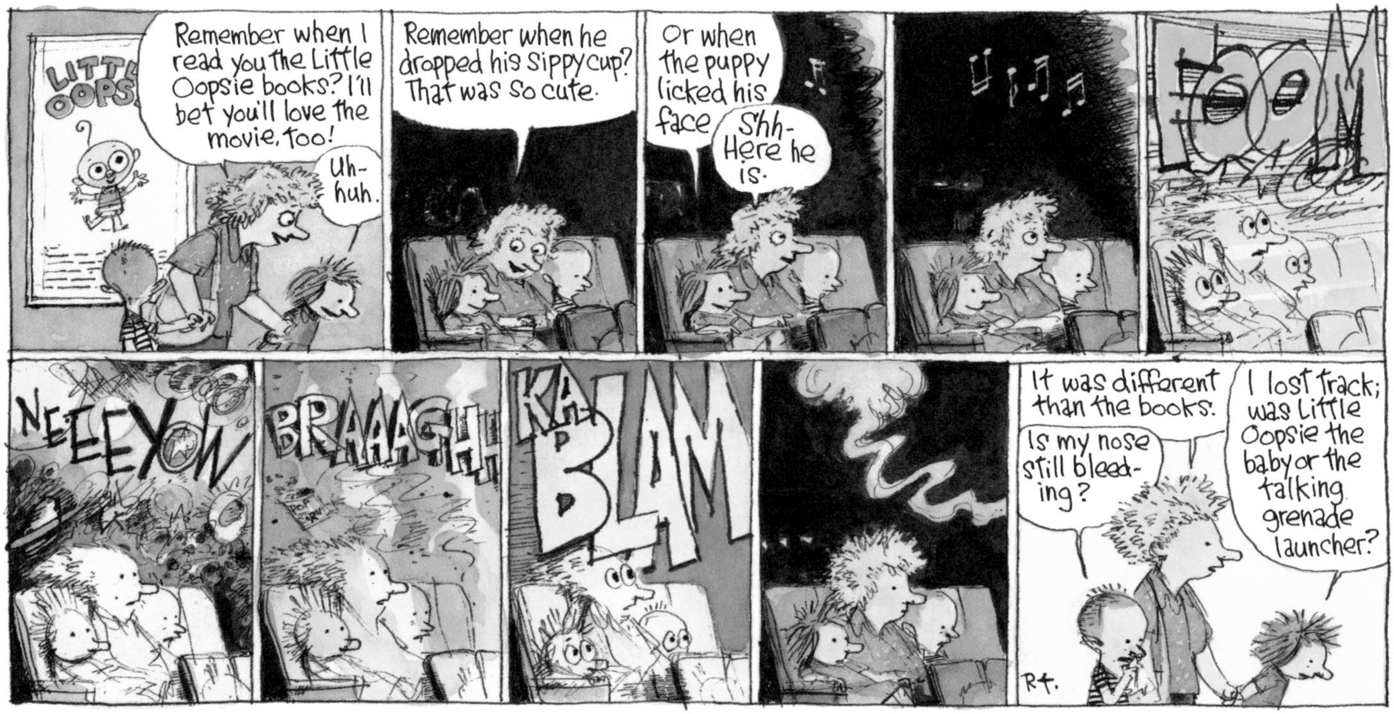
LITTLE OOPS
Remember when I read you the Little Oopsie books? I'll bet you'll love the movie, too!
Uh-huh.
Remember when he dropped his sippy cup? That was so cute.
Or when the puppy licked his face
Shh- Here he is.
FOOOM
NEEEYOW
BRAAAGH
KA-BLAM
It was different than the books.
Is my nose still bleed-ing?
I lost track; was Little Oopsie the baby or the talking grenade launcher?
R.T.

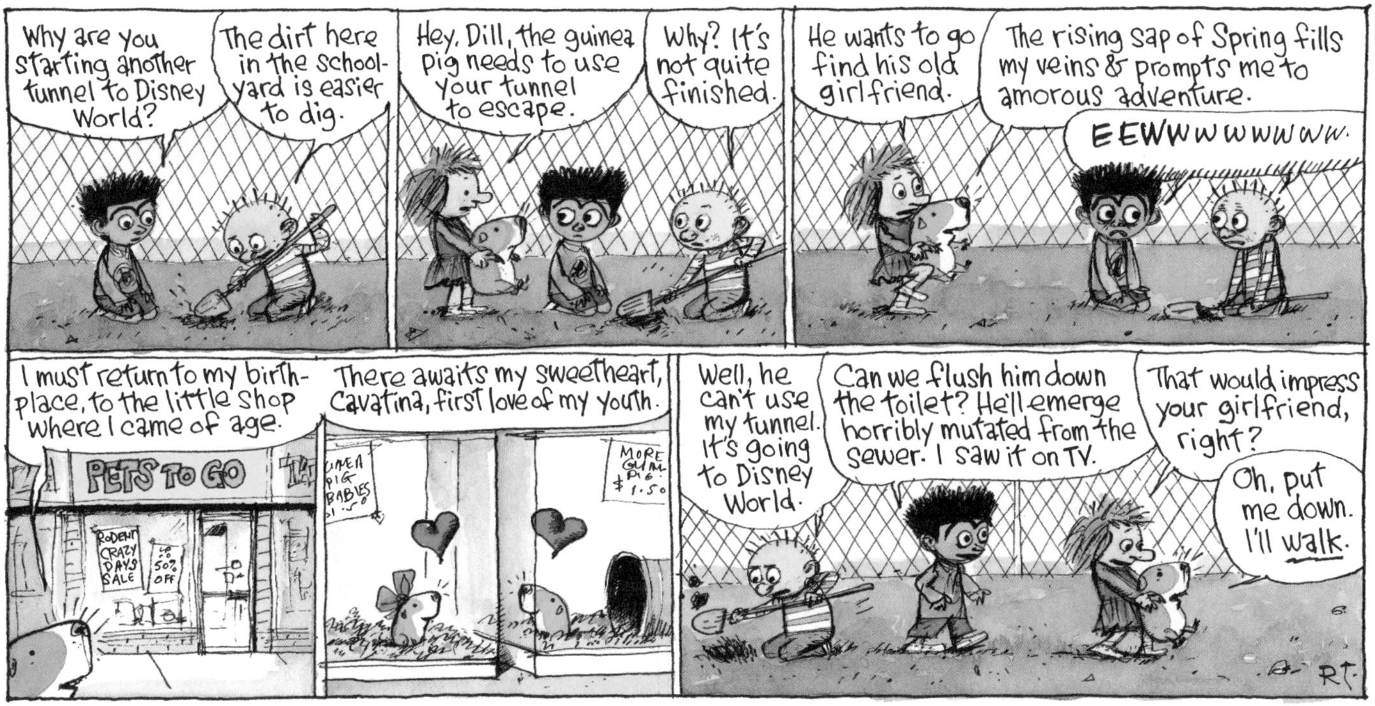
Why are you starting another tunnel to Disney World?
The dirt here in the schoolyard is easier to dig.
Hey, Dill, the guinea pig needs to use your tunnel to escape.
Why? It's not quite finished.
He wants to go find his old girlfriend.
The rising sap of Spring fills my veins & prompts me to amorous adventure.
EEWWWWWWWW.
I must return to my birthplace, to the little shop where I came of age.
PETS TO GO
RODENT CRAZY DAYS SALE
50% OFF
There awaits my sweetheart, Cavatina, first love of my youth.
Well, he can't use my tunnel. It's going to Disney World.
Can we flush him down the toilet? He'll emerge horribly mutated from the sewer. I saw it on TV.
That would impress your girlfriend, right?
Oh, put me down. I'll walk.
RT.

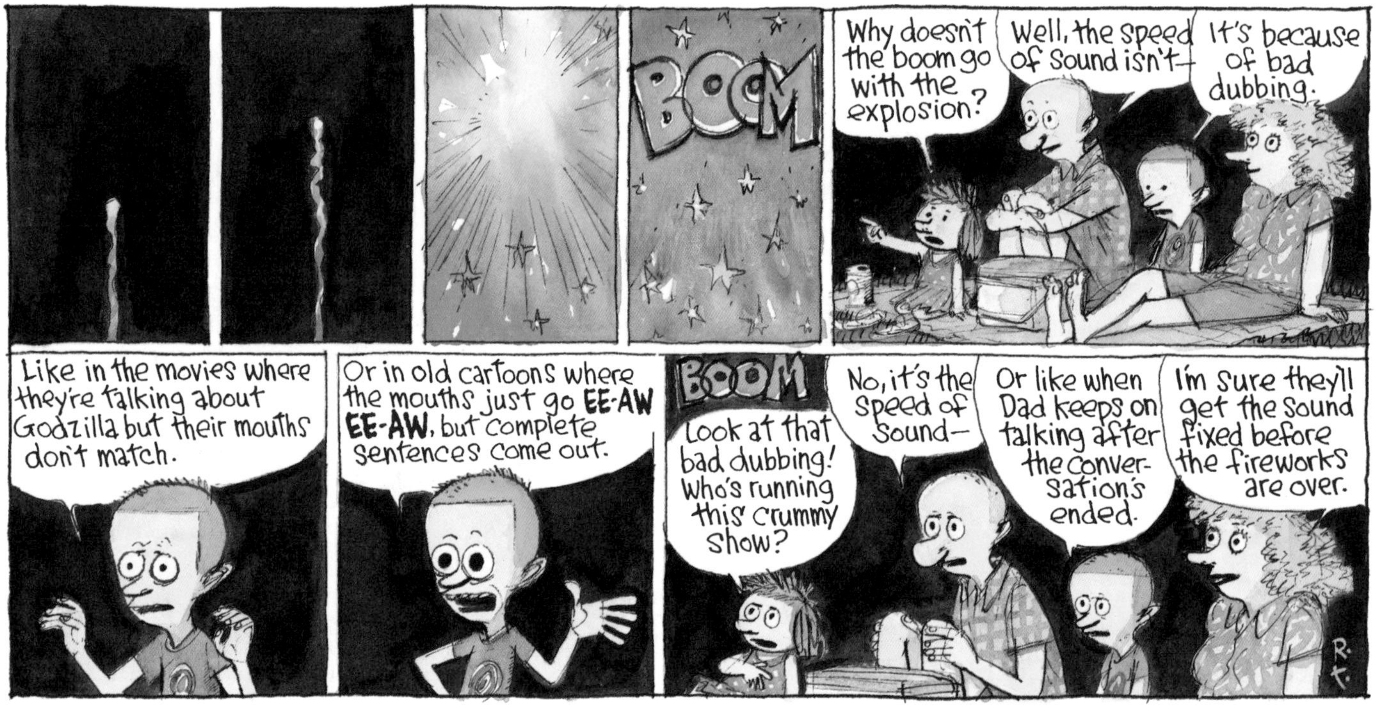
BOOM
Why doesn't the boom go with the explosion?
Well, the speed of sound isn't—
It's because of bad dubbing.
Like in the movies where they're talking about Godzilla but their mouths don't match.
Or in old cartoons where the mouths just go **EE-AW EE-AW**, but complete sentences come out.
BOOM
Look at that bad dubbing! Who's running this crummy show?
No, it's the speed of sound—
Or like when Dad keeps on talking after the conver-sation's ended.
I'm sure they'll get the sound fixed before the fireworks are over.
R.T.

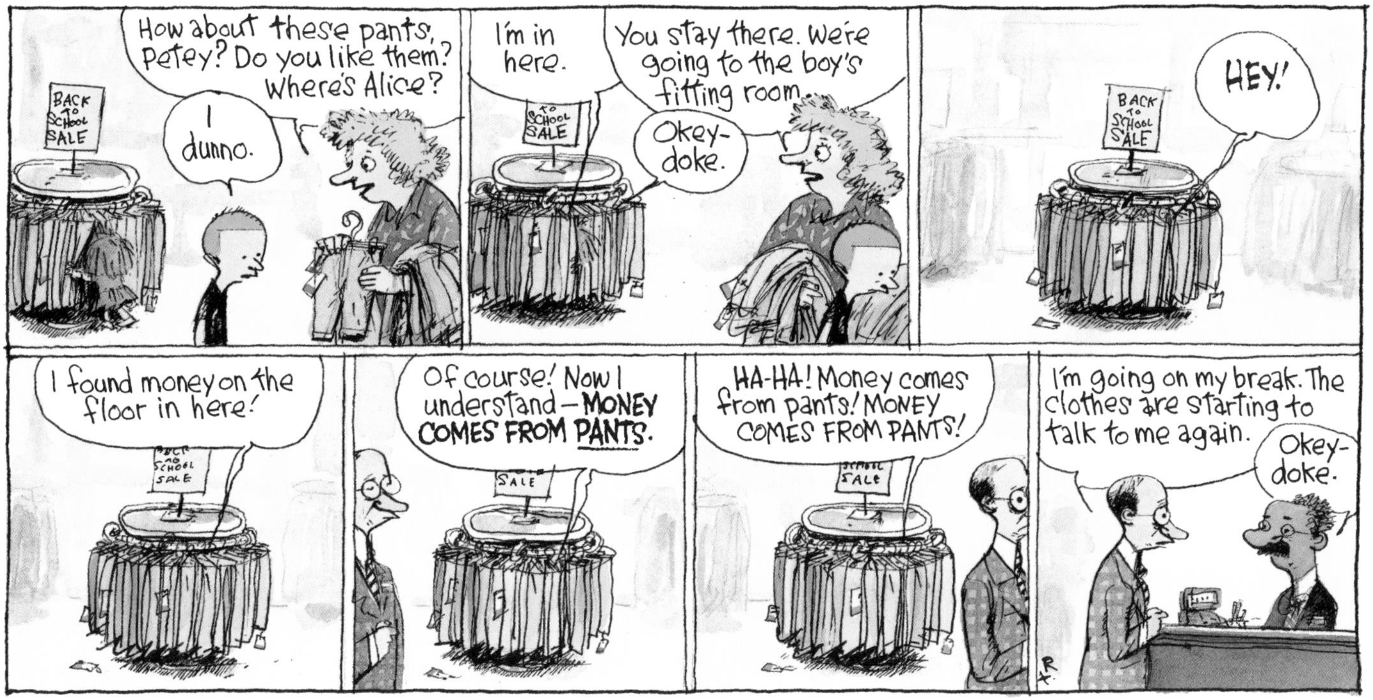
BACK TO SCHOOL SALE
How about these pants, Petey? Do you like them? Where's Alice?
I dunno.
I'm in here.
TO SCHOOL SALE
You stay there. We're going to the boy's fitting room.
Okey-doke.
BACK TO SCHOOL SALE
HEY!
I found money on the floor in here!
SCHOOL SALE
Of course! Now I understand—MONEY COMES FROM PANTS.
SALE
HA-HA! Money comes from pants! MONEY COMES FROM PANTS!
SCHOOL SALE
I'm going on my break. The clothes are starting to talk to me again.
Okey-doke.
R

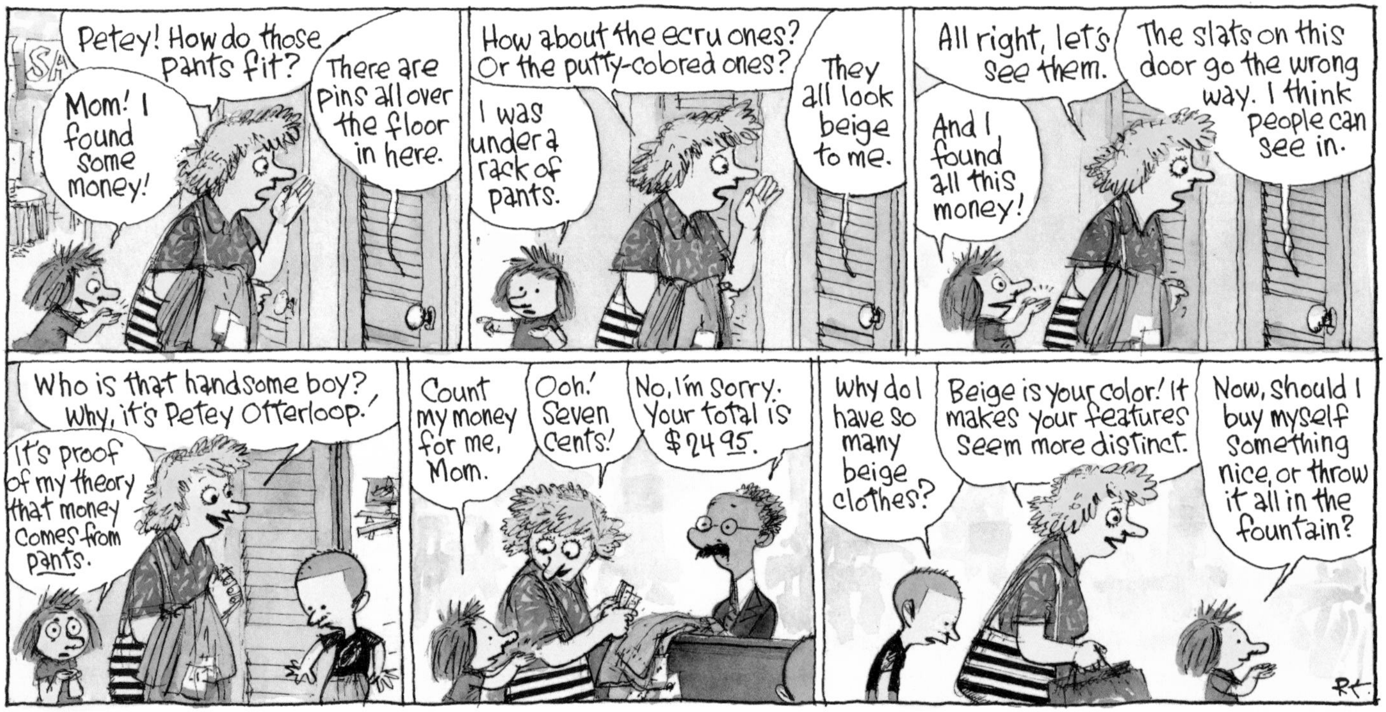

Petey! How do those pants fit?
Mom! I found some money!
There are pins all over the floor in here.
How about the ecru ones? Or the putty-colored ones?
I was under a rack of pants.
They all look beige to me.
All right, let's see them.
And I found all this money!
The slats on this door go the wrong way. I think people can see in.
Who is that handsome boy? Why, it's Petey Otterloop!
It's proof of my theory that money comes from pants.
Count my money for me, Mom.
Ooh! Seven cents!
No, I'm sorry. Your total is $24.95.
Why do I have so many beige clothes?
Beige is your color! It makes your features seem more distinct.
Now, should I buy myself something nice, or throw it all in the fountain?
RF

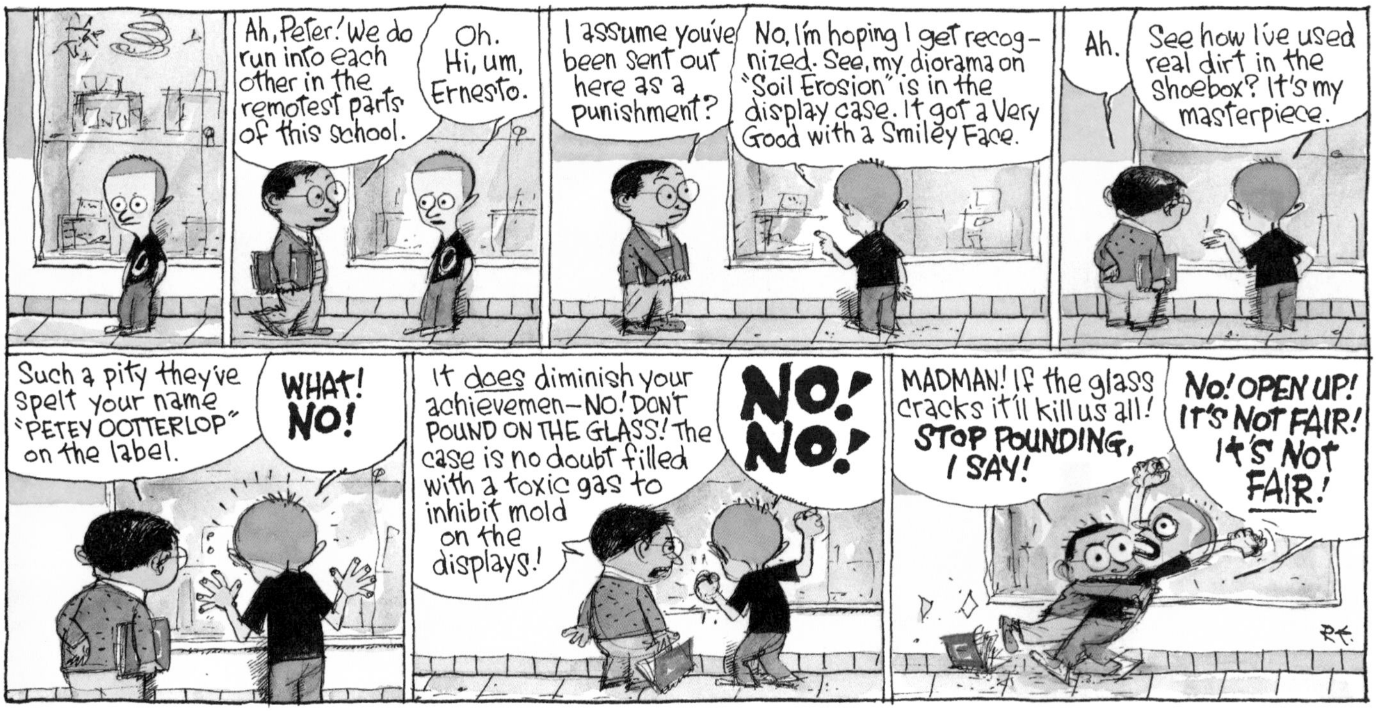

Ah, Peter! We do run into each other in the remotest parts of this school.
Oh. Hi, um, Ernesto.
I assume you've been sent out here as a punishment?
No, I'm hoping I get recognized. See, my diorama on "Soil Erosion" is in the display case. It got a Very Good with a Smiley Face.
Ah.
See how I've used real dirt in the shoebox? It's my masterpiece.
Such a pity they've spelt your name "PETEY OOTTERLOP" on the label.
WHAT! NO!
It does diminish your achievemen—NO! DON'T POUND ON THE GLASS! The case is no doubt filled with a toxic gas to inhibit mold on the displays!
NO! NO!
MADMAN! If the glass cracks it'll kill us all! STOP POUNDING, I SAY!
No! OPEN UP! IT'S NOT FAIR! IT'S NOT FAIR!

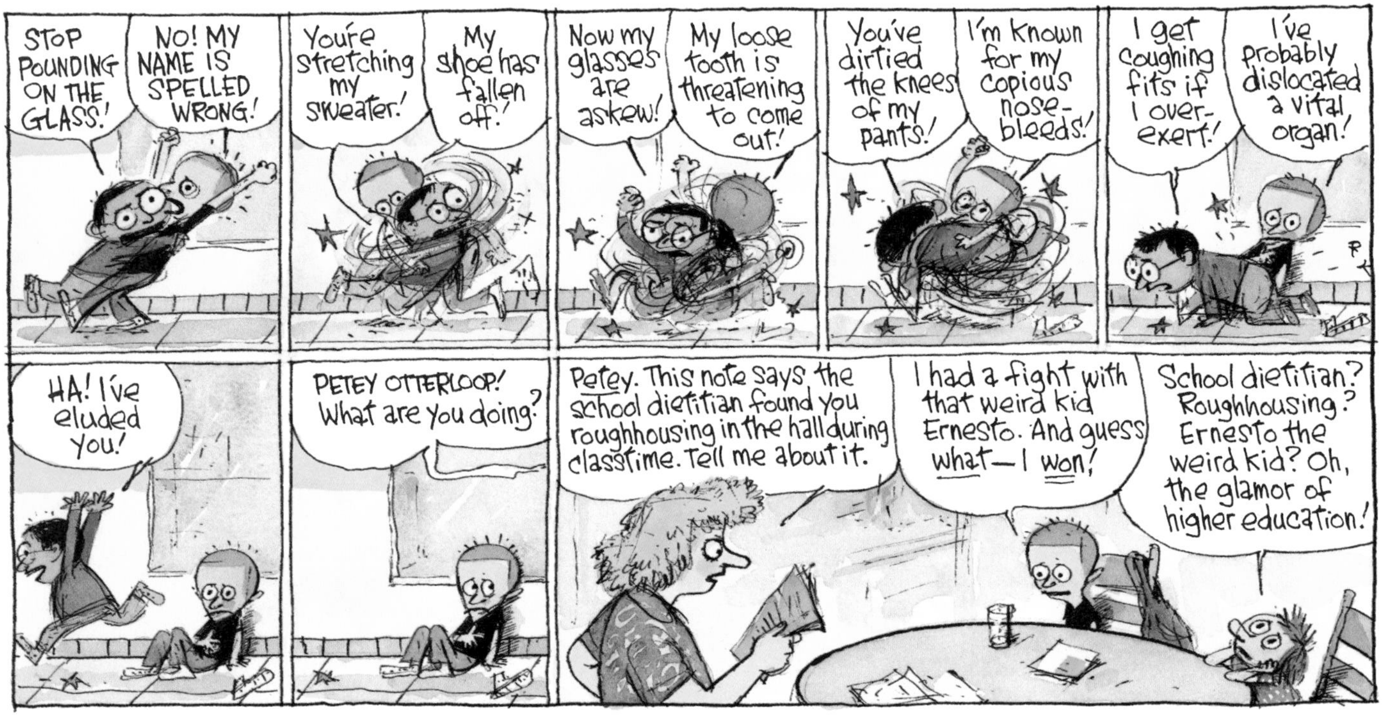
STOP POUNDING ON THE GLASS!
NO! MY NAME IS SPELLED WRONG!
You're stretching my sweater!
My shoe has fallen off!
Now my glasses are askew!
My loose tooth is threatening to come out!
You've dirtied the knees of my pants!
I'm known for my copious nose-bleeds!
I get coughing fits if I over-exert!
I've probably dislocated a vital organ!
HA! I've eluded You!
PETEY OTTERLOOP! What are you doing?
Petey. This note says the school dietitian found you roughhousing in the hall during classtime. Tell me about it.
I had a fight with that weird kid Ernesto. And guess what—I won!
School dietitian? Roughhousing? Ernesto the weird kid? Oh, the glamor of higher education!

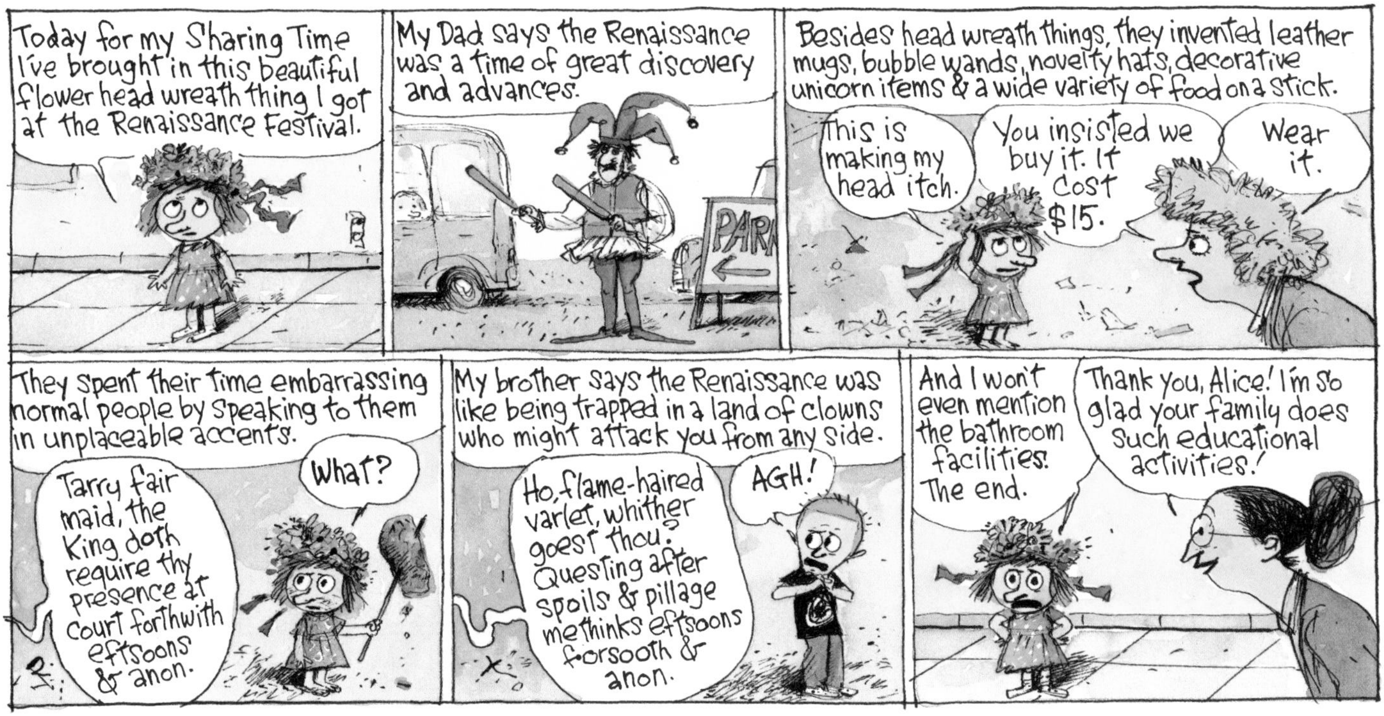
Today for my Sharing Time I've brought in this beautiful flower head wreath thing I got at the Renaissance Festival.
My Dad says the Renaissance was a time of great discovery and advances.
PARK
Besides head wreath things, they invented leather mugs, bubble wands, novelty hats, decorative unicorn items & a wide variety of food on a stick.
This is making my head itch.
You insisted we buy it. It cost $15.
Wear it.
They spent their time embarrassing normal people by speaking to them in unplaceable accents.
Tarry fair maid, the King doth require thy presence at court forthwith eftsoons & anon.
What?
My brother says the Renaissance was like being trapped in a land of clowns who might attack you from any side.
Ho, flame-haired varlet, whither goest thou? Questing after spoils & pillage methinks eftsoons forsooth & anon.
AGH!
And I won't even mention the bathroom facilities! The end.
Thank you, Alice! I'm so glad your family does such educational activities!

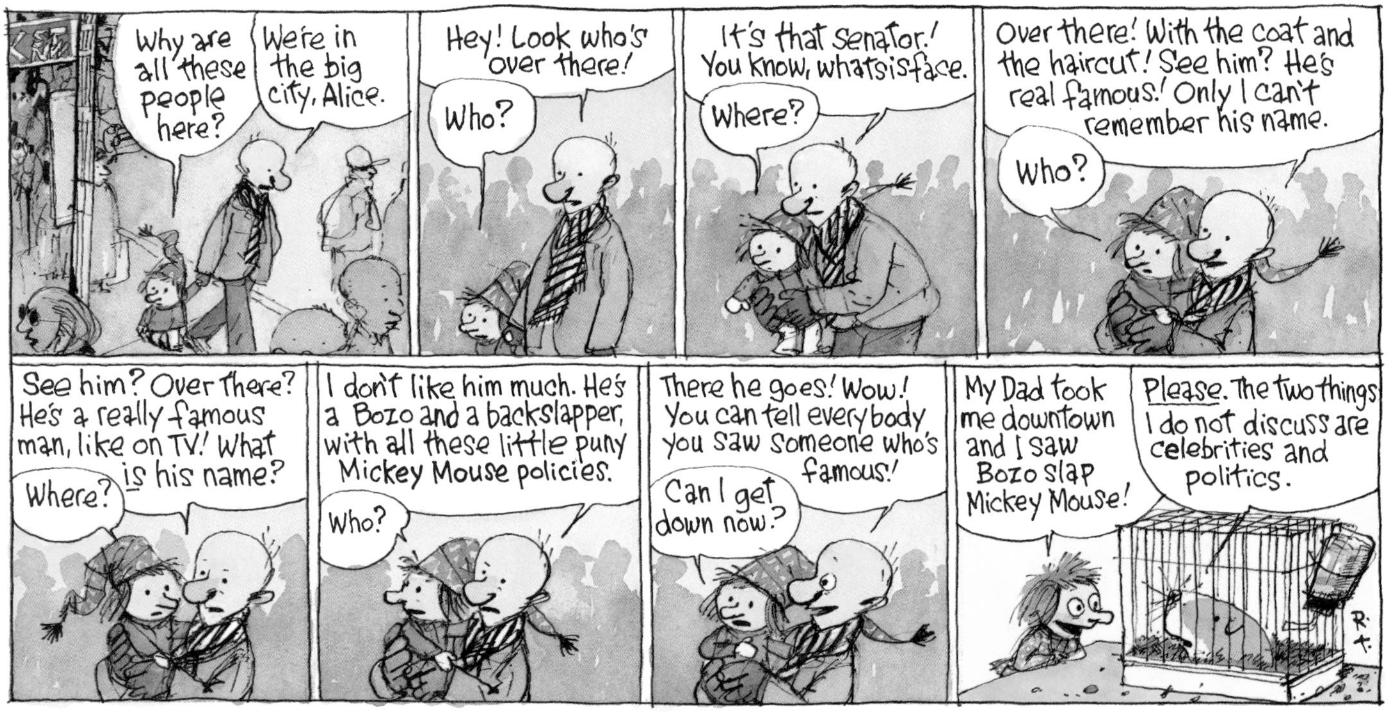
Why are all these people here?
We're in the big city, Alice.
Hey! Look who's over there!
Who?
It's that senator! You know, whatsisface.
Where?
Over there! With the coat and the haircut! See him? He's real famous! Only I can't remember his name.
Who?
See him? Over there? He's a really famous man, like on TV! What is his name?
Where?
I don't like him much. He's a Bozo and a backslapper, with all these little puny Mickey Mouse policies.
Who?
There he goes! Wow! You can tell everybody you saw someone who's famous!
Can I get down now?
My Dad took me downtown and I saw Bozo slap Mickey Mouse!
Please. The two things I do not discuss are celebrities and politics.
R. T.

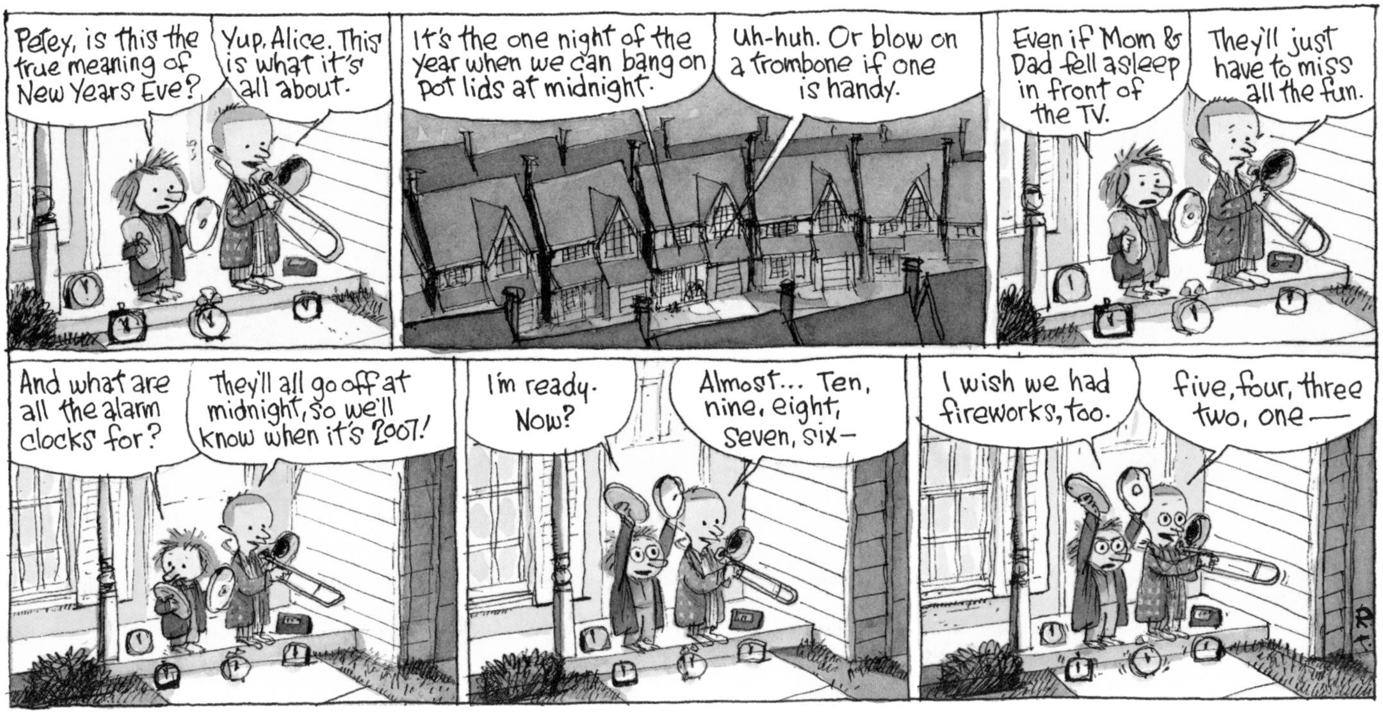
Petey, is this the true meaning of New Years Eve?
Yup, Alice. This is what it's all about.
It's the one night of the year when we can bang on pot lids at midnight.
Uh-huh. Or blow on a trombone if one is handy.
Even if Mom & Dad fell asleep in front of the TV.
They'll just have to miss all the fun.
And what are all the alarm clocks for?
They'll all go off at midnight, so we'll know when it's 2007!
I'm ready. Now?
Almost... Ten, nine, eight, seven, six—
I wish we had fireworks, too.
five, four, three two, one—

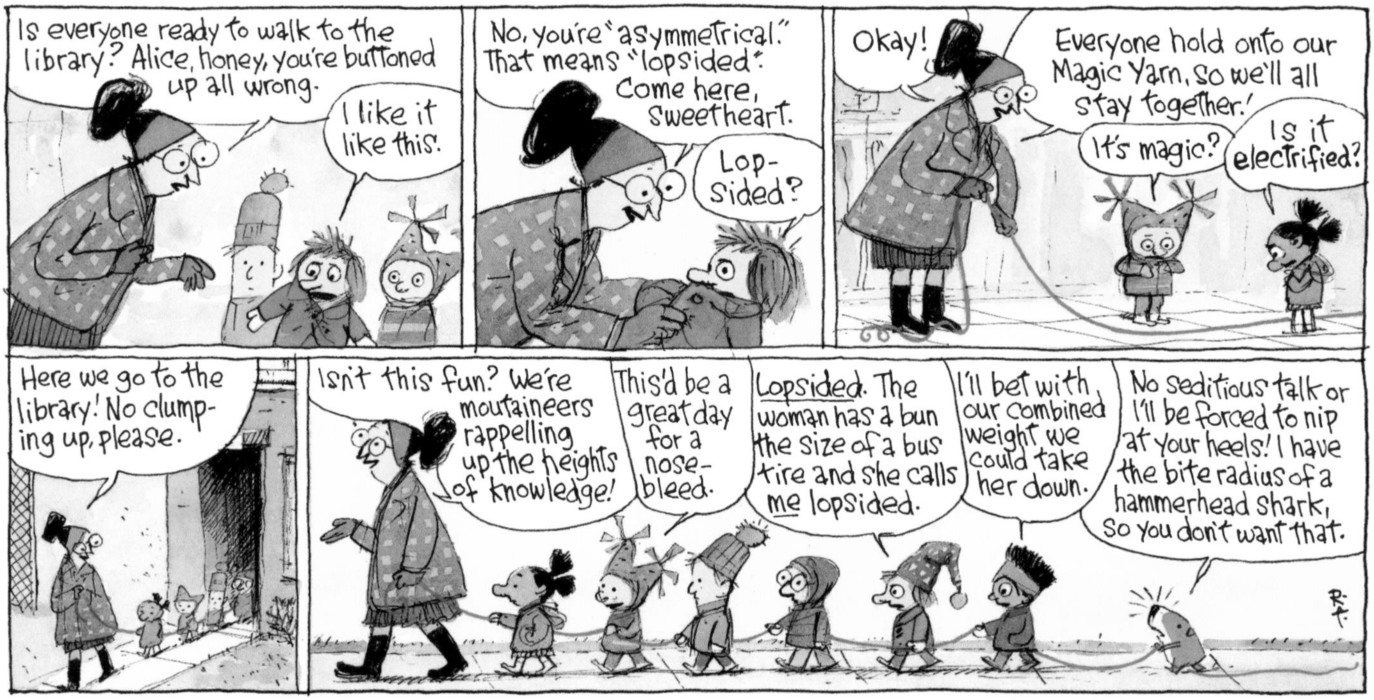
Is everyone ready to walk to the library? Alice, honey, you're buttoned up all wrong.
I like it like this.
No, you're "asymmetrical." That means "lopsided." Come here, sweetheart.
Lop-sided?
Okay!
Everyone hold onto our Magic Yarn, so we'll all stay together!
It's magic?
Is it electrified?
Here we go to the library! No clumping up, please.
Isn't this fun? We're moutaineers rappelling up the heights of knowledge!
This'd be a great day for a nose-bleed.
Lopsided. The woman has a bun the size of a bus tire and she calls me lopsided.
I'll bet with our combined weight we could take her down.
No seditious talk or I'll be forced to nip at your heels! I have the bite radius of a hammerhead shark, so you don't want that.
R.T.

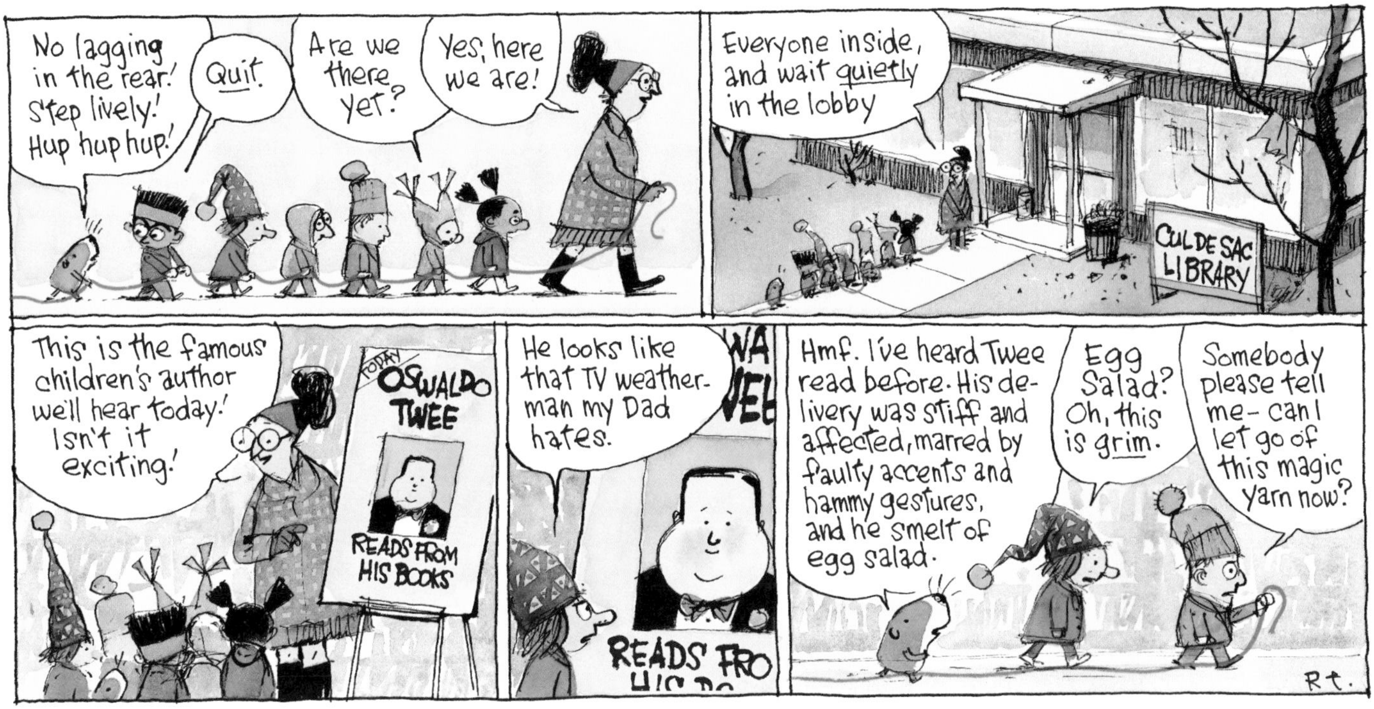
No lagging in the rear! Step lively! Hup hup hup!
Quit.
Are we there yet?
Yes, here we are!
Everyone inside, and wait quietly in the lobby
CUL DE SAC LIBRARY
This is the famous children's author we'll hear today! Isn't it exciting!
TODAY OSWALDO TWEE
READS FROM HIS BOOKS
He looks like that TV weatherman my Dad hates.
READS FRO
Hmf. I've heard Twee read before. His delivery was stiff and affected, marred by faulty accents and hammy gestures, and he smelt of egg salad.
Egg Salad? Oh, this is grim.
Somebody please tell me—can I let go of this magic yarn now?
Rt.

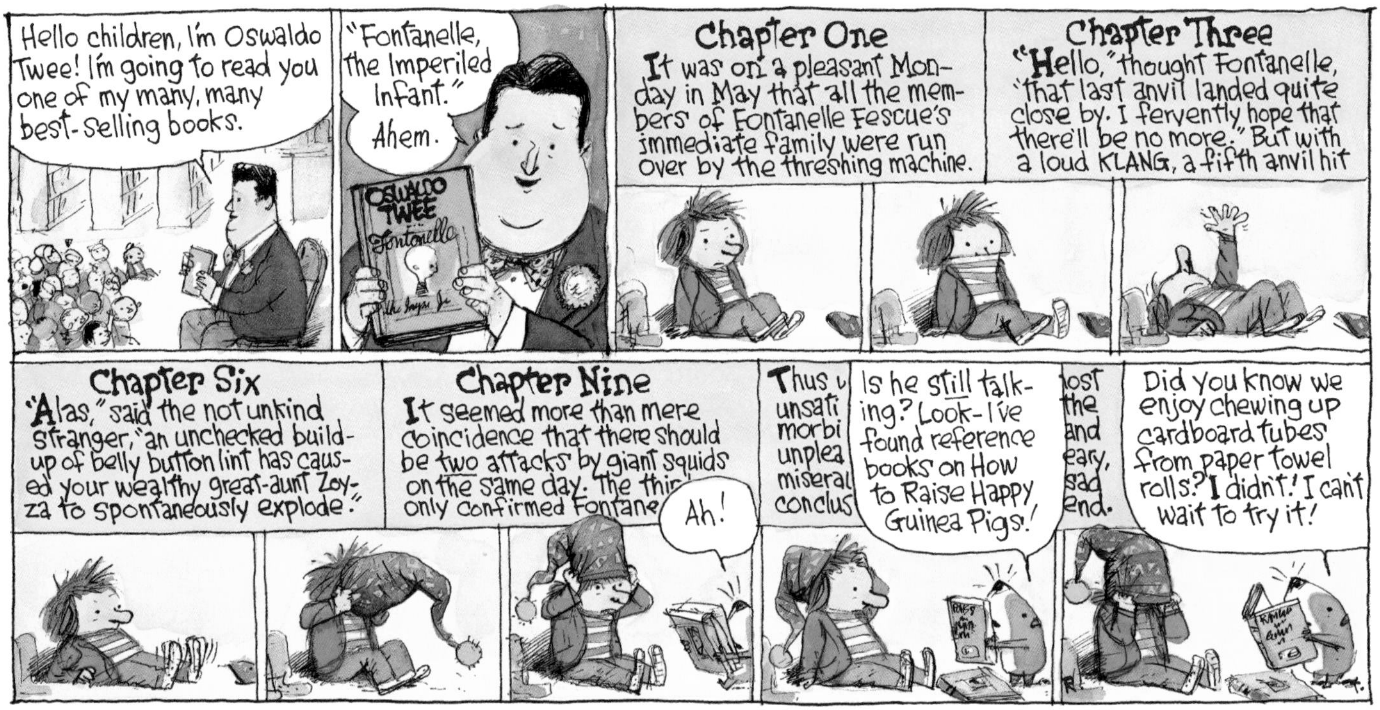
Hello children, I'm Oswaldo Twee! I'm going to read you one of my many, many best-selling books.
"Fontanelle, the Imperiled Infant."
Ahem.
OSWALDO TWEE
Fontanelle
Chapter One
It was on a pleasant Monday in May that all the members of Fontanelle Fescue's immediate family were run over by the threshing machine.
Chapter Three
"Hello," thought Fontanelle, "that last anvil landed quite close by. I fervently hope that there'll be no more." But with a loud KLANG, a fifth anvil hit
Chapter Six
"Alas," said the not unkind stranger, "an unchecked build-up of belly button lint has caused your wealthy great-aunt Zoyza to spontaneously explode."
Chapter Nine
It seemed more than mere coincidence that there should be two attacks by giant squids on the same day. The thir only confirmed Fontane
Ah!
Is he still talking? Look-I've found reference books on How to Raise Happy Guinea Pigs!
Did you know we enjoy chewing up cardboard tubes from paper towel rolls? I didn't! I can't wait to try it!

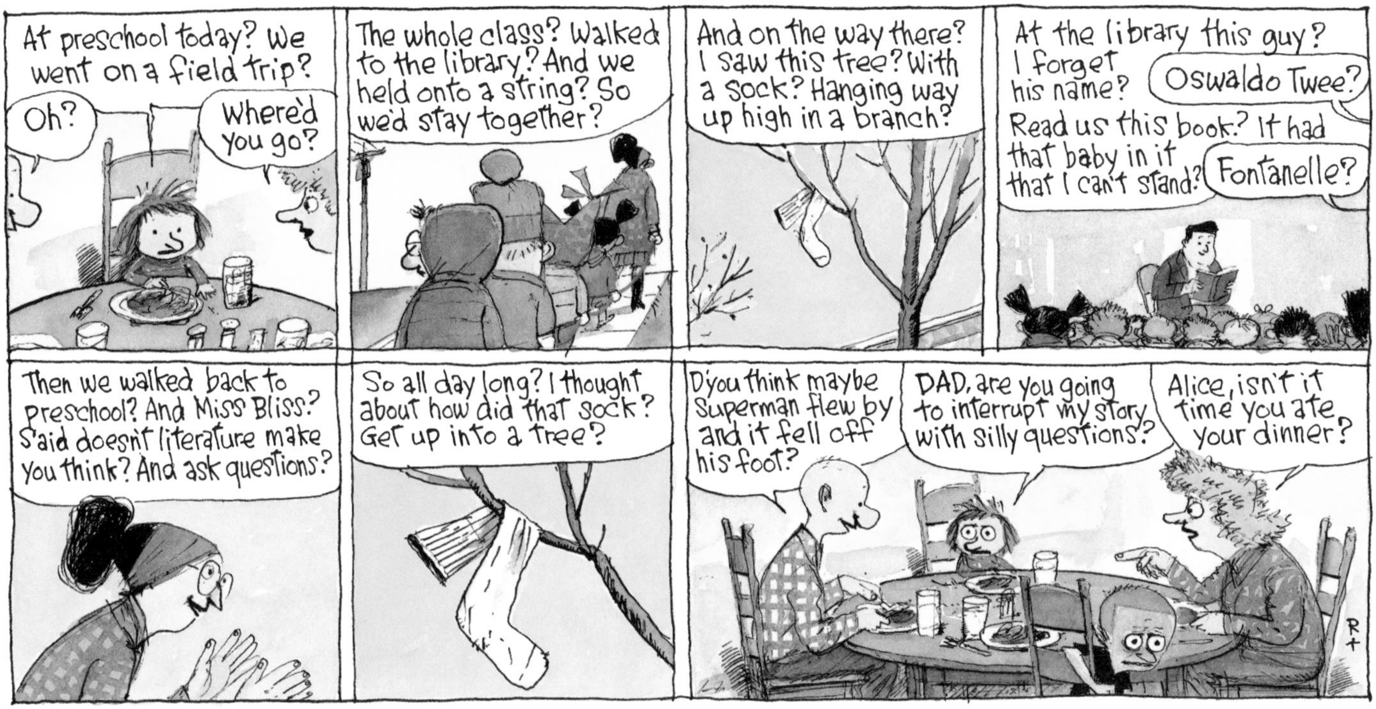
At preschool today? We went on a field trip?
Oh?
Where'd you go?
The whole class? Walked to the library? And we held onto a string? So we'd stay together?
And on the way there? I saw this tree? With a sock? Hanging way up high in a branch?
At the library this guy? I forget his name?
Oswaldo Twee?
Read us this book? It had that baby in it that I can't stand?
Fontanelle?
Then we walked back to preschool? And Miss Bliss? S'aid doesn't literature make you think? And ask questions?
So all day long? I thought about how did that sock? Get up into a tree?
D'you think maybe Superman flew by and it fell off his foot?
DAD, are you going to interrupt my story with silly questions?
Alice, isn't it time you ate your dinner?
R+

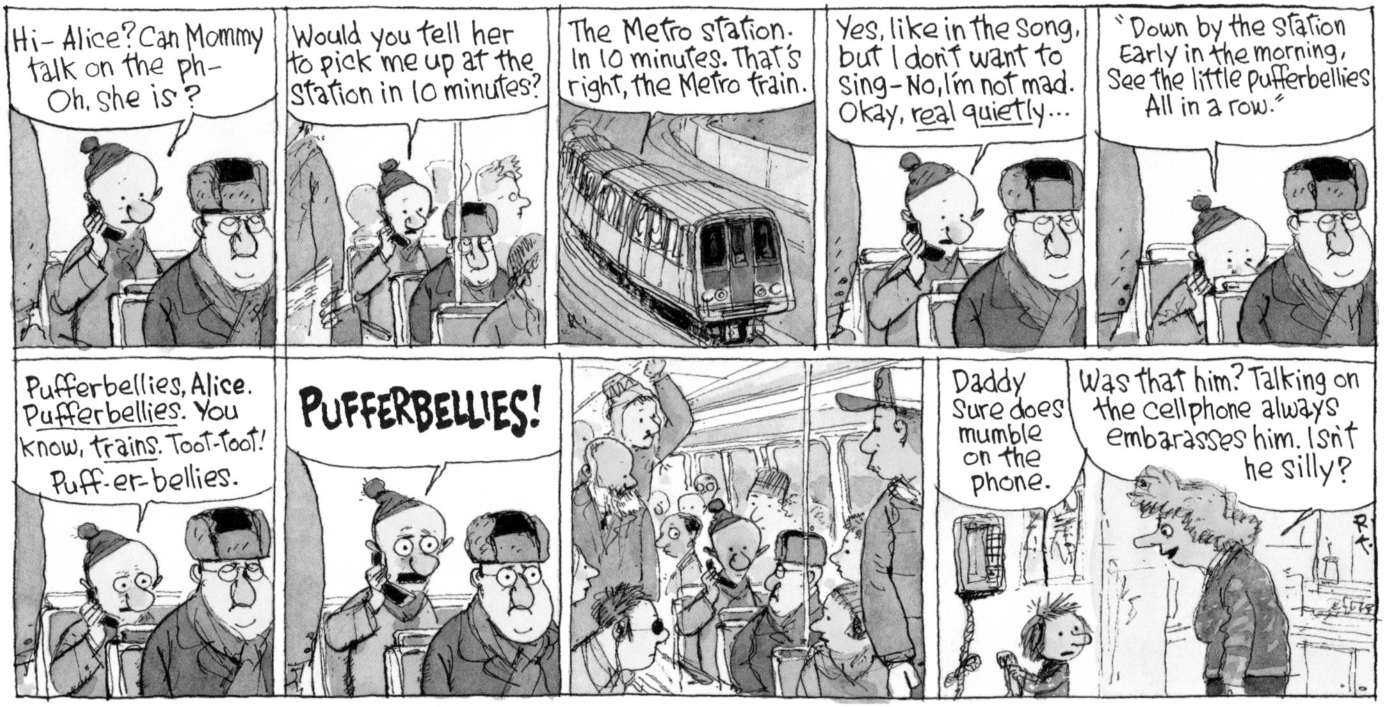
Hi- Alice? Can Mommy talk on the ph- Oh, she is?
Would you tell her to pick me up at the station in 10 minutes?
The Metro station. In 10 minutes. That's right, the Metro train.
Yes, like in the song, but I don't want to sing- No, I'm not mad. Okay, real quietly...
"Down by the station Early in the morning, See the little pufferbellies All in a row."
Pufferbellies, Alice. Pufferbellies. You know, trains. Toot-toot! Puff-er-bellies.
PUFFERBELLIES!
Daddy sure does mumble on the phone.
Was that him? Talking on the cellphone always embarasses him. Isn't he silly?

Panel 1: Mom! On TV the man said it might snow! Can we go sledding?

Don't get your hopes up, Alice, it's supposed to be just a few flakes.

At school they said that Eskimos have lots of words for snow.

Panel 2: Really? Like what, Petey?

Well, like they have a word for snow that's not too deep, or snow that's real deep, or snow that's a little deep in some places, or snow that's slushy, or snow that squeaks when you walk on it...

Panel 3: I've heard that's not true. Eskimos have only a few words for—

SSH. It's the first thing from school he's remembered in weeks.

Or snow that looks weird, or snow that smells funny, or snow that makes you vaguely uneasy...

Panel 4: Petey said Eskimos have names for all the snow.

Who's that one?

That's Timmy! C'mon Timmy! Stick! STICK!

45

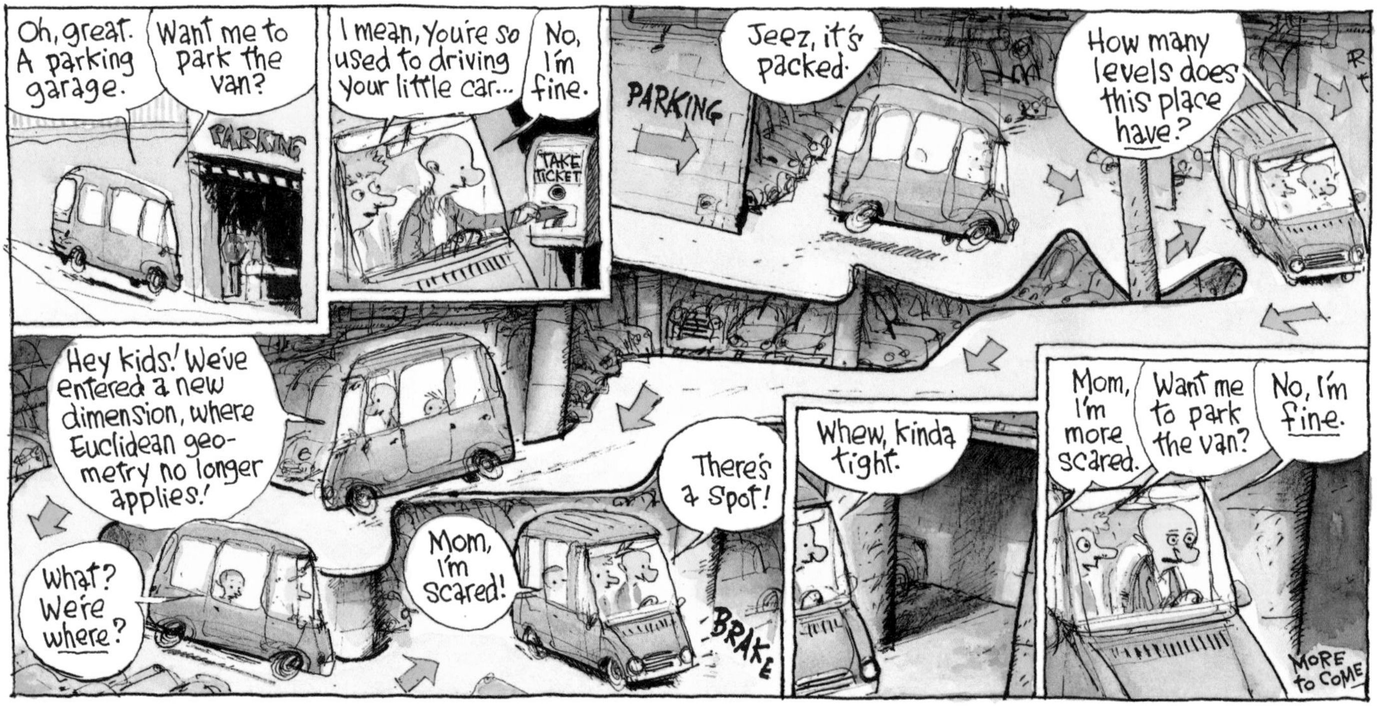
Oh, great. A parking garage.
Want me to park the van?
PARKING
I mean, You're so used to driving your little car...
No, I'm fine.
TAKE TICKET
PARKING
Jeez, it's packed.
How many levels does this place have?
Hey kids! We've entered a new dimension, where Euclidean geometry no longer applies!
What? We're where?
Mom, I'm scared!
There's a spot!
BRAKE
Whew, kinda tight.
Mom, I'm more scared.
Want me to park the van?
No, I'm fine.
MORE TO COME

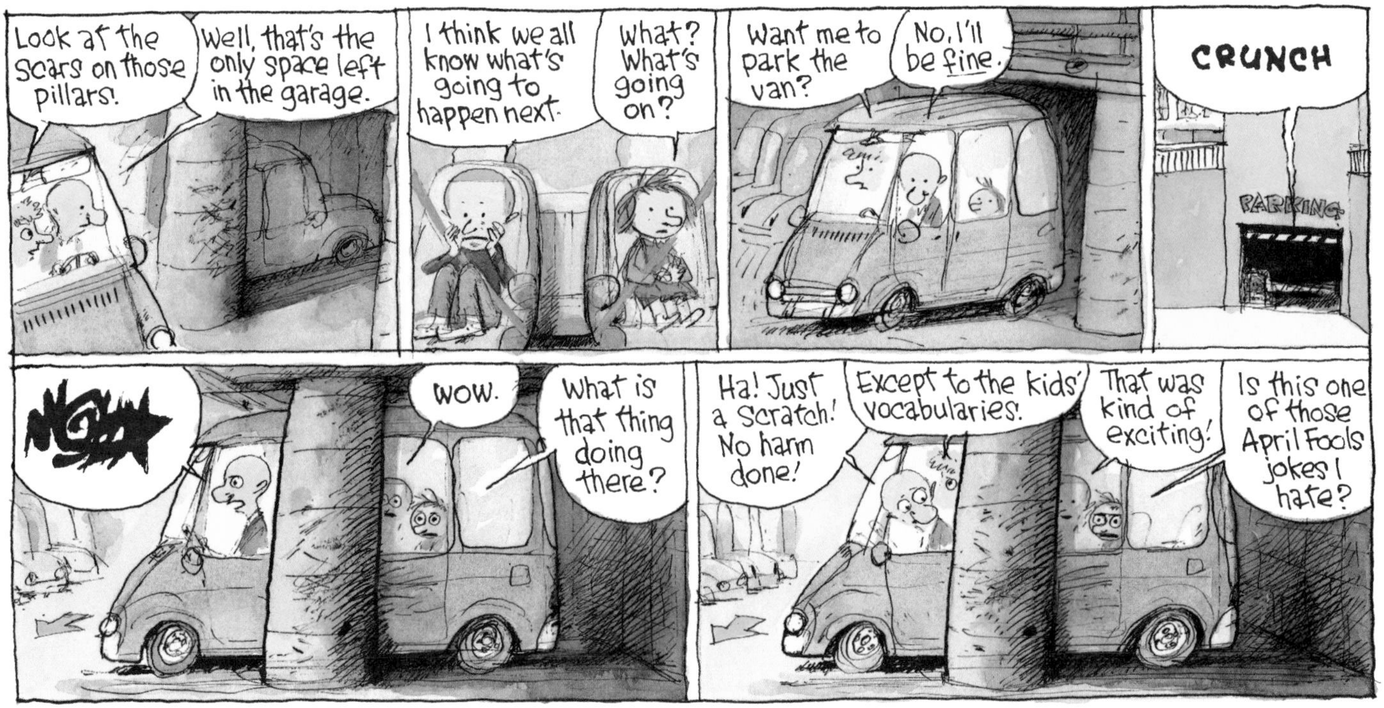
Look at the scars on those pillars!
Well, that's the only space left in the garage.
I think we all know what's going to happen next.
What? What's going on?
Want me to park the van?
No, I'll be fine.
CRUNCH
PARKING
WOW.
What is that thing doing there?
Ha! Just a scratch! No harm done!
Except to the kids' vocabularies.
That was kind of exciting!
Is this one of those April Fools jokes I hate?

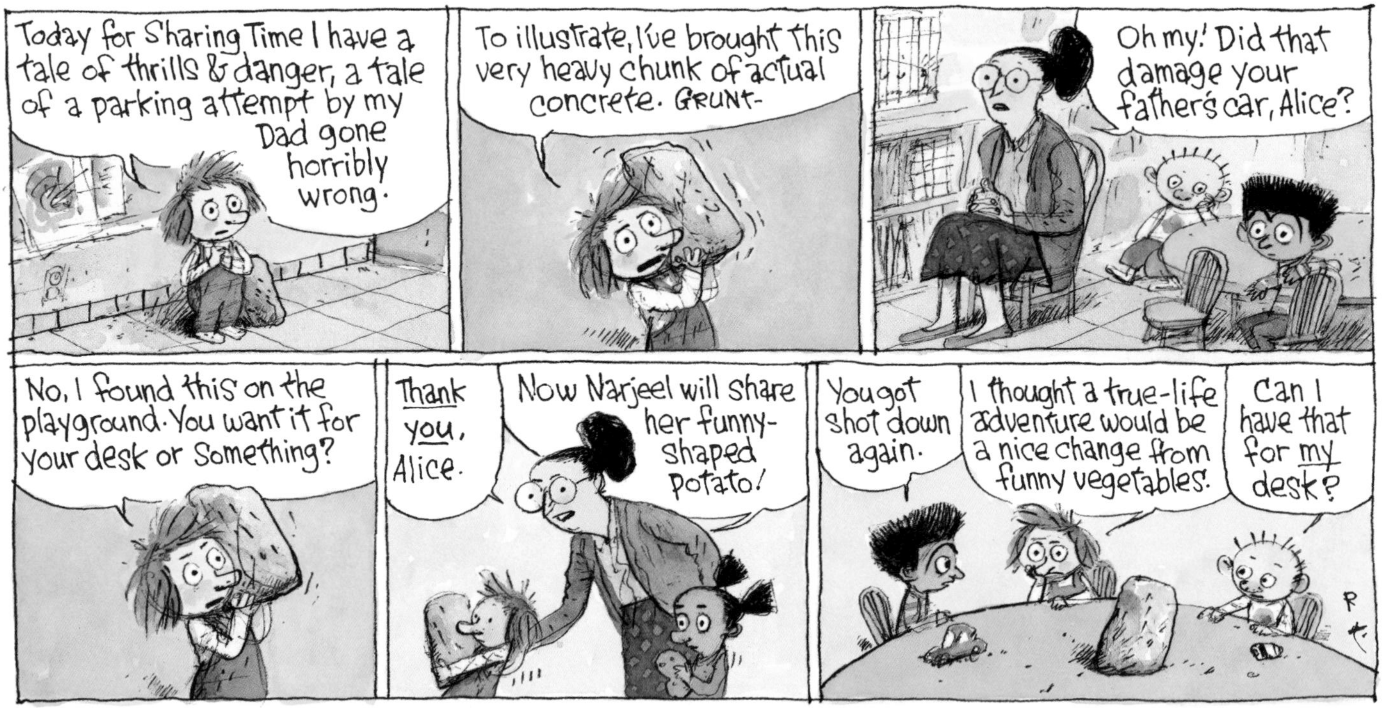
Today for Sharing Time I have a tale of thrills & danger, a tale of a parking attempt by my Dad gone horribly wrong.
To illustrate, I've brought this very heavy chunk of actual concrete. GRUNT-
Oh my! Did that damage your father's car, Alice?
No, I found this on the playground. You want it for your desk or something?
Thank you, Alice.
Now Narjeel will share her funny-shaped potato!
You got shot down again.
I thought a true-life adventure would be a nice change from funny vegetables.
Can I have that for my desk?

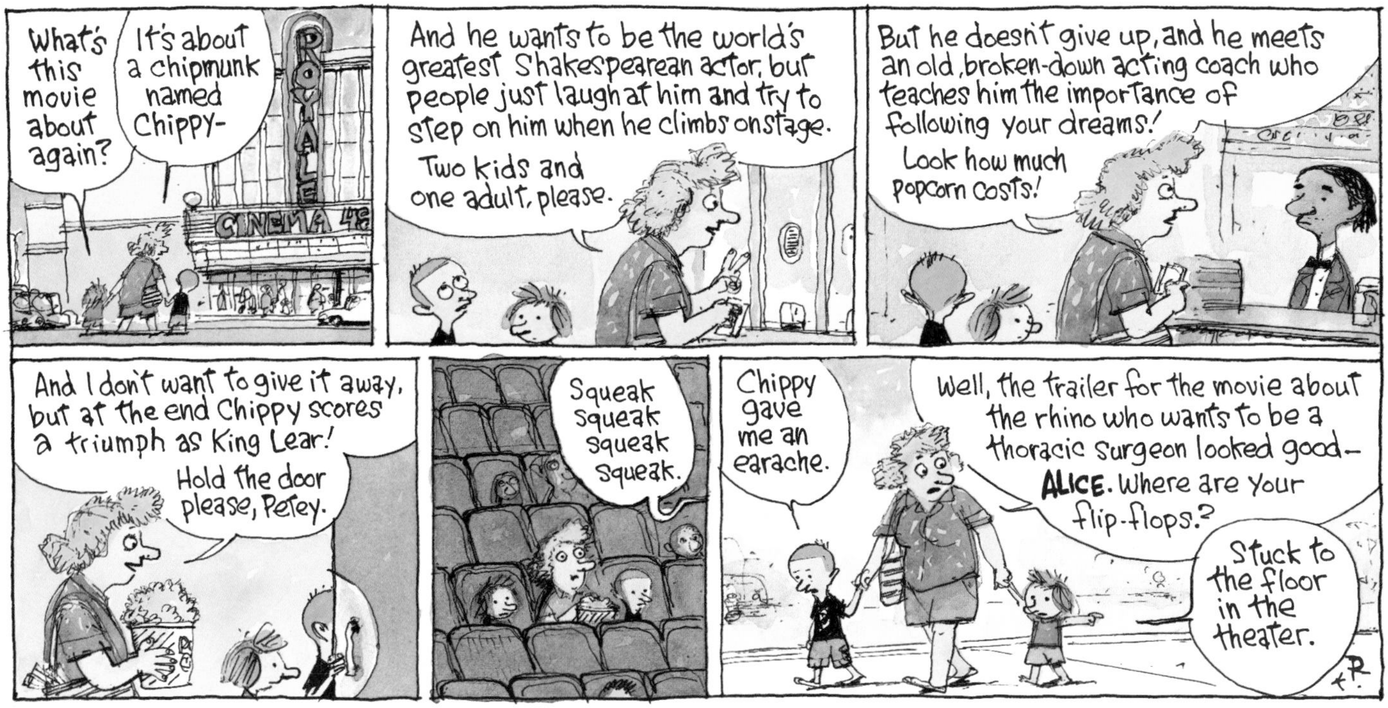
What's this movie about again?
It's about a chipmunk named Chippy-
ROYALE
CINEMA
And he wants to be the world's greatest Shakespearean actor, but people just laugh at him and try to step on him when he climbs onstage.
Two kids and one adult, please.
But he doesn't give up, and he meets an old, broken-down acting coach who teaches him the importance of following your dreams!
Look how much popcorn costs!
And I don't want to give it away, but at the end Chippy scores a triumph as King Lear!
Hold the door please, Petey.
Squeak squeak squeak squeak.
Chippy gave me an earache.
Well, the trailer for the movie about the rhino who wants to be a thoracic surgeon looked good– **ALICE.** Where are your flip-flops?
Stuck to the floor in the theater.

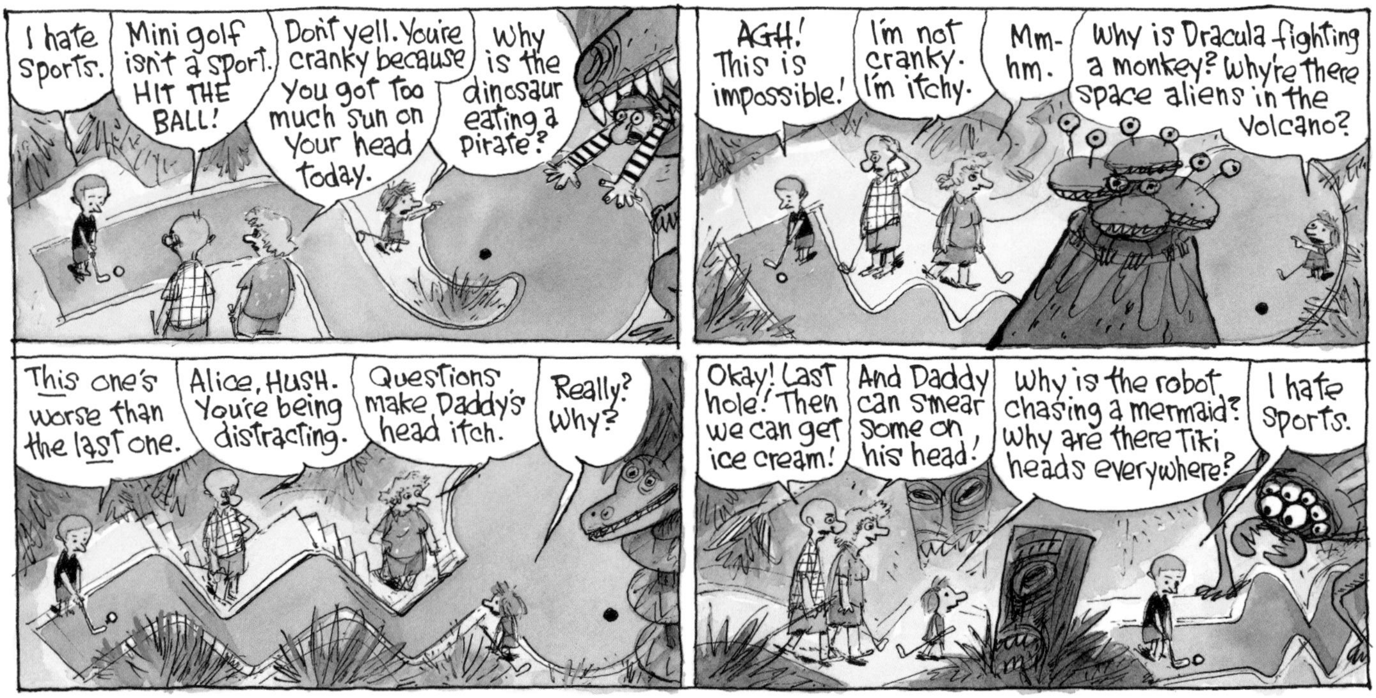
I hate sports.
Mini golf isn't a sport. HIT THE BALL!
Don't yell. You're cranky because you got too much sun on your head today.
Why is the dinosaur eating a pirate?
AGH! This is impossible!
I'm not cranky. I'm itchy.
Mm-hm.
Why is Dracula fighting a monkey? Why're there space aliens in the volcano?
This one's worse than the last one.
Alice, HUSH. You're being distracting.
Questions make Daddy's head itch.
Really? Why?
Okay! Last hole! Then we can get ice cream!
And Daddy can smear some on his head!
Why is the robot chasing a mermaid? Why are there Tiki heads everywhere?
I hate sports.

Panel 1: Good morning, Alice. It's your turn to make the morning announcements.

I know, Miss Bliss!

Panel 2: I'd like to cover some issues affecting me, like how few marshmallows were in my cereal at breakfast, and that dumb radio station my Mom listens to in the van.

Panel 3: No, we just need to hear the weather, how the class avocado plant is doing, and what the Shape of the Day is. Okay?

Panel 4: I think my lack of marshmallows is more interesting than that avocado plant.

Who am I to argue?

Panel 5: Good morning, class, this is Alice Otterloop with the announcements.

Panel 6: It will be mostly sunny today.

Panel 7: Our avocado plant, "Mr. Avocado Plant", is doing well.

Panel 8: The Triangle is the Shape of the Day.

Panel 9: AND MY CEREAL AT BREAKFAST HAD ONLY **THREE** MARSHMALLOWS AND THEY WERE **ALL GREEN!**

Panel 10: THANK YOU ALICE. CLASS, IT'S STORY TIME.

ADVANCED MOTHER GOOSE

Panel 11: Humpty Dumpty used caution & care, Instead of a wall He sat on a chair!

STORY TIME

Panel 12: See?

Panel 13: That was it?

Where's the drama? Where's the conflict?

How's this? Humpty Dumpty started to crack, 'Cause Humpty Dumpty Sat on a tack.

That's good! Did you write that?

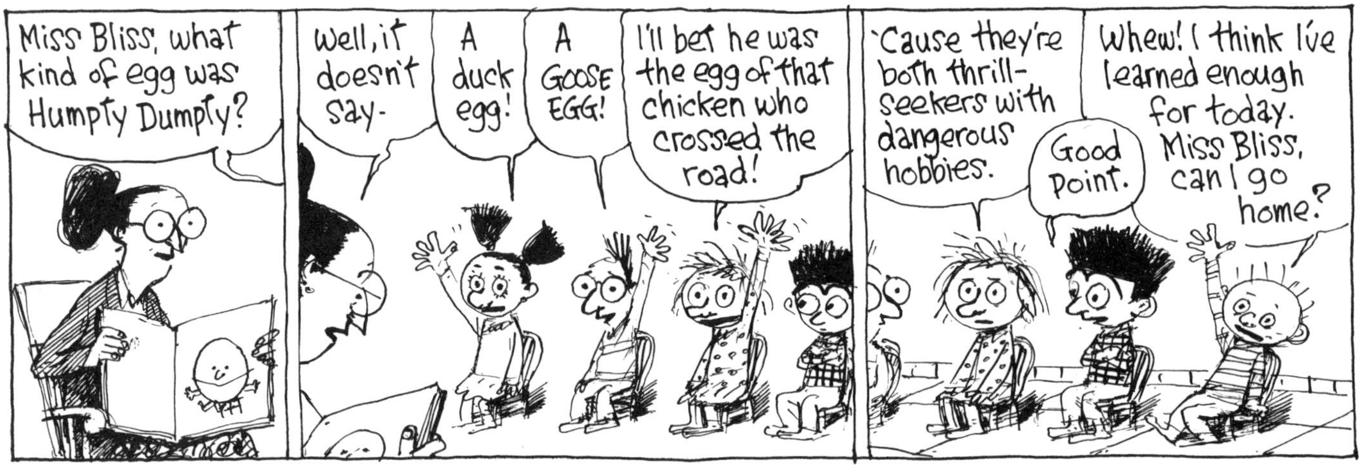
Miss Bliss, what kind of egg was Humpty Dumpty?
Well, it doesn't say-
A duck egg!
A GOOSE EGG!
I'll bet he was the egg of that chicken who crossed the road!
'Cause they're both thrill-seekers with dangerous hobbies.
Good Point.
Whew! I think I've learned enough for today. Miss Bliss, can I go home?

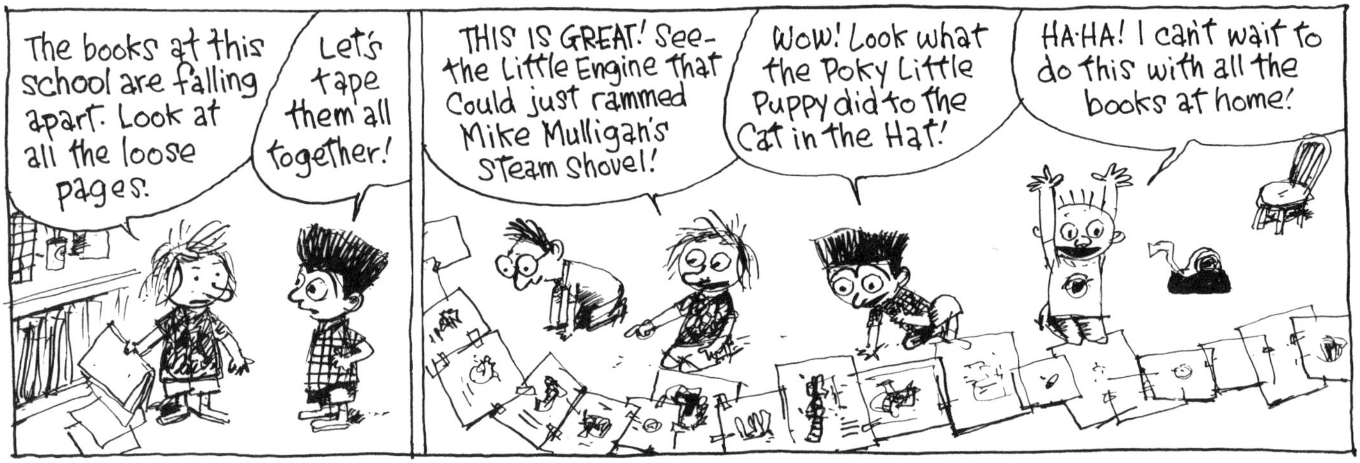
The books at this school are falling apart. Look at all the loose pages.
Let's tape them all together!
THIS IS GREAT! See- the Little Engine That Could just rammed Mike Mulligan's Steam Shovel!
WOW! Look what the Poky Little Puppy did to the Cat in the Hat!
HA-HA! I can't wait to do this with all the books at home!

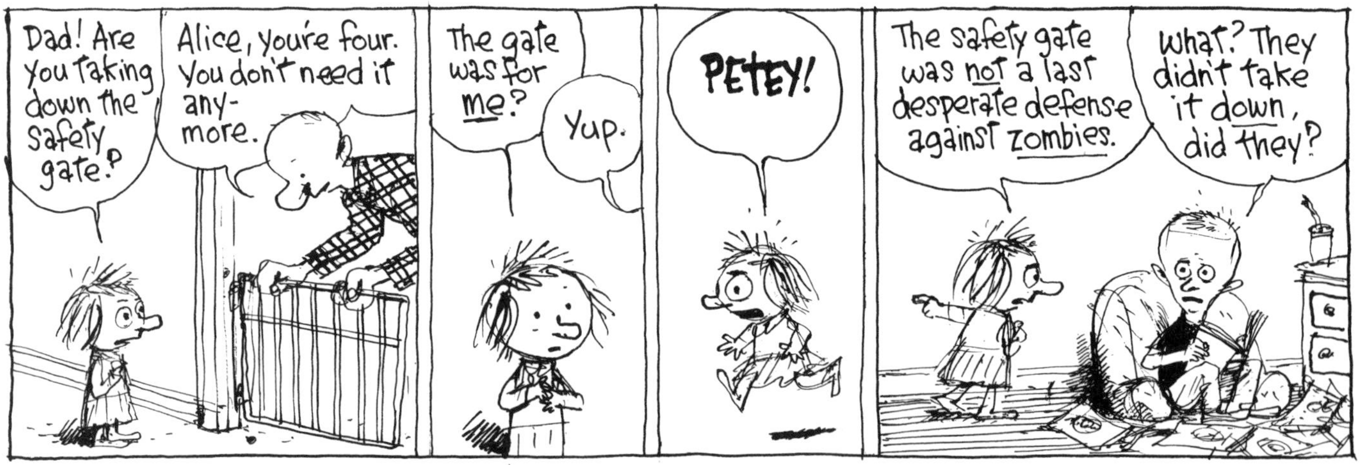
Dad! Are you taking down the safety gate?
Alice, you're four. You don't need it any-more.
The gate was for me?
Yup.
PETEY!
The safety gate was not a last desperate defense against zombies.
What? They didn't take it down, did they?

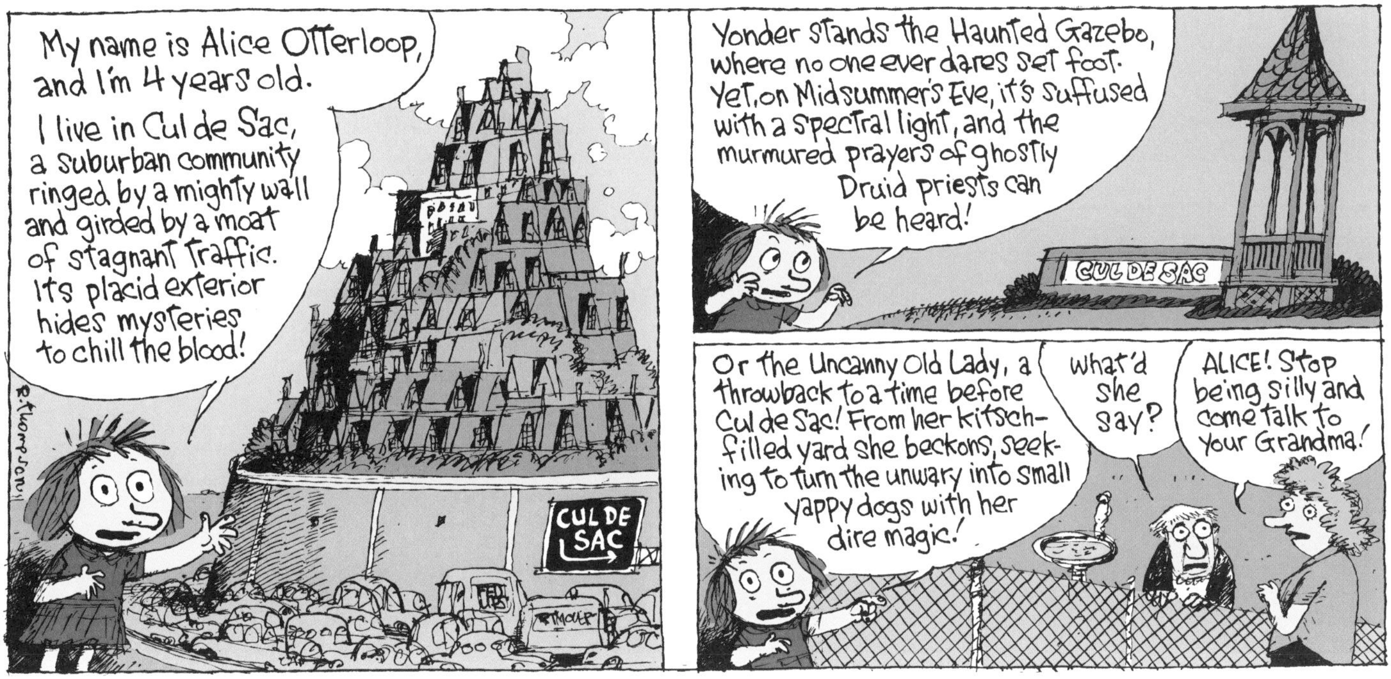
My name is Alice Otterloop, and I'm 4 years old.
I live in Cul de Sac, a suburban community ringed by a mighty wall and girded by a moat of stagnant traffic. Its placid exterior hides mysteries to chill the blood!
CUL DE SAC
Yonder stands the Haunted Gazebo, where no one ever dares set foot. Yet, on Midsummer's Eve, it's suffused with a spectral light, and the murmured prayers of ghostly Druid priests can be heard!
CUL DE SAC
Or the Uncanny Old Lady, a throwback to a time before Cul de Sac! From her kitsch-filled yard she beckons, seeking to turn the unwary into small yappy dogs with her dire magic!
What'd she say?
ALICE! Stop being silly and come talk to your Grandma!

Panel 1:
Why are there signs on everything in the classroom?

It's probably the end of the world.

Panel 2:
Why are there signs on everything in the classroom?

Miss Bliss is mocking us because we can't read.

Panel 3:
Why are there signs on everything in the classroom?

They're for Parents' Back-to School Night.

Panel 4:
I like your answer best.

Thanks! I use it a lot.

Panel 5 (middle strip):
To help your parents understand what we do in class, I've put these signs up.

PRINT MEDIA CENTER

SHOE TYING STRATEGY STATION

SHAPE RECOGNITION FACILITY.

I am *so* glad I can't read.

Cling to that small, bright shred of ignorance while you can.

HOW A GUINEA PIG WORKS

Panel 6:
Tonight your parents will all come here to Blisshaven Preschool.

Panel 7:
And they'll sit right in your chair!

Both parents at once? Can we come watch that?

Woo. And my dad's not a *small* man, either.

Panel 8:
You should see what he can do to a plastic lawn chair.

So our parents are coming here to play some grotesque version of musical chairs?

And we can't watch?

54

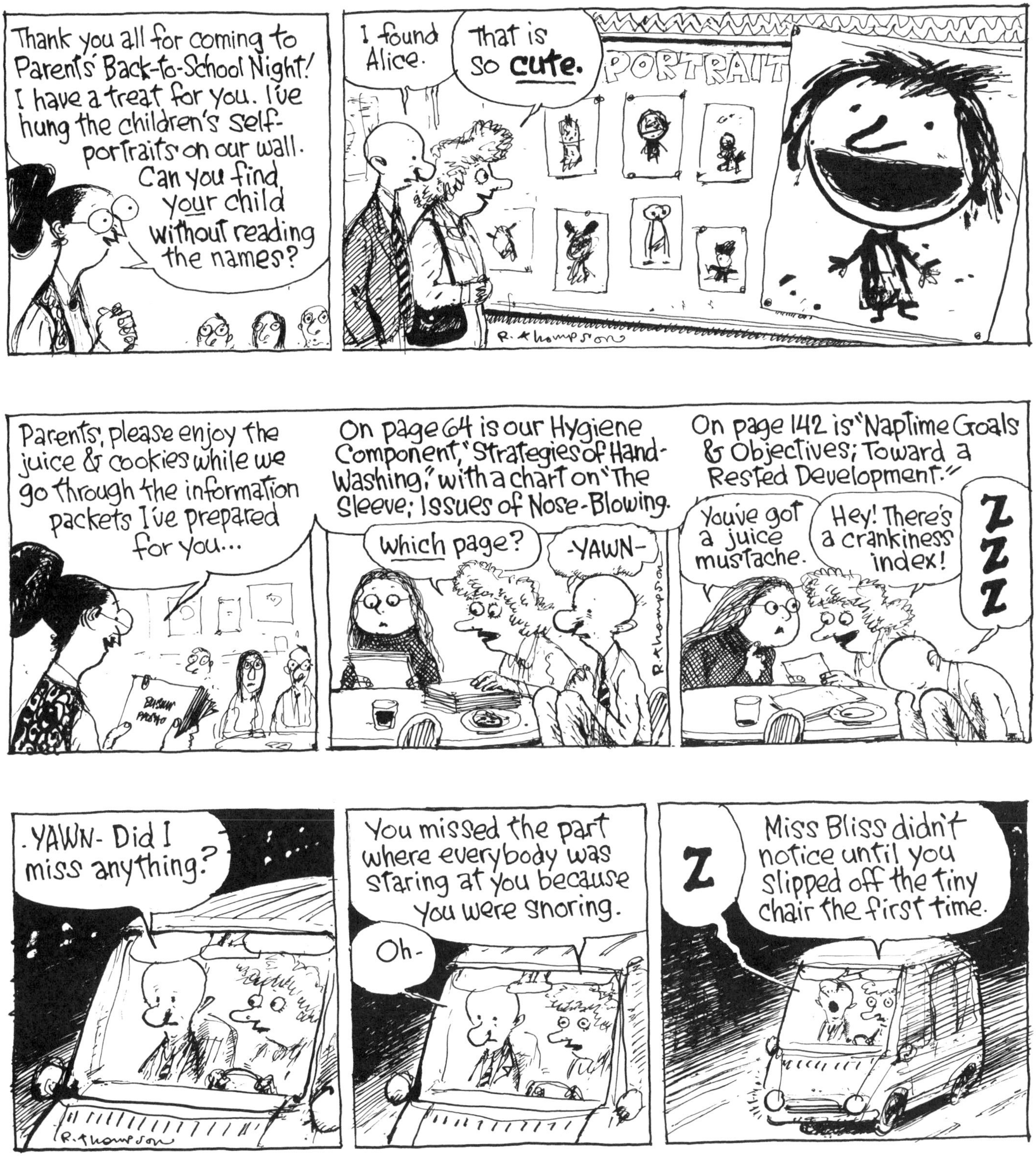

Thank you all for coming to Parents' Back-to-School Night! I have a treat for you. I've hung the children's self-portraits on our wall. Can you find your child without reading the names?
I found Alice.
That is so cute.
PORTRAIT
R. Thompson
Parents, please enjoy the juice & cookies while we go through the information packets I've prepared for you...
On page 64 is our Hygiene Component, "Strategies of Hand-Washing," with a chart on "The Sleeve; Issues of Nose-Blowing."
Which page?
-YAWN-
R. Thompson
On page 142 is "NapTime Goals & Objectives; Toward a Rested Development."
You've got a juice mustache.
Hey! There's a crankiness index!
Z Z Z
-YAWN- Did I miss anything?
R. Thompson
You missed the part where everybody was staring at you because you were snoring.
Oh-
Z
Miss Bliss didn't notice until you slipped off the tiny chair the first time.

This is the Blisshaven Academy, A Preschool, the scene of my daily toil.

That's the official crest. It shows a preschooler rampant on a field of green, clutching a crayon in each hand. Beneath is a banner with the school motto, "A Little Learning."

THE BLISSHAVEN ACADEMY
A LITTLE LEARNING
A PRESCHOOL

How do you know all this stuff?

My Mom read the school brochure to me.

And my brother Petey went here.

Petey did?

You can still see the scratches his fingernails made on the sidewalk when he was dragged into school one memorable Monday.

So much for my theory about the giant chicken.

R. Thompson

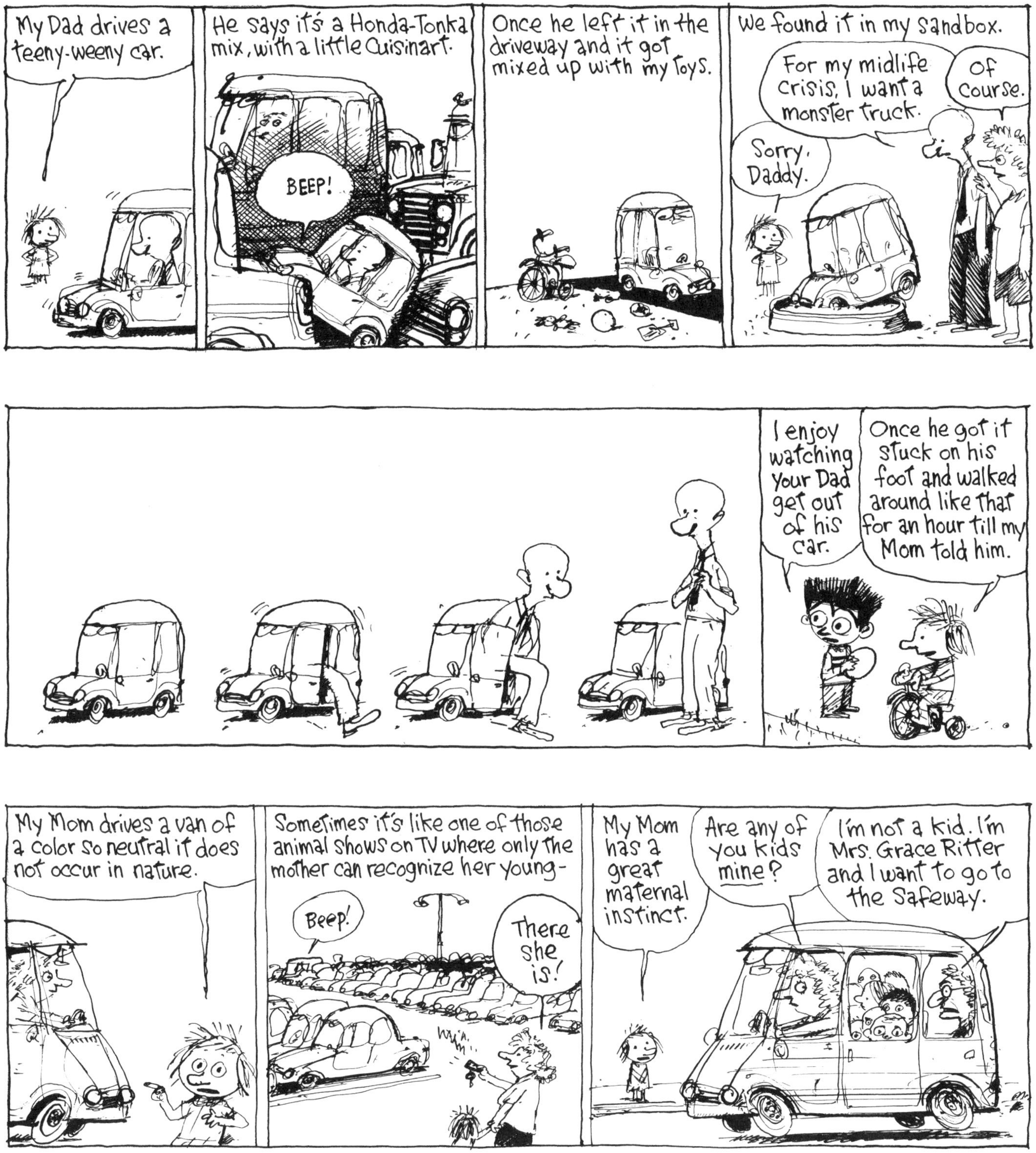

My Dad drives a teeny-weeny car.
He says it's a Honda-Tonka mix, with a little Cuisinart.
BEEP!
Once he left it in the driveway and it got mixed up with my toys.
We found it in my sandbox.
For my midlife crisis, I want a monster truck.
Of course.
Sorry, Daddy.
I enjoy watching your Dad get out of his car.
Once he got it stuck on his foot and walked around like that for an hour till my Mom told him.
My Mom drives a van of a color so neutral it does not occur in nature.
Sometimes it's like one of those animal shows on TV where only the mother can recognize her young-
Beep!
There she is!
My Mom has a great maternal instinct.
Are any of you kids mine?
I'm not a kid. I'm Mrs. Grace Ritter and I want to go to the Safeway.

Panel 1: Mine.

Panel 2: Mine.

Panel 3: Mine. | No.

Panel 4: Every day I test the boundaries of my domain. | Of course. We learn by grabbing.

Panel 1: Dill, want to climb on the big jungle gym? | Alice! Are you joking?

Panel 2: I've heard of kids getting lost in that thing for years at a time!

Panel 3: Then one day emerging unexpectedly from a tube slide, their bodies stooped with age, their gray beards brushing the ground... | Is that a yes or a no?

What is that? | A sign about a lady.

SALE

Why're there balloons? | Maybe it's her birthday.

FRANKL POTTS Realty

Should we get her a present? | Not a scarf. Looks like she's wearing six of 'em already. | I want a sign like that for my birthday.

SALE

R. Thompson

Ah, perfect!
Jeez, that's her worst one yet.
Aw, I think it's cute. She's only 4.
PIZZA 24
Photographs! You are so sentimental.
Yeah? Comic strips are supposed to be funny. You aren't funny.
DIET PLAN
And you're bitter because I'll go into a photo album, but you'll just go in the trash!
Ah, I hope your magnet degausses.
BE QUIET, OR I'LL EAT YOU!
Oh, I wouldn't do that.
LI'L STEP
R. Thompson

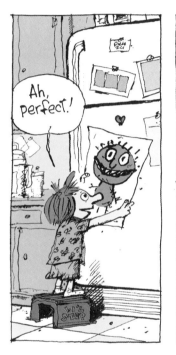

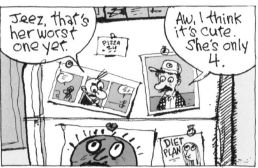

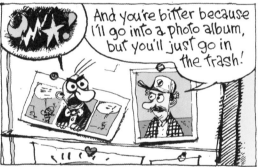

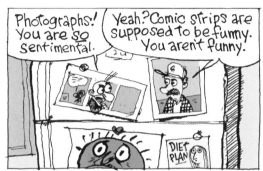

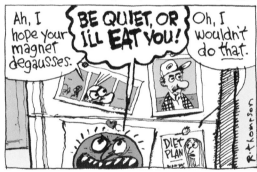

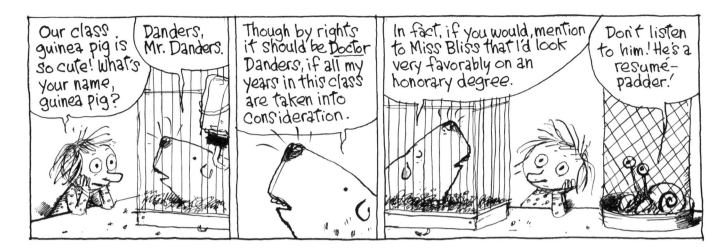

Panel 1: Our class guinea pig is so cute! What's your name, guinea pig?

Panel 2: Danders, Mr. Danders.

Panel 3: Though by rights it should be Doctor Danders, if all my years in this class are taken into consideration.

Panel 4: In fact, if you would, mention to Miss Bliss that I'd look very favorably on an honorary degree.

Panel 5: Don't listen to him! He's a resumé-padder!

Panel 6: I hadn't realized guinea pigs hate hermit crabs.

Oh, yes—

Panel 7: In the wild, guinea pigs and hermit crabs are deadly enemies. They engage in vicious battles lasting for <u>days</u>.

Panel 8: I saw one of those on a TV nature show. It was real pathetic.

OH! IF THESE BARS DID NOT CONSTRAIN ME YOU'D SEE SOMETHING EPIC!

HA!

Panel 9: What a cute rabbit! Does it have a name?

"Polyfill." My brother read it on the tag.

Panel 10: She's actually a doggie chew-toy that I rescued. If I hadn't, she would've been ripped to shreds, like on those animal TV shows with all the lions and the blood and guts all over the place.

Panel 11: Then the hyenas show up and it's—

Hey, Miss Bliss?

Panel 12: Adults never pay enough attention to me.

I have the opposite problem.

R. Thompson

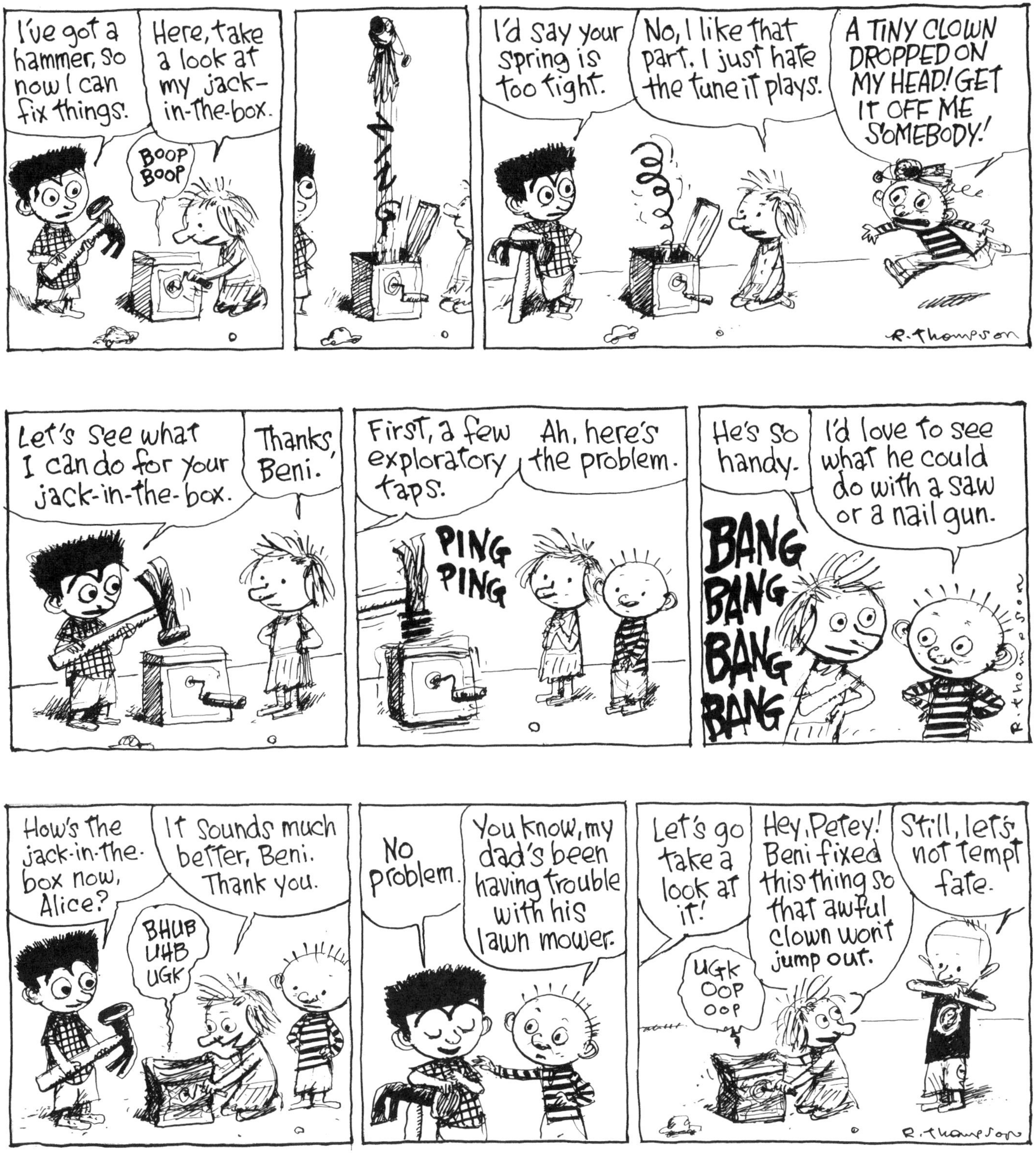
I've got a hammer, so now I can fix things!
Here, take a look at my jack-in-the-box.
BOOP BOOP
ZING
I'd say your spring is too tight.
No, I like that part. I just hate the tune it plays!
A TINY CLOWN DROPPED ON MY HEAD! GET IT OFF ME SOMEBODY!
R. Thompson
Let's see what I can do for your jack-in-the-box.
Thanks, Beni.
First, a few exploratory taps.
PING PING
Ah, here's the problem.
He's so handy.
BANG BANG BANG BANG BANG
I'd love to see what he could do with a saw or a nail gun.
R. Thompson
How's the jack-in-the-box now, Alice?
BHUB UHB UGK
It sounds much better, Beni. Thank you.
No problem.
You know, my dad's been having trouble with his lawn mower.
Let's go take a look at it!
UGK OOP OOP
Hey, Petey! Beni fixed this thing so that awful clown won't jump out.
Still, let's not tempt fate.
R. Thompson

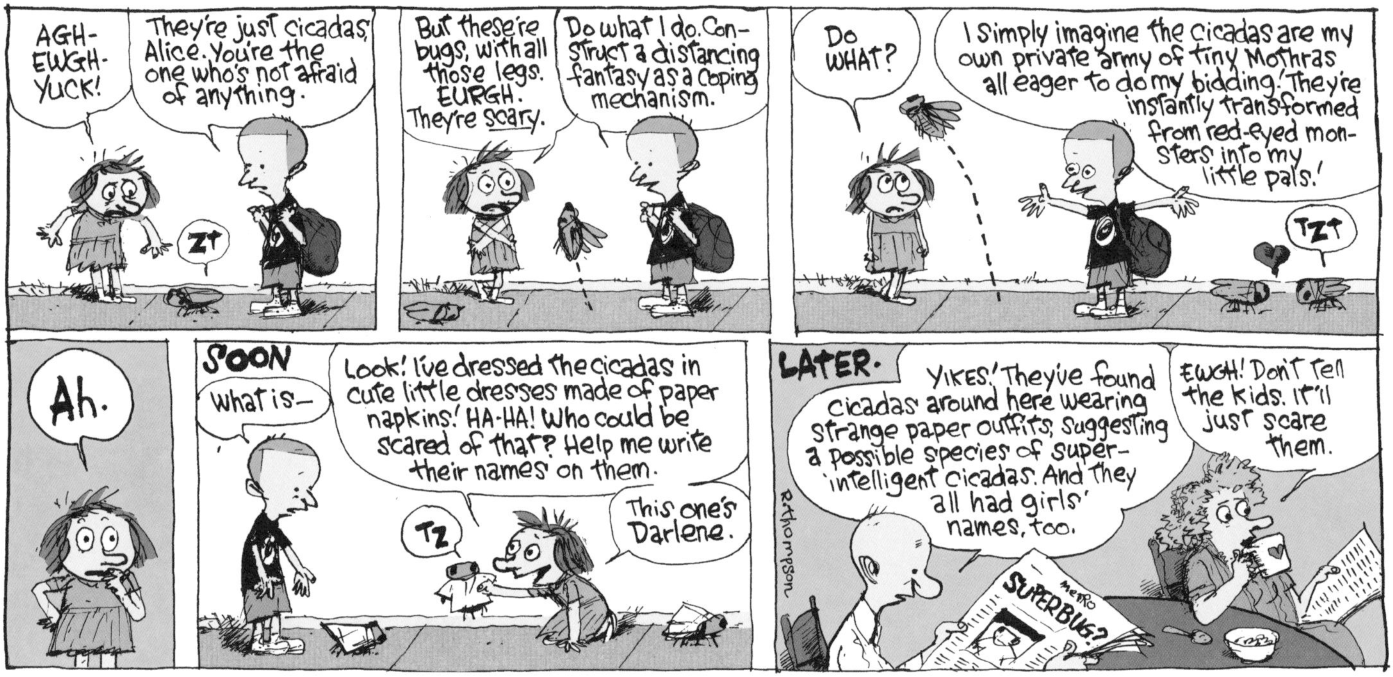
AGH-EWGH-YUCK!
They're just cicadas, Alice. You're the one who's not afraid of anything.
ZT
But these're bugs, with all those legs. EURGH. They're scary.
Do what I do. Construct a distancing fantasy as a coping mechanism.
Do WHAT?
I simply imagine the cicadas are my own private army of tiny Mothras all eager to do my bidding! They're instantly transformed from red-eyed monsters into my little pals!
TZT
Ah.
SOON
What is—
Look! I've dressed the cicadas in cute little dresses made of paper napkins! HA-HA! Who could be scared of that? Help me write their names on them.
TZ
This one's Darlene.
R.Thompson
LATER.
YIKES! They've found cicadas around here wearing strange paper outfits, suggesting a possible species of super-intelligent cicadas. And they all had girls' names, too.
METRO
SUPERBUG?
EWGH! Don't tell the kids. It'll just scare them.

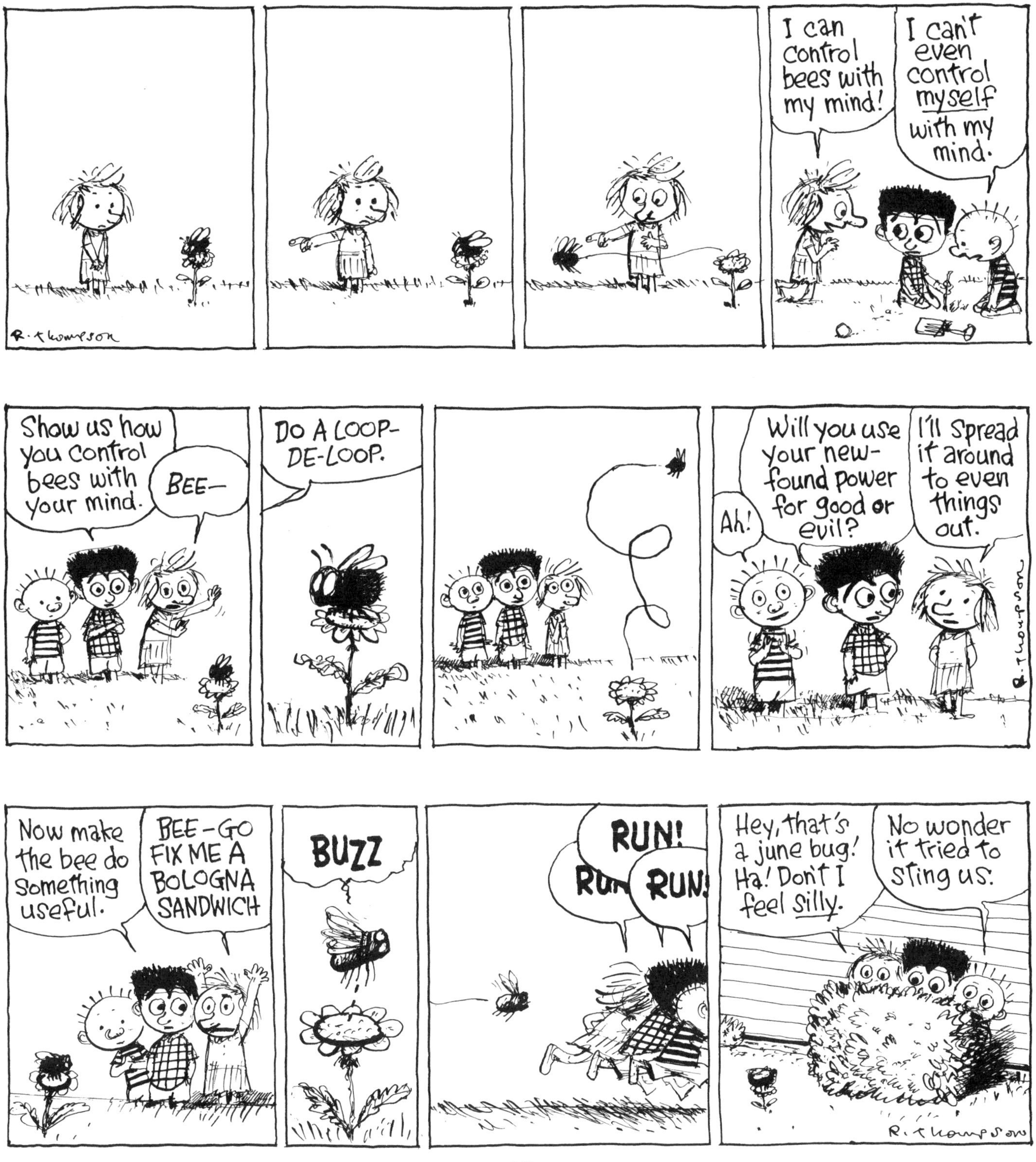
R. Thompson
I can control bees with my mind!
I can't even control myself with my mind.
Show us how you control bees with your mind.
BEE—
DO A LOOP-DE-LOOP.
Ah!
Will you use your new-found power for good or evil?
I'll spread it around to even things out.
R. Thompson
Now make the bee do something useful.
BEE—GO FIX ME A BOLOGNA SANDWICH
BUZZ
RUN!
RUN!
RUN!
Hey, that's a june bug! Ha! Don't I feel silly.
No wonder it tried to sting us.
R. Thompson

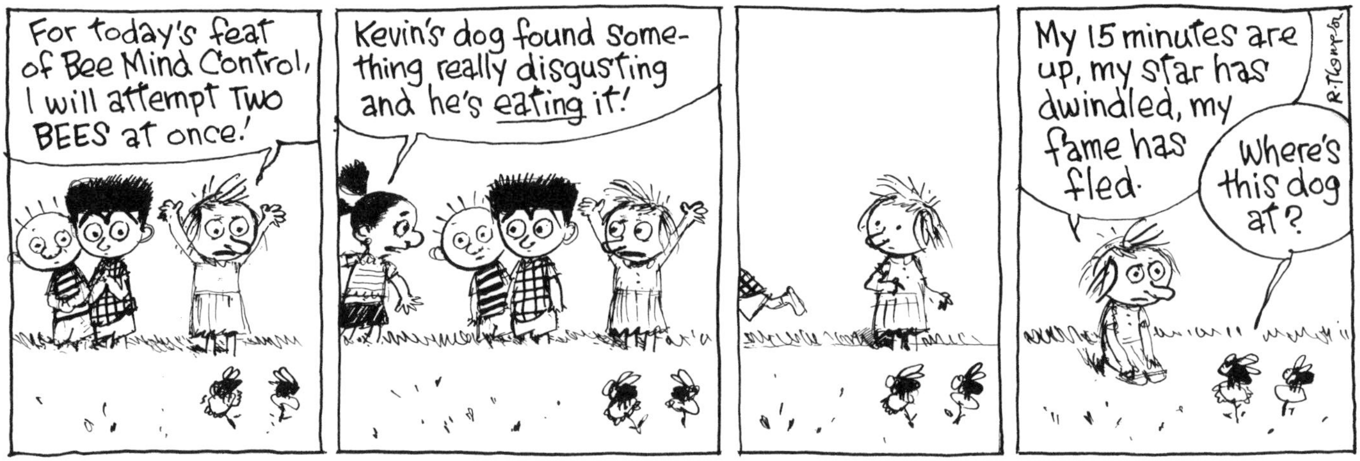
For today's feat of Bee Mind Control, I will attempt TWO BEES at once!
Kevin's dog found something really disgusting and he's eating it!
My 15 minutes are up, my star has dwindled, my fame has fled.
Where's this dog at?

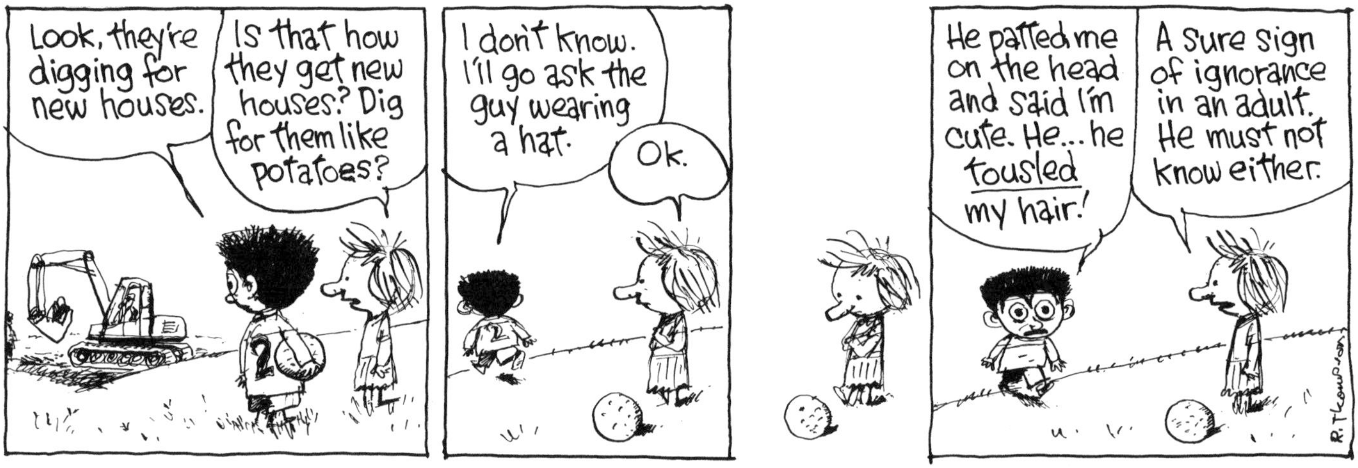
Look, they're digging for new houses.
Is that how they get new houses? Dig for them like potatoes?
I don't know. I'll go ask the guy wearing a hat.
Ok.
He patted me on the head and said I'm cute. He... he tousled my hair!
A sure sign of ignorance in an adult. He must not know either.

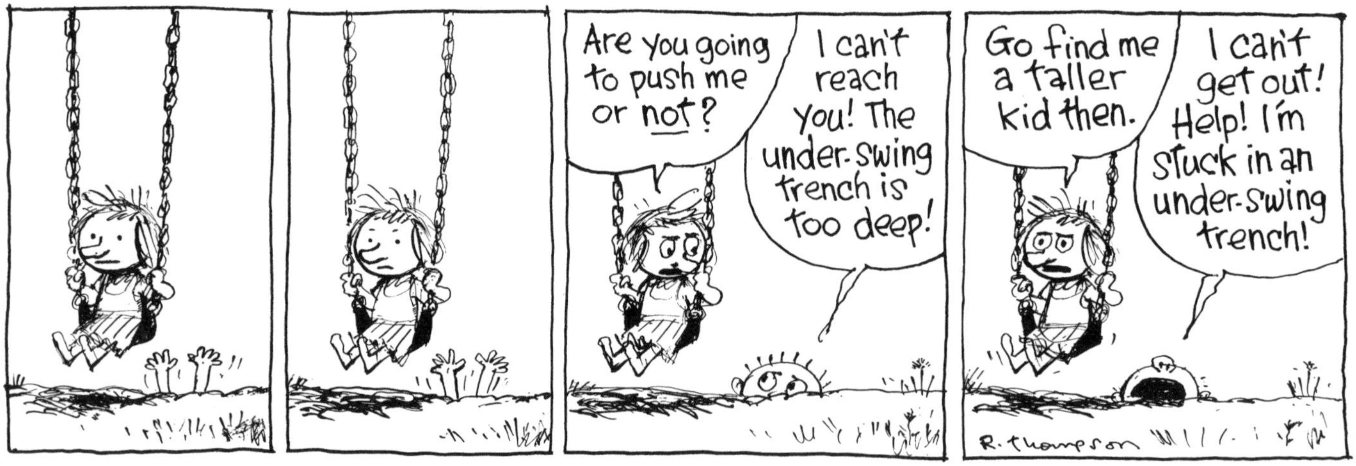
Are you going to push me or not?
I can't reach you! The under-swing trench is too deep!
Go find me a taller kid then.
I can't get out! Help! I'm stuck in an under-swing trench!
R. Thompson

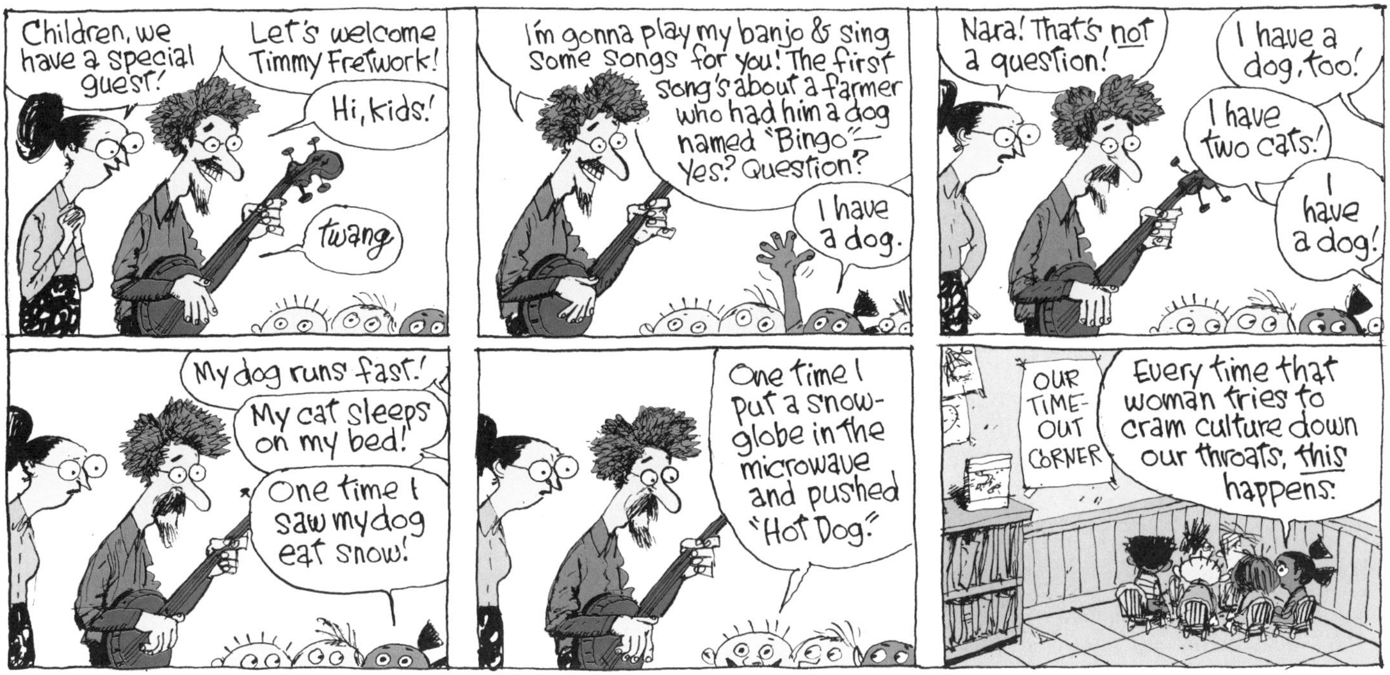
Children, we have a special guest!
Let's welcome Timmy Fretwork!
Hi, kids!
twang
I'm gonna play my banjo & sing some songs for you! The first song's about a farmer who had him a dog named "Bingo"— Yes? Question?
I have a dog.
Nara! That's not a question!
I have a dog, too!
I have two cats!
I have a dog!
My dog runs fast!
My cat sleeps on my bed!
One time I saw my dog eat snow!
One time I put a snow-globe in the microwave and pushed "Hot Dog."
OUR TIME-OUT CORNER
Every time that woman tries to cram culture down our throats, this happens.

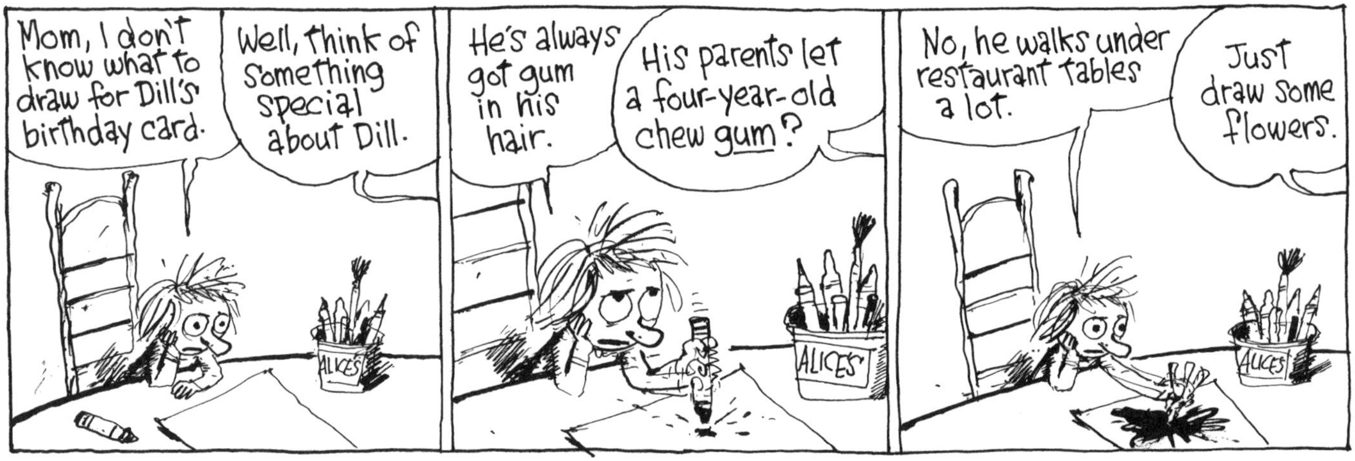
Mom, I don't know what to draw for Dill's birthday card.
Well, think of something special about Dill.
He's always got gum in his hair.
His parents let a four-year-old chew gum?
No, he walks under restaurant tables a lot.
Just draw some flowers.
ALICE'S

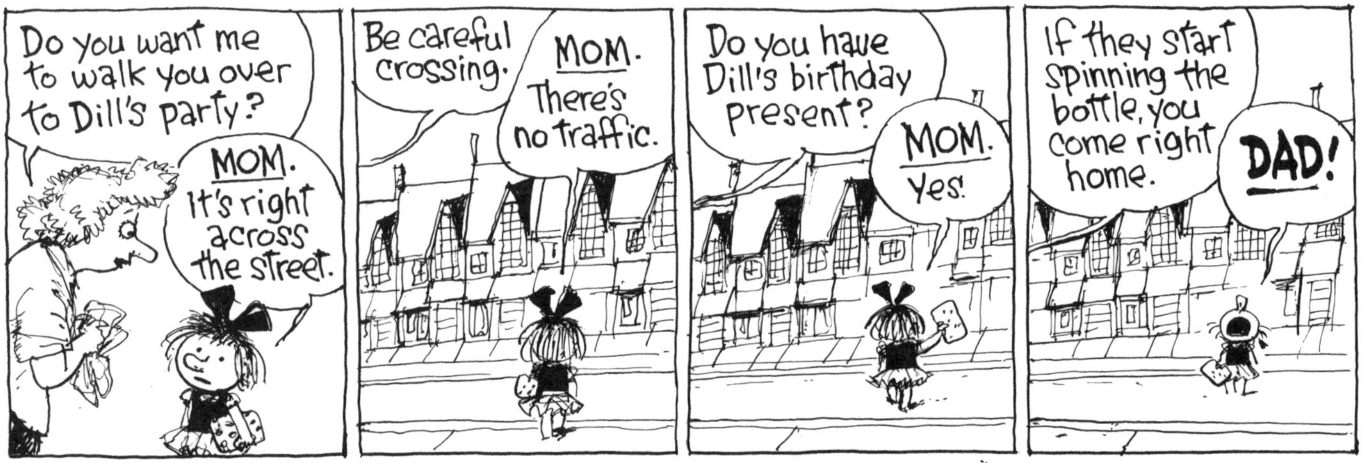
Do you want me to walk you over to Dill's party?
MOM. It's right across the street.
Be careful crossing.
MOM. There's no traffic.
Do you have Dill's birthday present?
MOM. Yes!
If they start spinning the bottle, you come right home.
DAD!

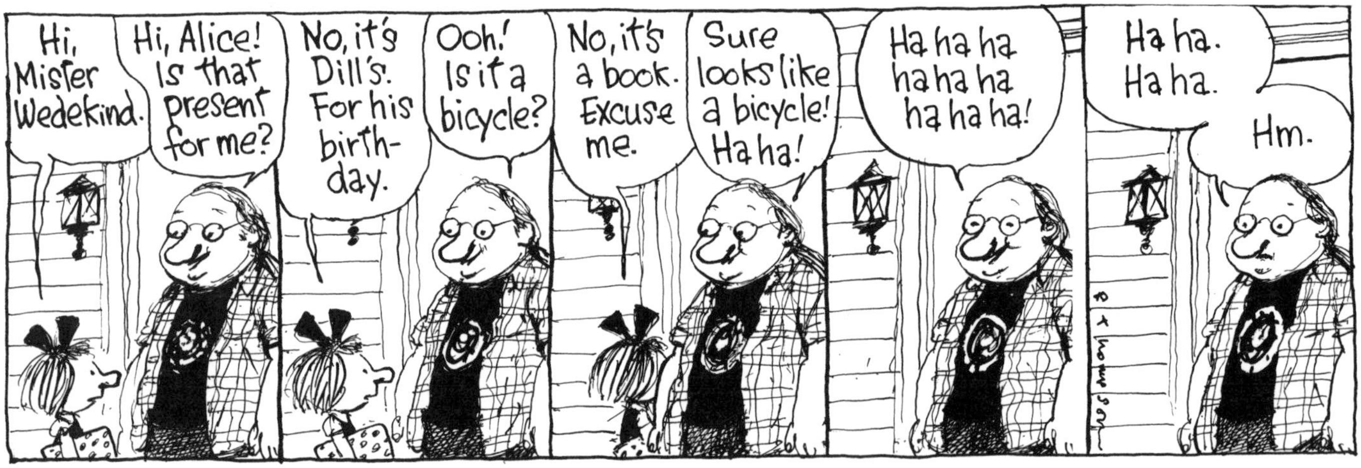
Hi, Mister Wedekind.
Hi, Alice! Is that present for me?
No, it's Dill's. For his birth-day.
Ooh! Is it a bicycle?
No, it's a book. Excuse me.
Sure looks like a bicycle! Ha ha!
Ha ha ha ha ha ha ha ha ha!
Ha ha. Ha ha.
Hm.

Panel 1:
Happy Birthday, Dill.
Hi, Alice! Here's your goodie bag.

Panel 2:
Where is everybody?
They, um, they...

Panel 3:
Did you give them their goodie bags and they all went home?
Uh-huh.

Panel 4:
You confused them! You're supposed to give out the goodie bags LAST!
I'm not very good at this...

Panel 5:
What do we do now?
Here's a birthday party game! I'll put a sticker on your head.

Panel 6:
Why?
Now I'll put one on my head, and we'll ask questions to find out what's on them!

Panel 7:
Okay. Why have you got a duck stuck on your head?
I don't know. What are you doing with a frog stuck on yours?

Panel 8:
That was fun.
Wait, who won? The winner gets a plastic whistle.

Panel 9:
Alice! You're home already! How was Dill's party?
Awful.

Panel 10:
Nobody else was there, the games were boring, his mom made his birthday cake a CARROT CAKE. Ick.

Panel 11:
And look what's in the goodie bag— a little package of soy sauce, some frilly toothpicks and a teenie-weenie bottle of shampoo.

Panel 12:
What are those things all over you?
Dill and I got into a sticker fight and I won! That part was great!

67

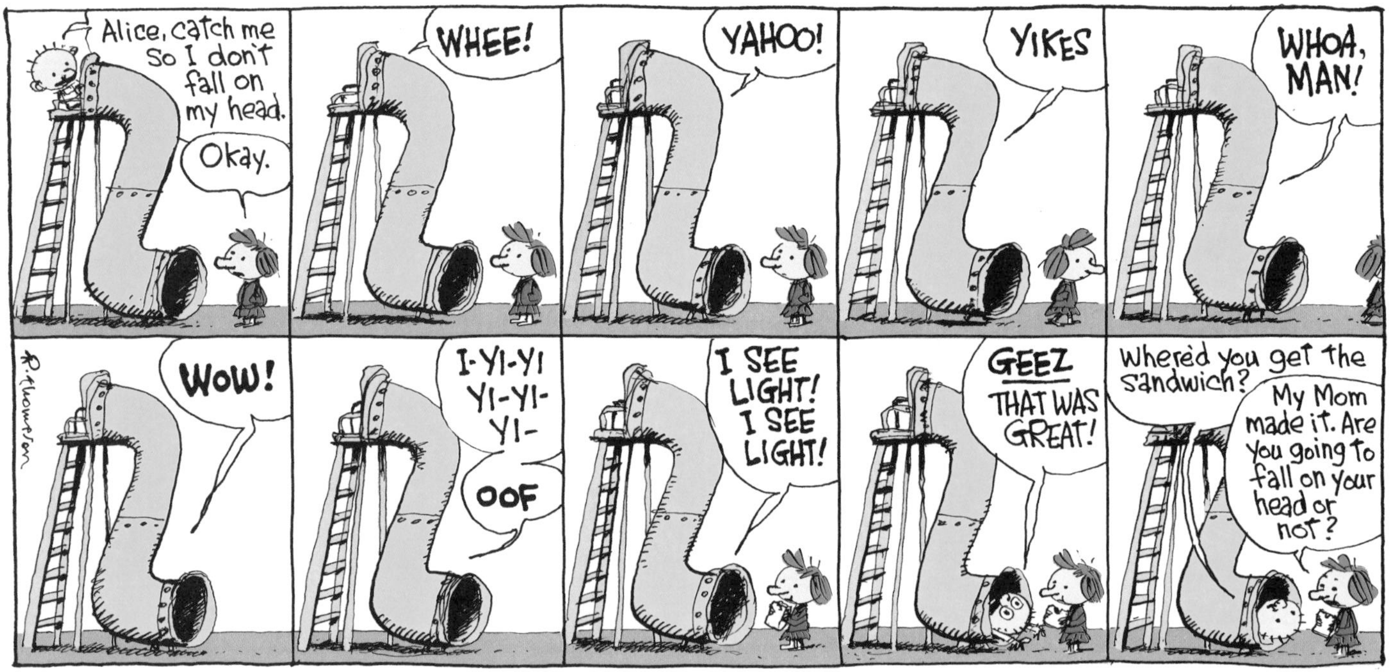
Alice, catch me so I don't fall on my head.
Okay.
WHEE!
YAHOO!
YIKES
WHOA, MAN!
WOW!
I-YI-YI YI-YI-YI-
OOF
I SEE LIGHT! I SEE LIGHT!
GEEZ THAT WAS GREAT!
Where'd you get the sandwich?
My Mom made it. Are you going to fall on your head or not?

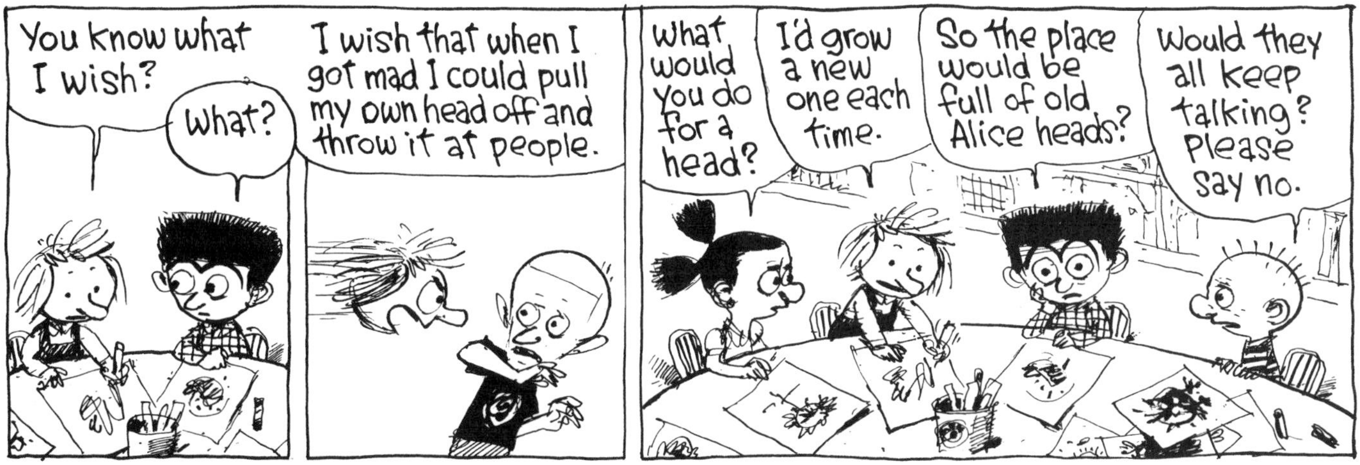
You know what I wish?
What?
I wish that when I got mad I could pull my own head off and throw it at people.
What would you do for a head?
I'd grow a new one each time.
So the place would be full of old Alice heads?
Would they all keep talking? Please say no.

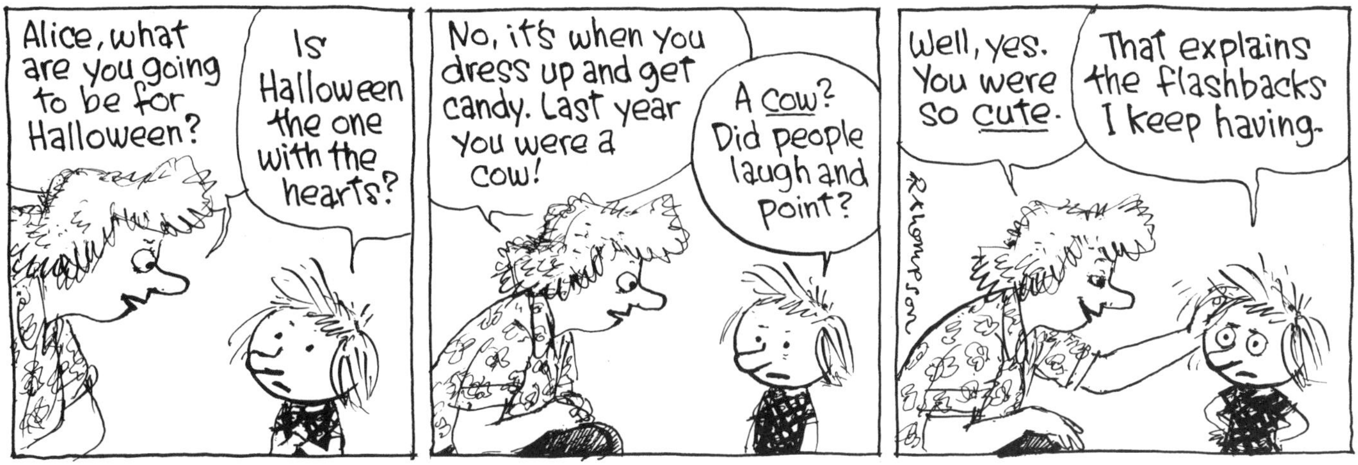
Alice, what are you going to be for Halloween?
Is Halloween the one with the hearts?
No, it's when you dress up and get candy. Last year you were a cow!
A cow? Did people laugh and point?
Well, yes. You were so cute.
That explains the flashbacks I keep having.

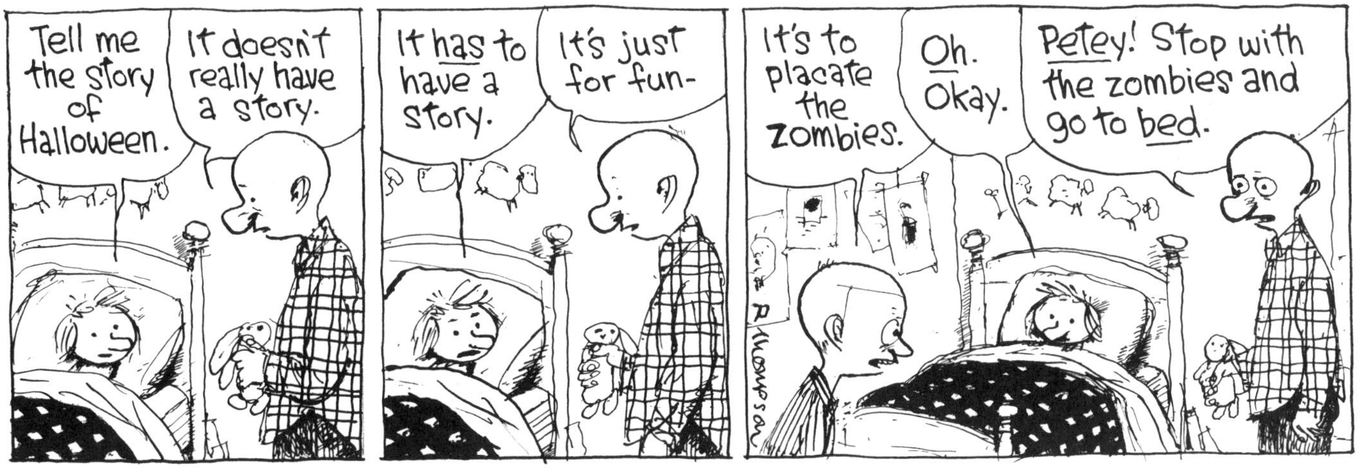
Tell me the story of Halloween.
It doesn't really have a story.
It has to have a story.
It's just for fun.
It's to placate the zombies.
Oh. Okay.
Petey! Stop with the zombies and go to bed.

Panel 1: "I want to be this for Halloween." "What?"

Panel 2: "It's a crayon sharpener shaped like a cat. It's my favorite thing!" "I'll tape it to my head."

Panel 3: "There! Tell me I don't look scary." "I don't think you've grasped the possibilities of Halloween."

R. Thompson

Panel 4: "I want to be this for Halloween." "What?"

Panel 5: "Princess Fairyqueen, Queen of all the Fairy Princesses. She's my favorite thing."

To all my friends, Princess Queen

Panel 6: "Um, okay. We can make a costume—" "And the wings have to really fly. And the wand really shoots a death ray."

R. Thompson

Panel 7: "I'm going like this for Halloween."

Panel 8:

BOO!

Panel 9: "It's dignified yet expressive."

Panel 10: "How about 'Boo,' no exclamation point?" "Even better!"

R. Thompson

Look, Petey! Mom finally finished my costume! See? I'm Princess Fairyqueen!

Who's that?

Princess Fairyqueen! She's the star of those TV cartoons! Plus she's got books, DVDs, CDs, a weekly magazine, video games, lunchboxes, snacks, millions of toys—

She's on breakfast cereals, linens, shower curtains, sleepwear, active wear, athletic shoes, bandages, hats, scarves, baby items, a vast interactive web site, an airmail stamp in Pago Pago, a limited-edition SUV—

And a fast food franchise, theme parks, a cable network, a chain of children's hair salons, an ironic novel by Dave Eggers, cough syrup, an ice show—

This costume is too itchy. I want to be a kitty cat instead.

I'll go tell Mom.

"Tonight: A Fickle Four-Year-Old Brings the Economy to a Grinding Halt."

"In a Related Development, a Local Woman Heaves a Sewing Machine Through a Brick Wall."

You WHAT?

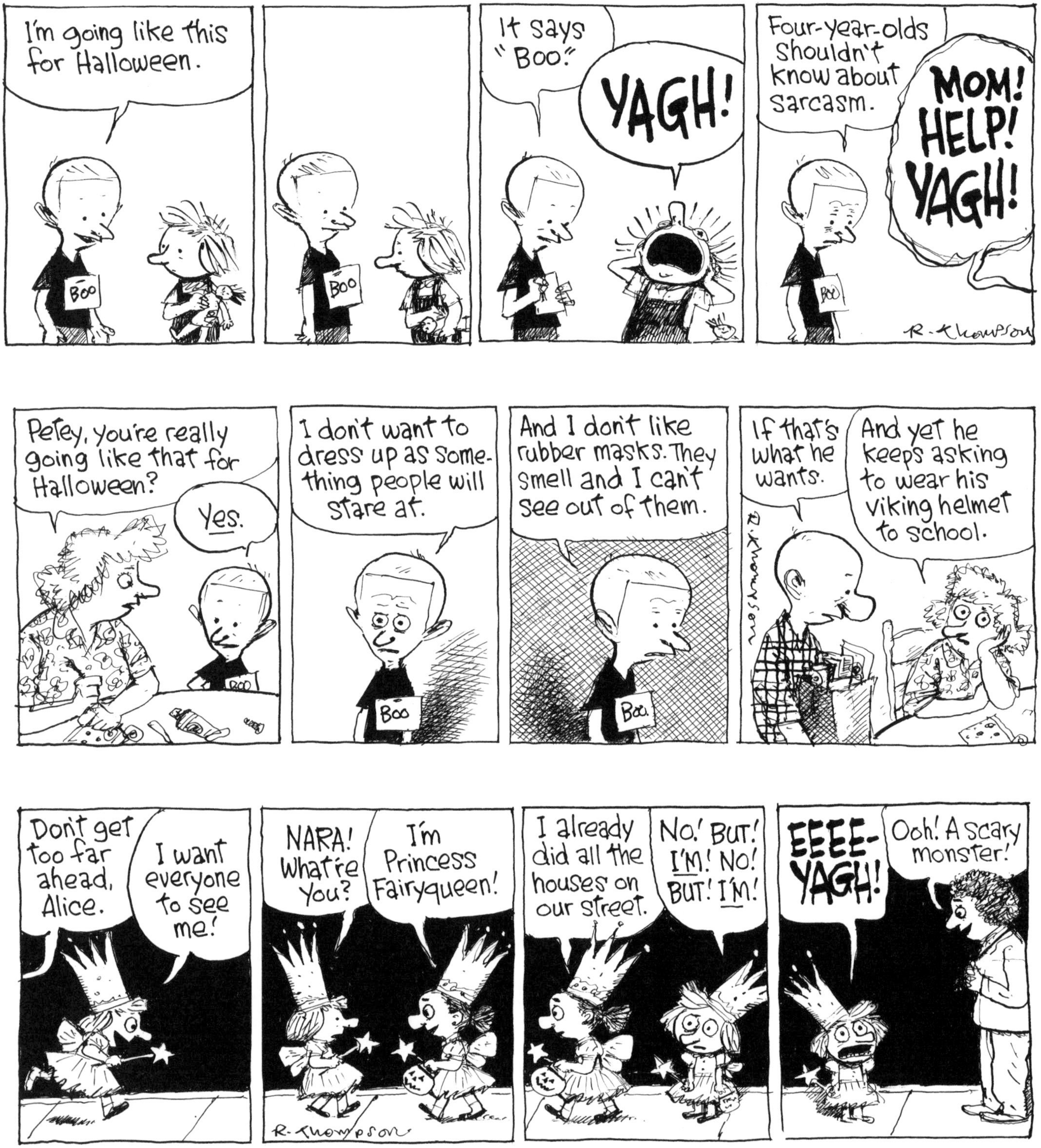
I'm going like this for Halloween.
It says "Boo."
YAGH!
Four-year-olds shouldn't know about sarcasm.
MOM! HELP! YAGH!
R. Thompson
Petey, you're really going like that for Halloween?
Yes.
Boo
I don't want to dress up as something people will stare at.
And I don't like rubber masks. They smell and I can't see out of them.
If that's what he wants.
And yet he keeps asking to wear his viking helmet to school.
R. Thompson
Don't get too far ahead, Alice.
I want everyone to see me!
NARA! What're you?
I'm Princess Fairyqueen!
R. Thompson
I already did all the houses on our street.
No! BUT! I'M! No! BUT! I'M!
EEEE-YAGH!
Ooh! A scary monster!

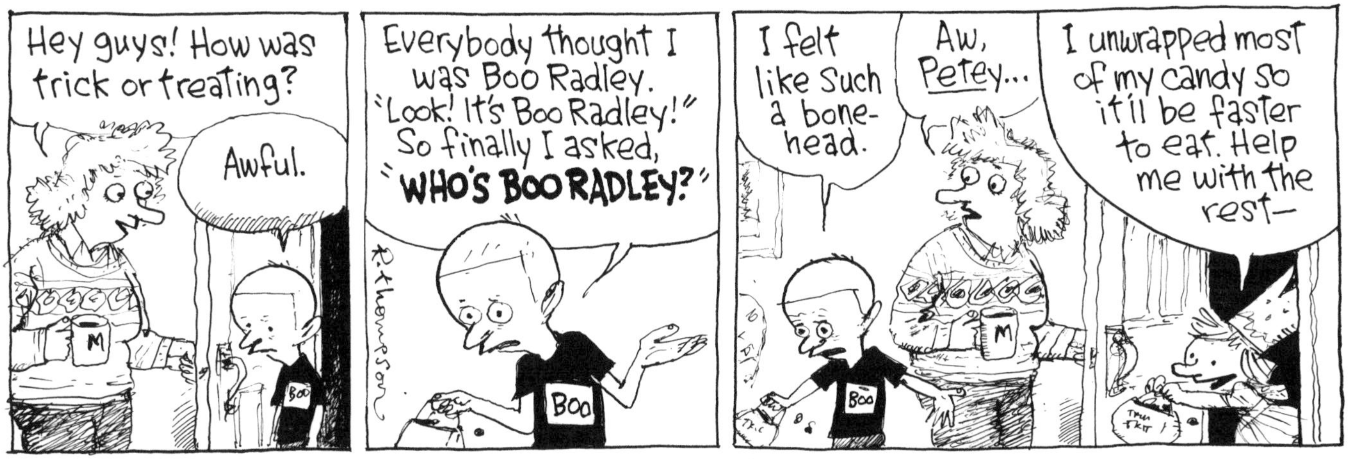
Hey guys! How was trick or treating?
Awful.
Everybody thought I was Boo Radley. "Look! It's Boo Radley!" So finally I asked, "WHO'S BOO RADLEY?"
I felt like such a bone-head.
Aw, Petey...
I unwrapped most of my candy so it'll be faster to eat. Help me with the rest—

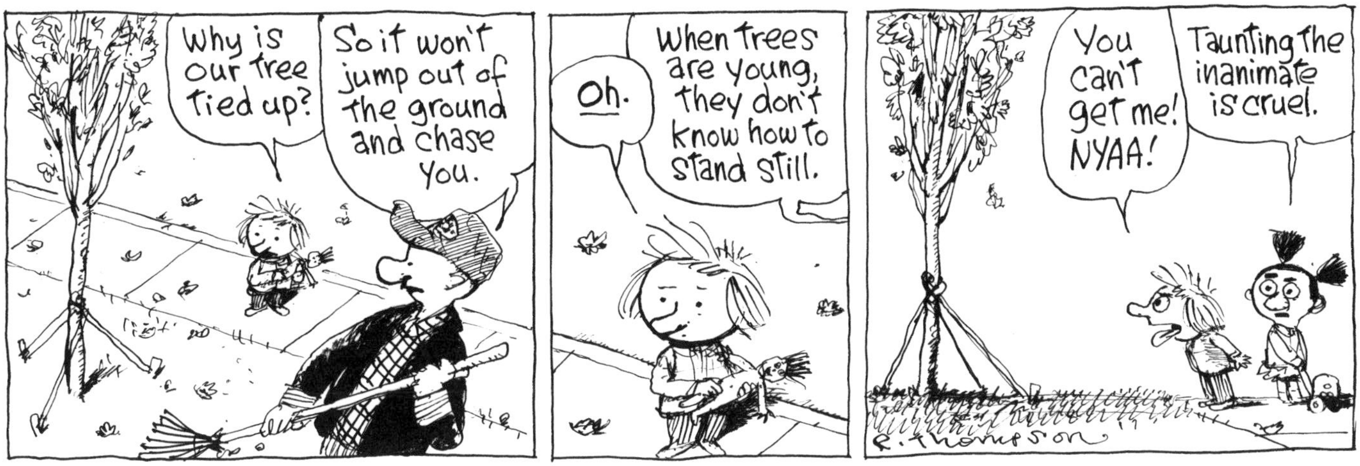
Why is our tree tied up?
So it won't jump out of the ground and chase you.
Oh.
When trees are young, they don't know how to stand still.
You can't get me! NYAA!
Taunting the inanimate is cruel.

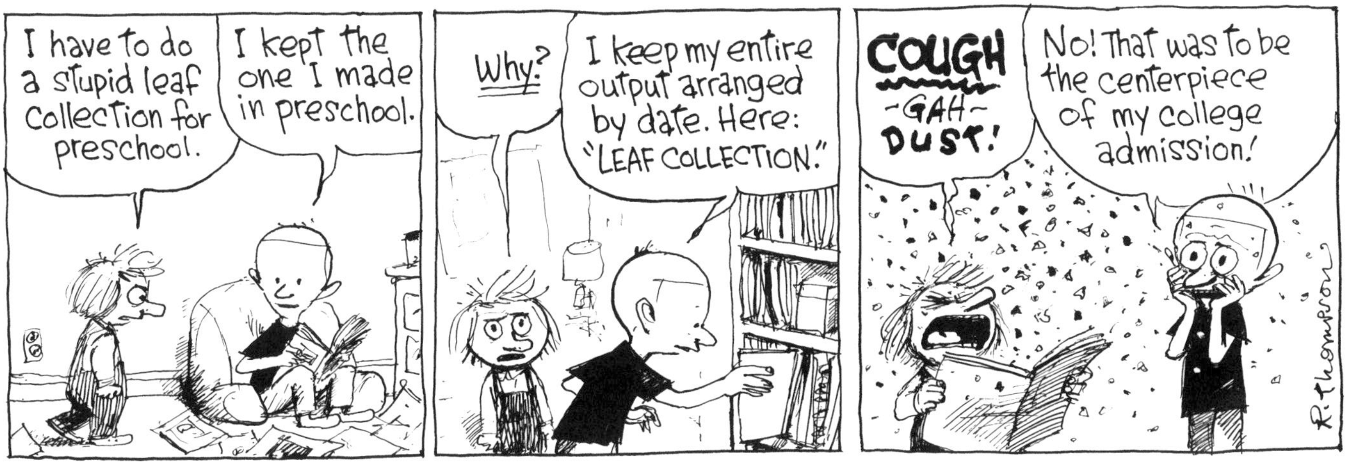
I have to do a stupid leaf collection for preschool.
I kept the one I made in preschool.
Why?
I keep my entire output arranged by date. Here: "LEAF COLLECTION."
COUGH -GAH- DUST!
No! That was to be the centerpiece of my college admission!

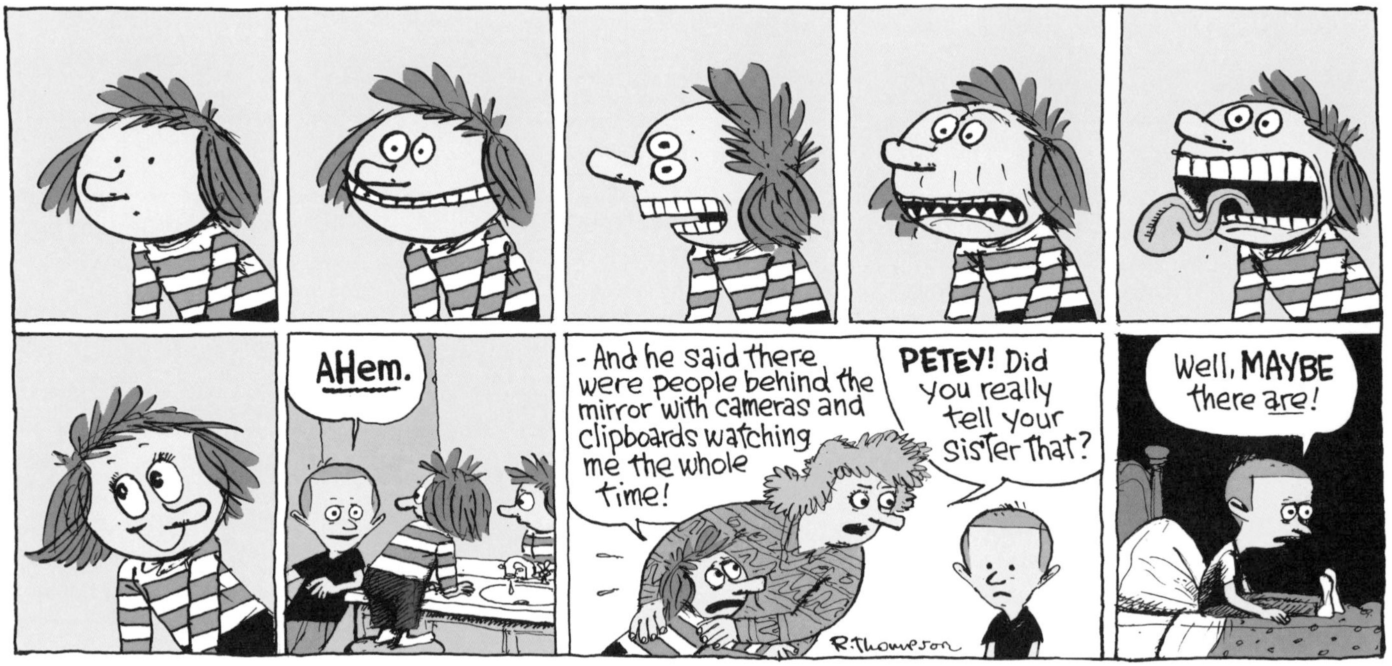
AHem.
- And he said there were people behind the mirror with cameras and clipboards watching me the whole time!
PETEY! Did you really tell your sister that?
Well, MAYBE there are!
R. Thompson

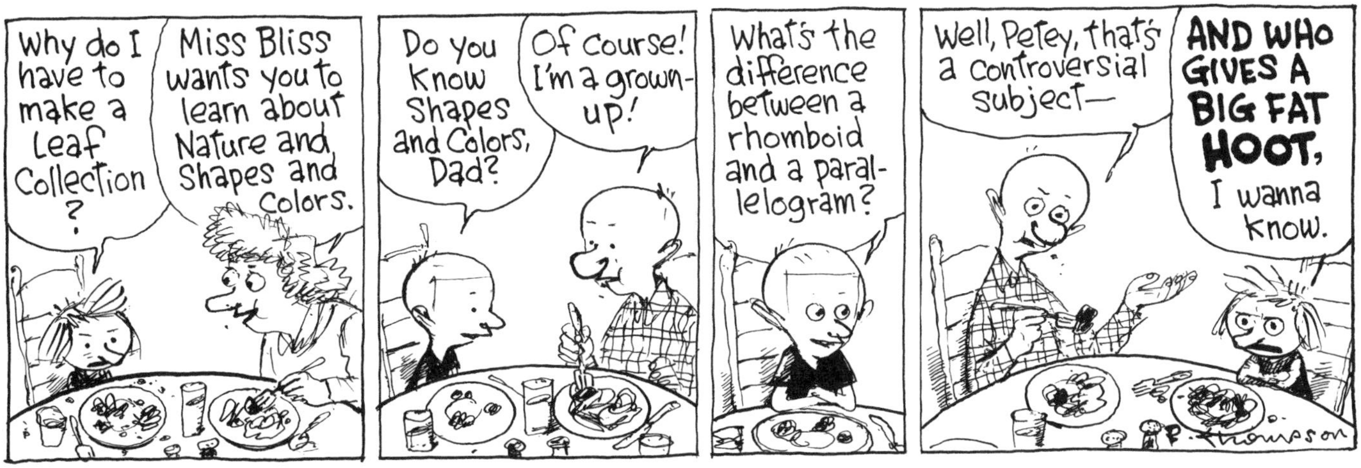
Why do I have to make a Leaf Collection?
Miss Bliss wants you to learn about Nature and Shapes and Colors.
Do you know Shapes and Colors, Dad?
Of course! I'm a grown-up!
What's the difference between a rhomboid and a parallelogram?
Well, Petey, that's a controversial subject—
AND WHO GIVES A BIG FAT HOOT, I wanna know.

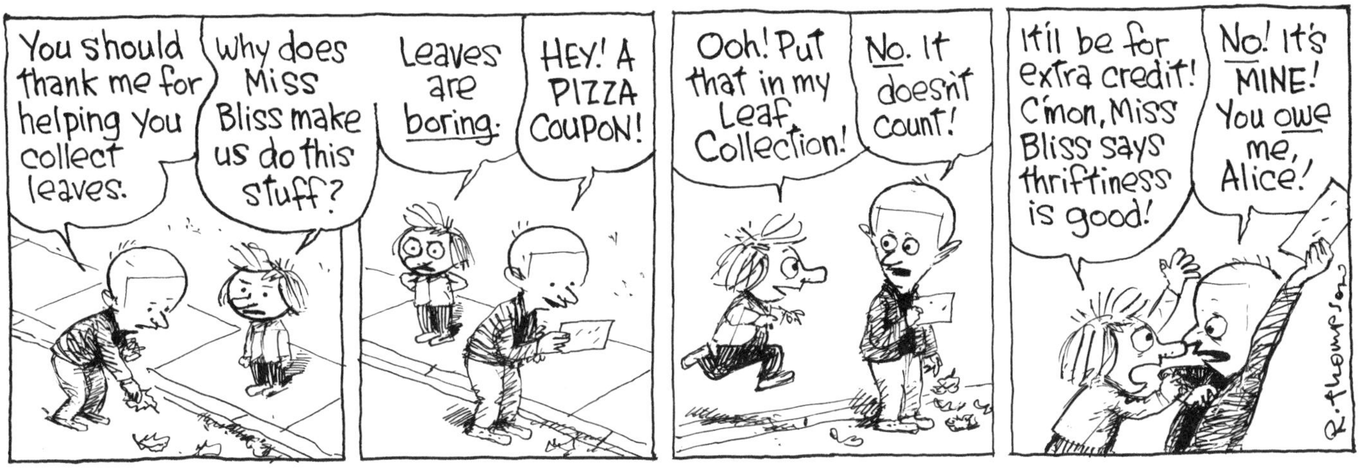
You should thank me for helping you collect leaves.
Why does Miss Bliss make us do this stuff?
Leaves are boring.
HEY! A PIZZA COUPON!
Ooh! Put that in my Leaf Collection!
No. It doesn't count!
It'll be for extra credit! C'mon, Miss Bliss says thriftiness is good!
No! It's MINE! You owe me, Alice!

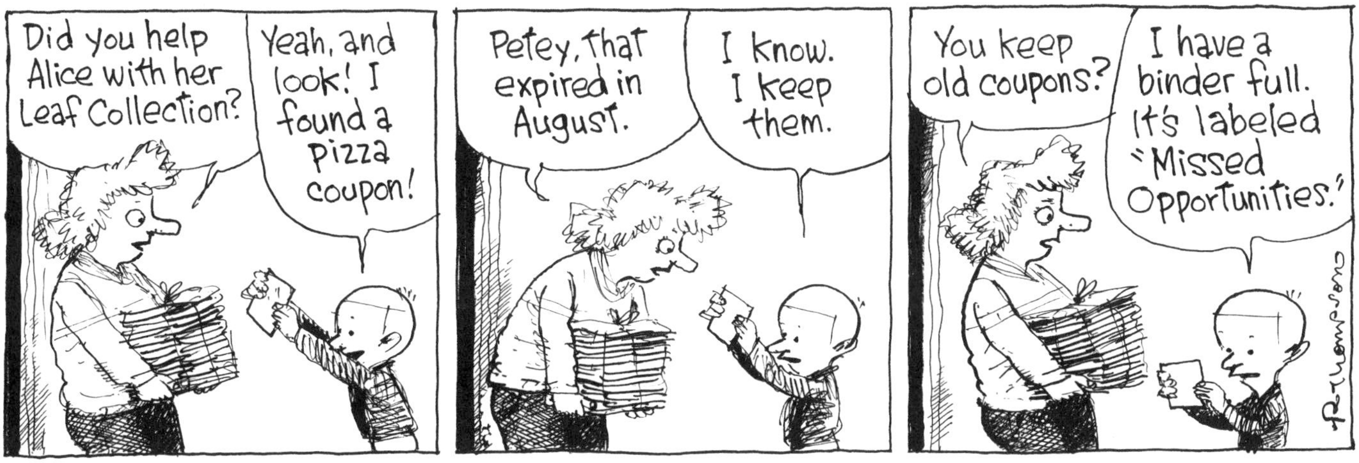
Did you help Alice with her Leaf Collection?
Yeah, and look! I found a pizza coupon!
Petey, that expired in August.
I know. I keep them.
You keep old coupons?
I have a binder full. It's labeled "Missed Opportunities."

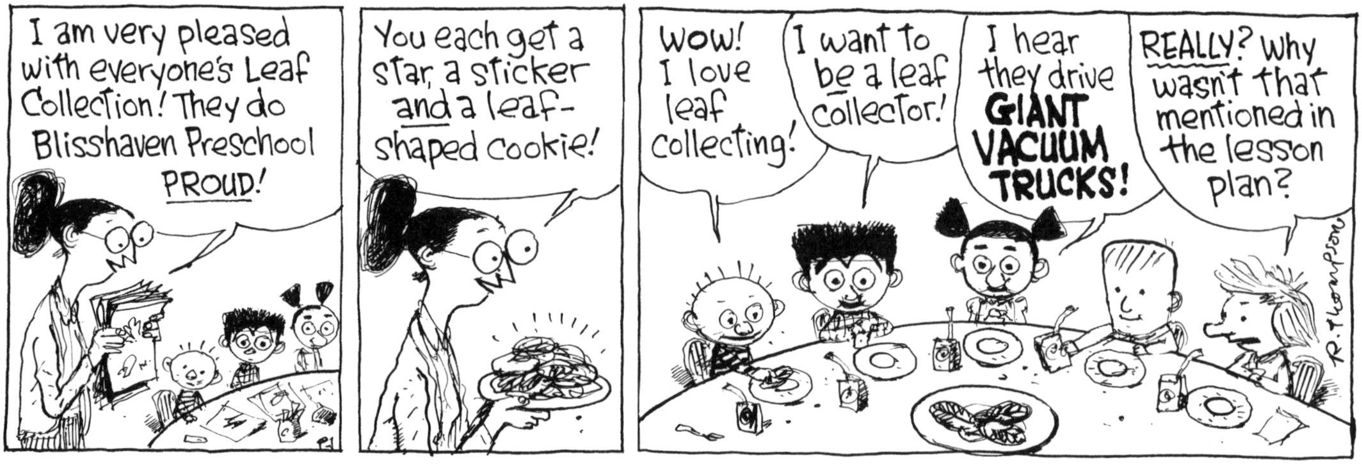
I am very pleased with everyone's Leaf Collection! They do Blisshaven Preschool PROUD!
You each get a star, a sticker and a leaf-shaped cookie!
WOW! I love leaf collecting!
I want to be a leaf collector!
I hear they drive GIANT VACUUM TRUCKS!
REALLY? Why wasn't that mentioned in the lesson plan?
R. Thompson

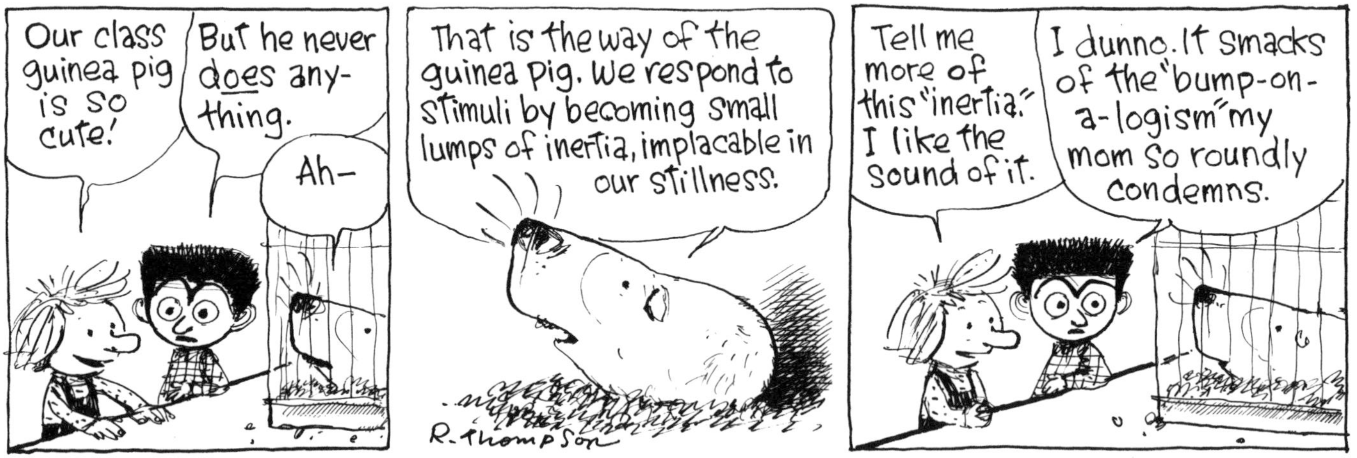
Our class guinea pig is so cute!
But he never does anything.
Ah-
That is the way of the guinea pig. We respond to stimuli by becoming small lumps of inertia, implacable in our stillness.
R. Thompson
Tell me more of this "inertia." I like the sound of it.
I dunno. It smacks of the "bump-on-a-logism" my mom so roundly condemns.

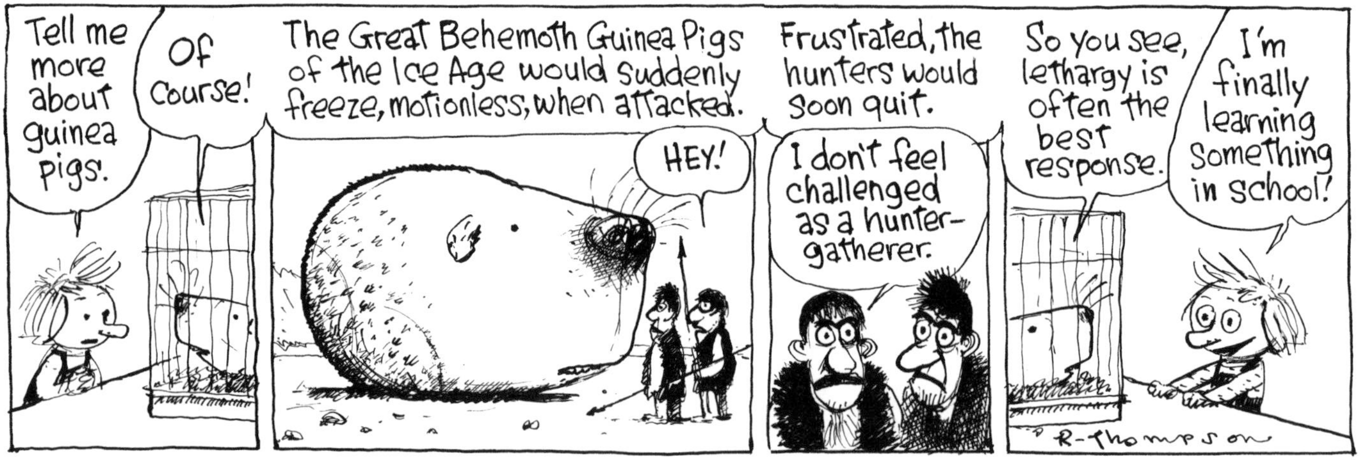
Tell me more about guinea pigs.
Of course!
The Great Behemoth Guinea Pigs of the Ice Age would suddenly freeze, motionless, when attacked.
HEY!
Frustrated, the hunters would soon quit.
I don't feel challenged as a hunter-gatherer.
So you see, lethargy is often the best response.
I'm finally learning something in school!
R. Thompson

Today we're going to use a new communication tool in class! It's called a "Talking Stick."
OOH!
See? It has ribbons and glitter on it to make it special! Whoever holds it speaks while the rest of the class listens attentively.
Who has something to say? Alice? Here, you may be the first to use the Talking Stick!
Yes, Miss Bliss!
OKAY, STAND BACK! I'M DOING THE TALKING! DON'T TRY ANYTHING FUNNY 'CAUSE I HAVE A STICK!
R. Thompson
Miss Bliss, do you swing it like a hammer or like a baseball bat?
Thank you, Alice, you may sit down please!

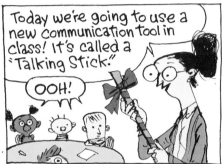

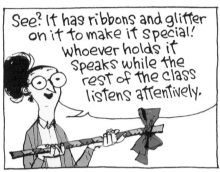

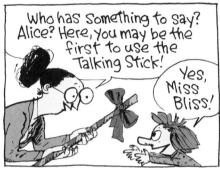

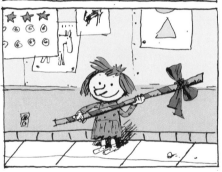

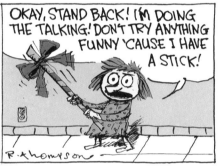

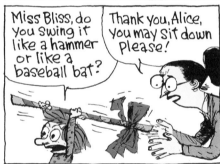

Panel 1: Maybe Dill has something to say and he'd like to hold the Talking Stick.

Yes, Miss Bliss!

Panel 2: HI, I'M MR. STICKY THE TALKING STICK! I'M SURE GLAD I'M NOT STILL GROWING OUT OF SOME STUPID TREE—

Panel 3: WITH A COUPLE OF STUPID BIRDS SITTING ON M—

GRAB

Panel 4: She took it away because "Mr. Sticky" is a dumb name.

PHOOEY.

Panel 5: I think this class still does not know the purpose of the Talking Stick.

Panel 6: The Talking Stick is about deference, respect and taking turns, the keys to civilized discourse.

Panel 7: Look! I made my own Talking Stick!

Me, too, out of a popsicle stick!

Mine has a ribbon!

Mine has a ribbon and glitter! So my Talking Stick is the loudest!

Panel 8: Alice, look. Here's how you can write your own name.

Panel 9: There! **LS**! It's like code for Alice!

REALLY? Let me try—

Panel 10: LS

I did it! HA HA HA!

Panel 11: Will just anyone be able to read this? Am I at risk of identity theft?

There's always that danger.

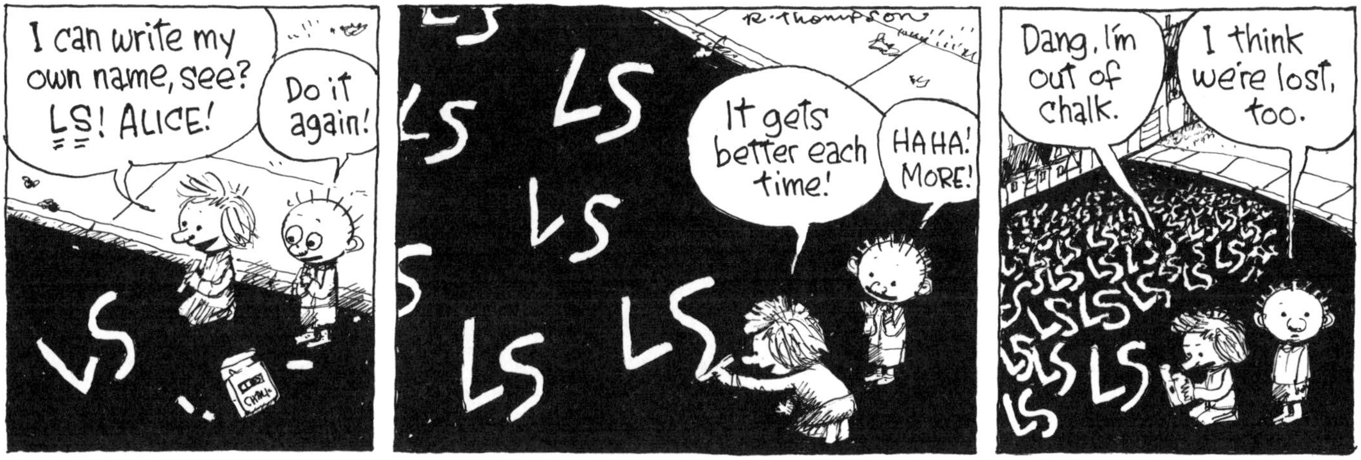
I can write my own name, see? LS! ALICE!
Do it again!
It gets better each time!
HAHA! MORE!
Dang, I'm out of chalk.
I think we're lost, too.

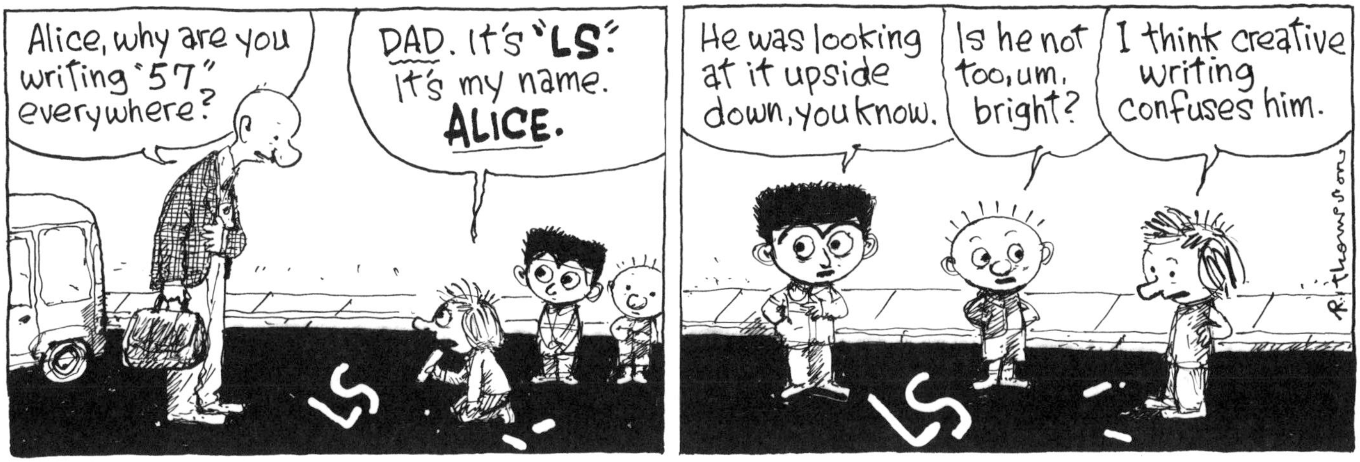
Alice, why are you writing "57" everywhere?
DAD. It's "LS". It's my name. ALICE.
He was looking at it upside down, you know.
Is he not too, um, bright?
I think creative writing confuses him.

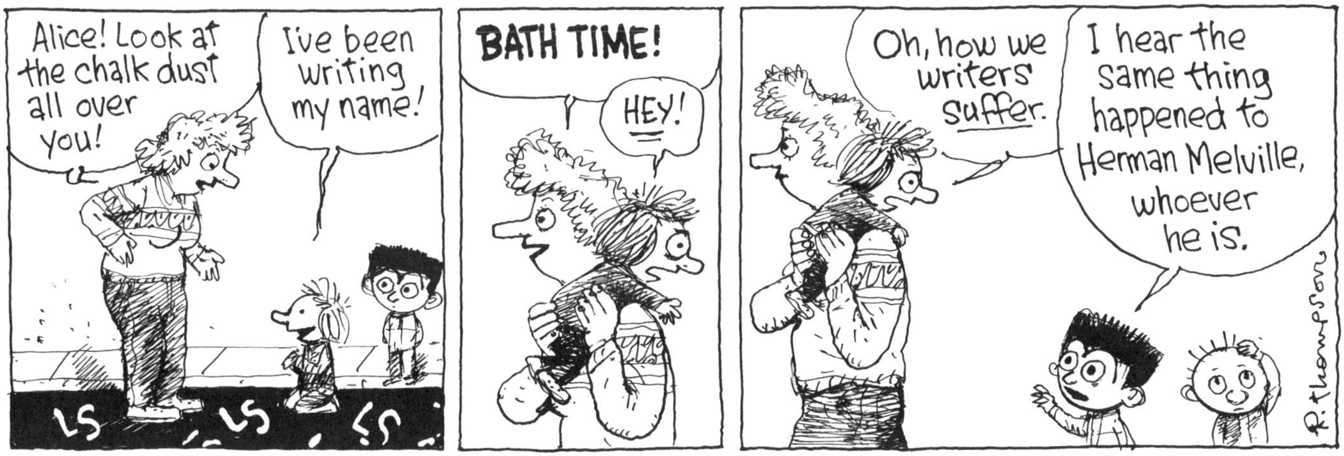
Alice! Look at the chalk dust all over you!
I've been writing my name!
BATH TIME!
HEY!
Oh, how we writers suffer.
I hear the same thing happened to Herman Melville, whoever he is.

Panel 1: "Petey, what's that?" "It's my school project on Thanksgiving. It didn't go so well."

Panel 2: "Why?" "Instead of the FIRST Thanksgiving, I did a diorama of the THIRD Thanksgiving, when they were all getting on each other's nerves."

Panel 3: "See, they're standing around in an awkward silence. And look, everyone hates the stuffing, and the turkey came out dry."

Panel 4: "The Native Americans are sitting at a separate table because all the pilgrims are talking about football. And who cares about that?"

Panel 5: "Ha! It's great! I always love your work!" "Well, my teacher says it didn't fall within the parameters of the assignment. Now it just makes me cringe."

Panel 6: "Would it help if I took it outside and ran over it with my tricycle?" "Sure. Back up over it a few times, too."

R. Thompson

Panel 1: We're going to my Grandma's for Thanksgiving.

Panel 2: She has a dog I'm scared of named Big Shirley.

Panel 3: Petey says Big Shirley probably ate Grandpa.

Panel 4: My grandma tells filthy jokes in Spanish.

Petey also says Grandma puts dog kibble in the stuffing.

Panel 5: My Grandma used to wave at traffic all day.

Panel 6: Then she got tired of traffic. Now she throws deviled eggs at it.

Panel 7: Grandma's got a good arm, too.

Grandma! It's us!

You people need a more distinctive car.

Panel 8: Hi, Grandma! We're here for Thanksgiving Dinner!

Panel 9: Show her the food.

Look, Grandma! Food! FOOOOOD! We bring food! Friends!

Panel 10: Alice! Stop THAT!

You can come in, but those better not be beets.

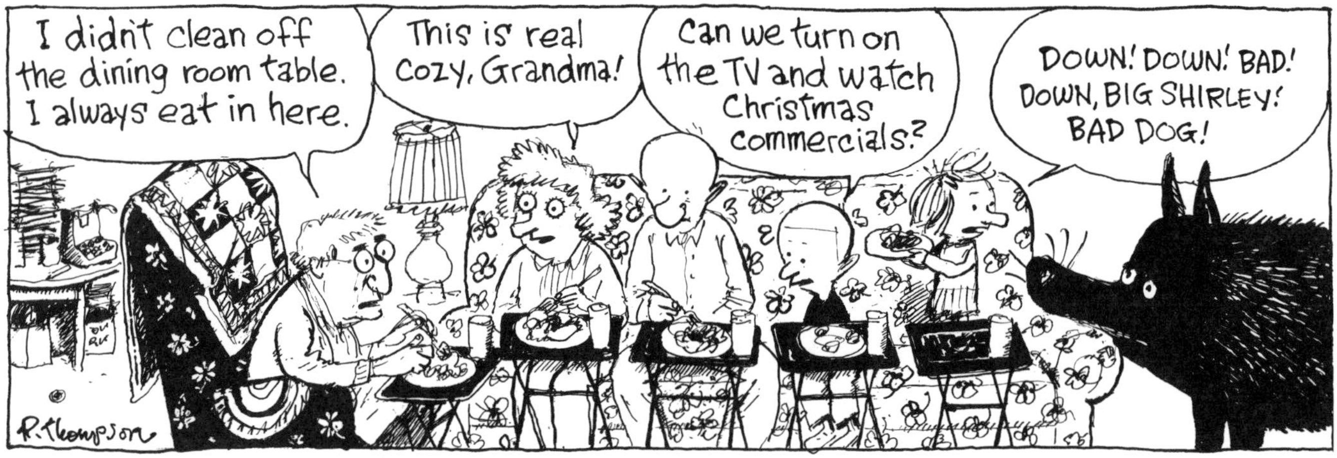
I didn't clean off the dining room table. I always eat in here.
This is real cozy, Grandma!
Can we turn on the TV and watch Christmas commercials?
DOWN! DOWN! BAD! DOWN, BIG SHIRLEY! BAD DOG!
R. Thompson

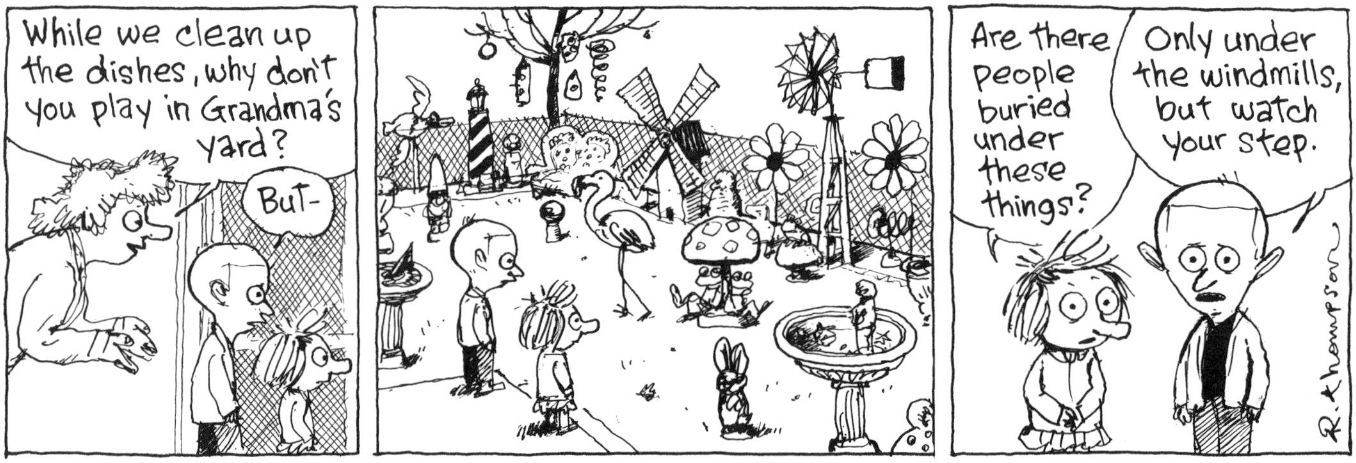
While we clean up the dishes, why don't you play in Grandma's yard?
But-
Are there people buried under these things?
Only under the windmills, but watch your step.
R. Thompson

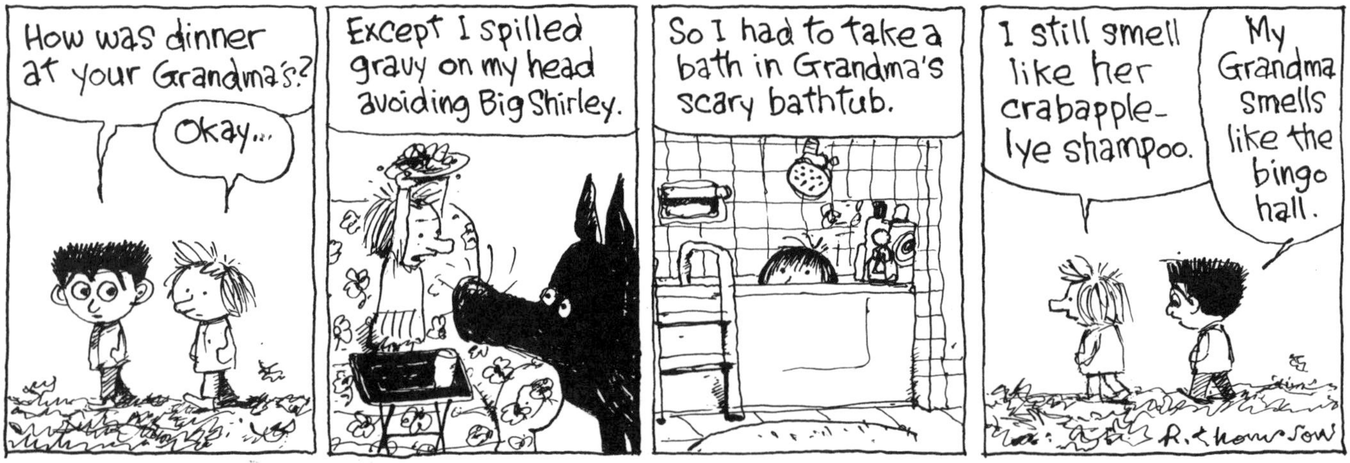
How was dinner at your Grandma's?
Okay...
Except I spilled gravy on my head avoiding Big Shirley.
So I had to take a bath in Grandma's scary bathtub.
I still smell like her crabapple-lye shampoo.
My Grandma smells like the bingo hall.
R. Thompson

Petey, what're those?
They're "comic strips," examples of a mighty, yet dying art form.
Read this one to me.
Well, see the cat says-
Is he happy or sad?
I don't know yet.
I think he's sad.
Okay. He says—
He's sad because the last cat here is eating pie.
No! He-
Yes he is! He hates the cat in the last box on the end! If he wasn't in a box too, he'd go beat up that cat and take his pie!
ALICE! IT'S ALL THE SAME CAT! SEE? THEY'RE ALL HIM!
Actually, I think he's a girl cat.
Maybe it's just as well comic strips are a dying art form.
R. Thompson

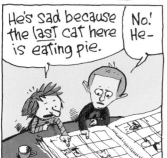

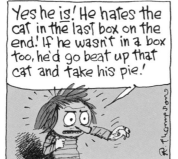

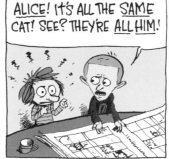

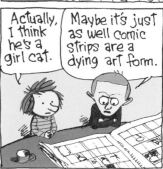

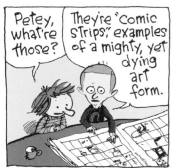

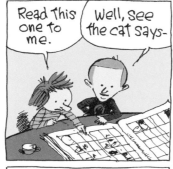

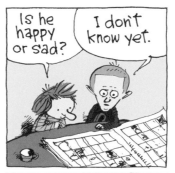

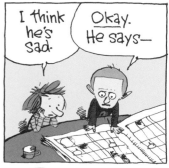

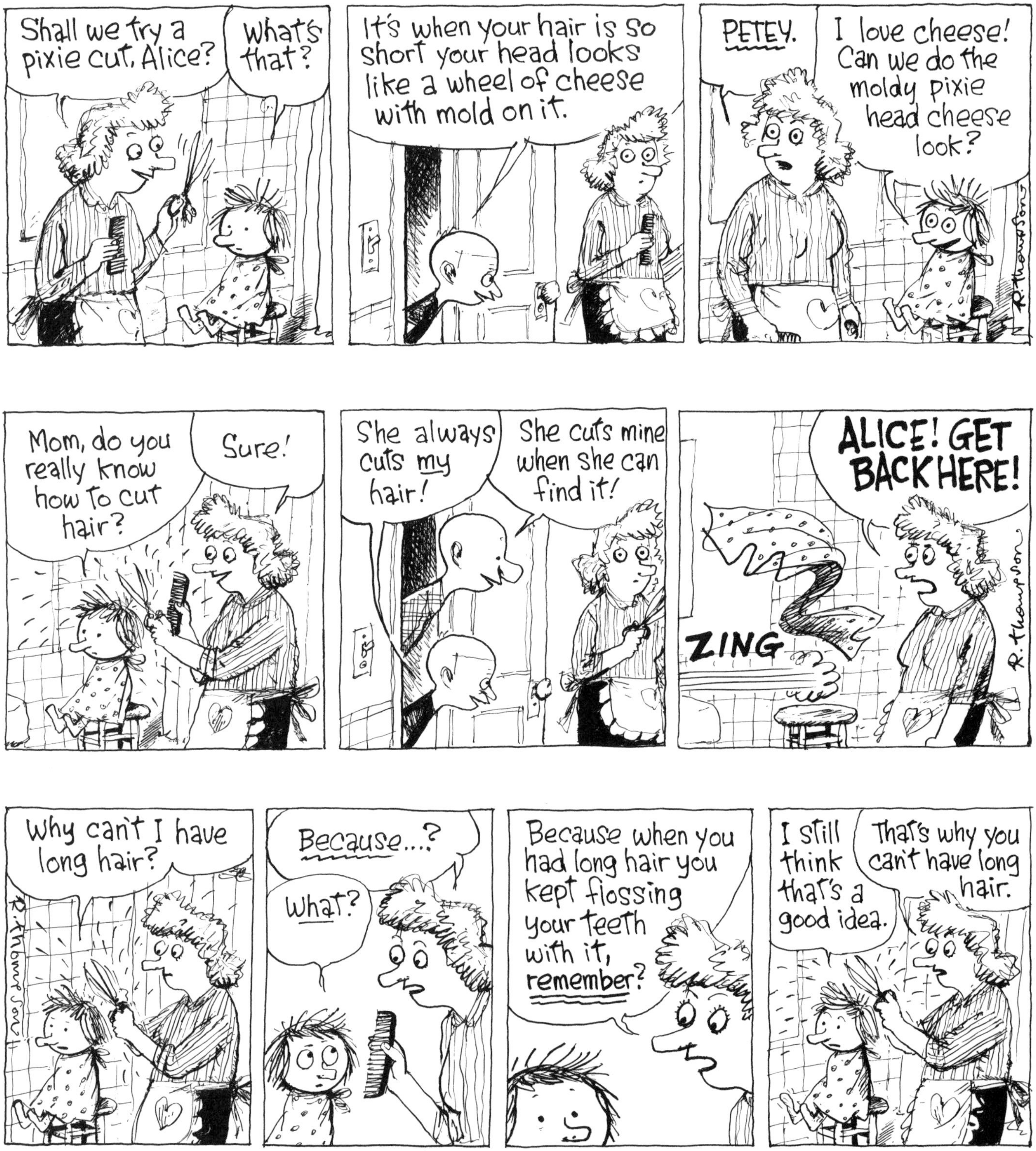
Shall we try a pixie cut, Alice?
What's that?
It's when your hair is so short your head looks like a wheel of cheese with mold on it.
PETEY.
I love cheese! Can we do the moldy pixie head cheese look?
R. Thompson
Mom, do you really know how to cut hair?
Sure!
She always cuts my hair!
She cuts mine when she can find it!
ALICE! GET BACK HERE!
ZING
R. Thompson
Why can't I have long hair?
R. Thompson
Because...?
What?
Because when you had long hair you kept flossing your teeth with it, remember?
I still think that's a good idea.
That's why you can't have long hair.

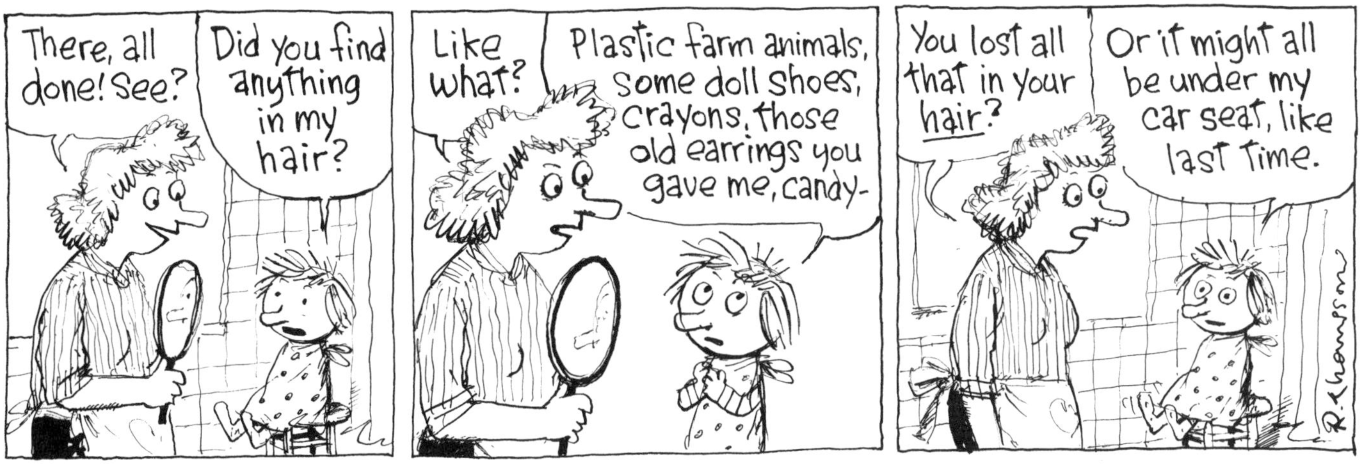
There, all done! See?
Did you find anything in my hair?
Like what?
Plastic farm animals, some doll shoes, crayons, those old earrings you gave me, candy-
You lost all that in your hair?
Or it might all be under my car seat, like last time.

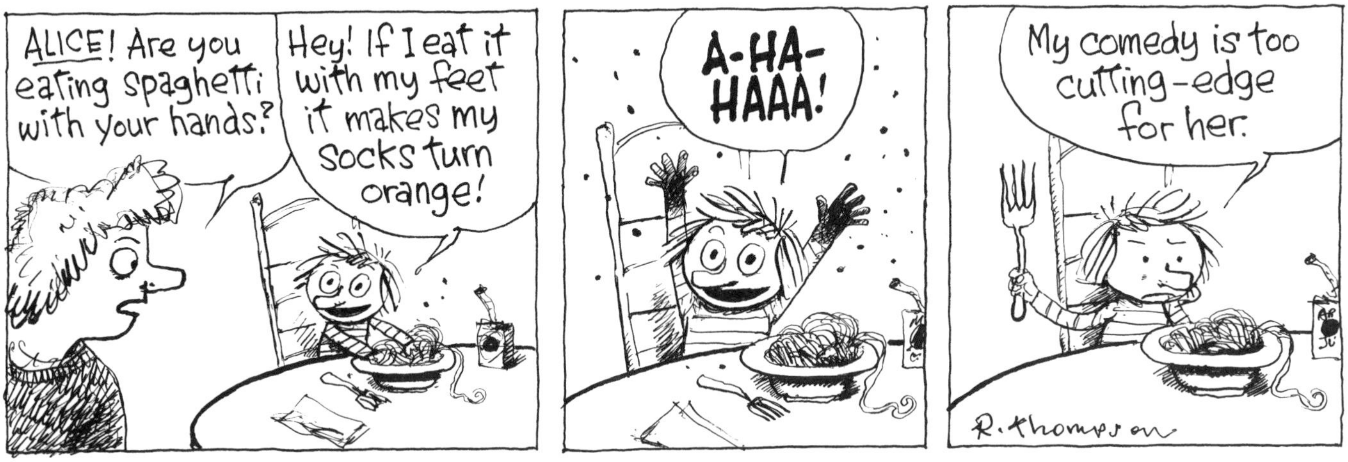
ALICE! Are you eating spaghetti with your hands?
Hey! If I eat it with my feet it makes my socks turn orange!
A-HA-HAAA!
My comedy is too cutting-edge for her.

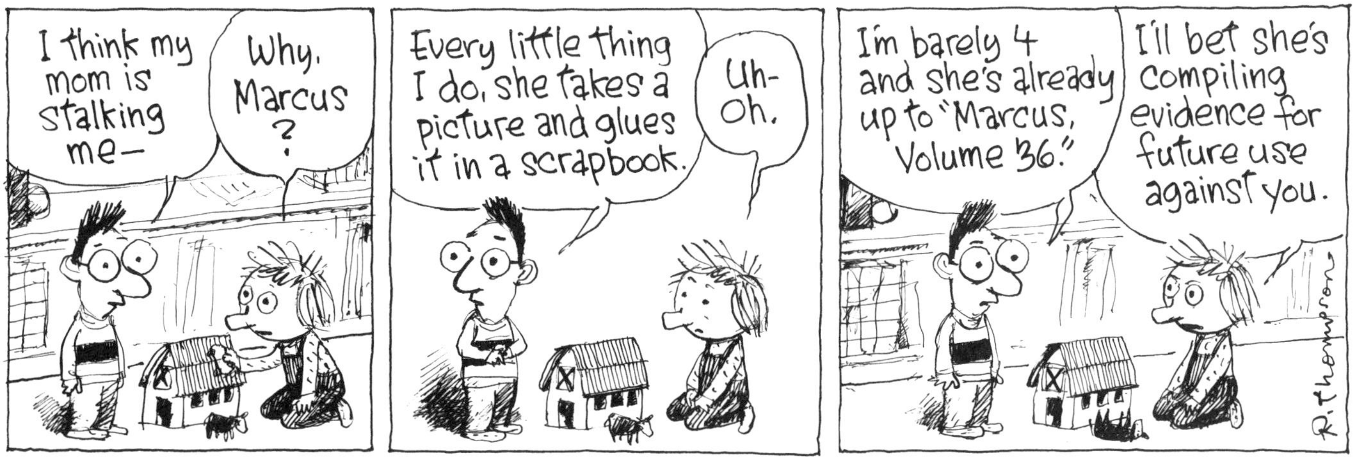
I think my mom is stalking me–
Why, Marcus?
Every little thing I do, she takes a picture and glues it in a scrapbook.
Uh-Oh.
I'm barely 4 and she's already up to "Marcus, Volume 36."
I'll bet she's compiling evidence for future use against you.

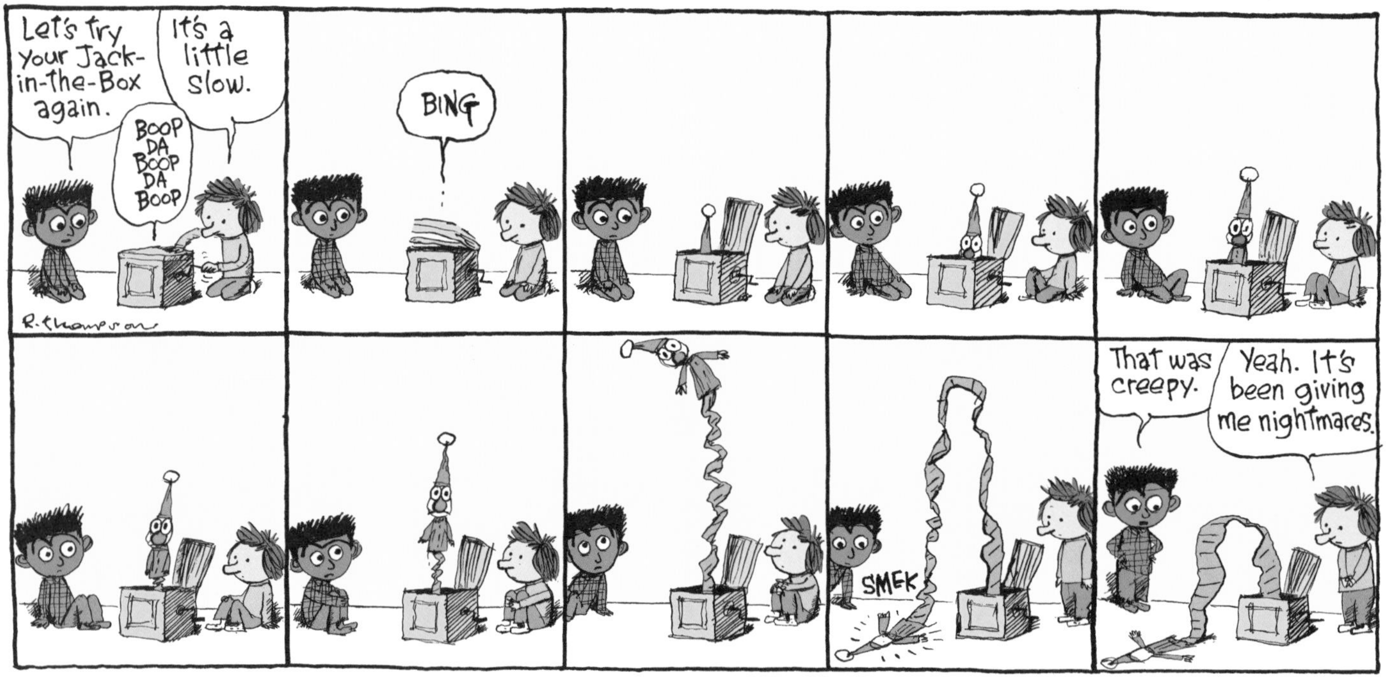
Let's try your Jack-in-the-Box again.
BOOP DA BOOP DA BOOP
It's a little slow.
R. Thompson
BING
SMEK
That was creepy.
Yeah. It's been giving me nightmares.

Panel 1: Alice! Stop gobbling your food so fast.

Panel 2: Watch Petey. He eats nice and slow.

Panel 3: I don't like the bites to collide going down...

Panel 4: They might pile up dangerously in the stomach.

I should watch _that_?

Watch. Don't listen.

Panel 5: My mom's van is "in the shop."

She's selling her van?

Panel 6: _Huh?_

If it's in the shop, it must be for sale.

Panel 7: But I've got a stash of old candy and fast food hidden under the back seat!

Oh, that'll sell _fast_.

Panel 8: My dad drove me to school in his little tiny car.

How was that?

Panel 9: Hey, Dad! Drive into the classroom and do donuts around Miss Bliss, OK?

Panel 10: It was no fun at _all_.

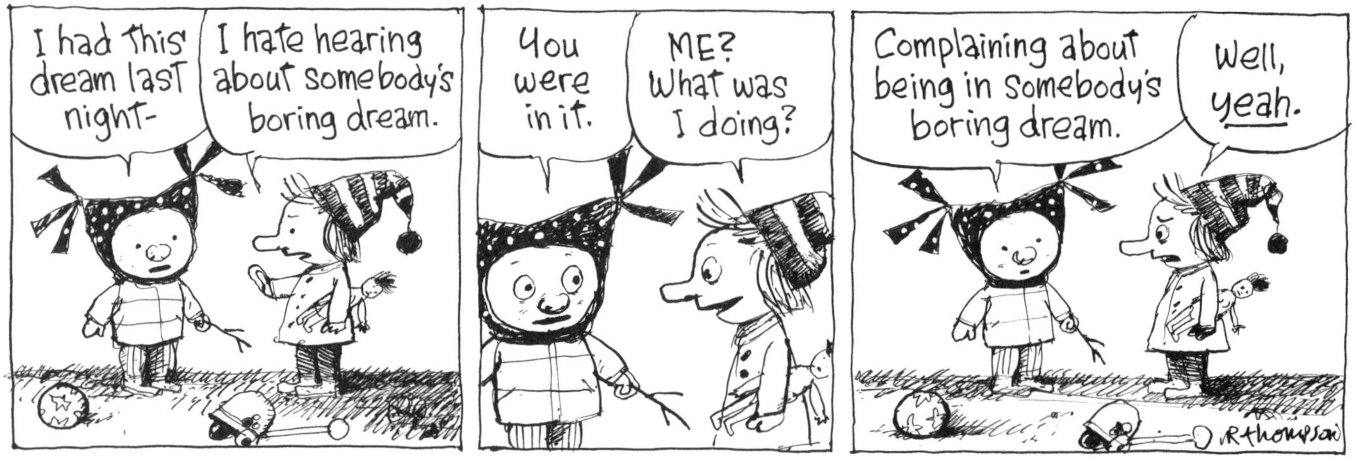
I had this dream last night-
I hate hearing about somebody's boring dream.
You were in it.
ME? What was I doing?
Complaining about being in somebody's boring dream.
Well, yeah.

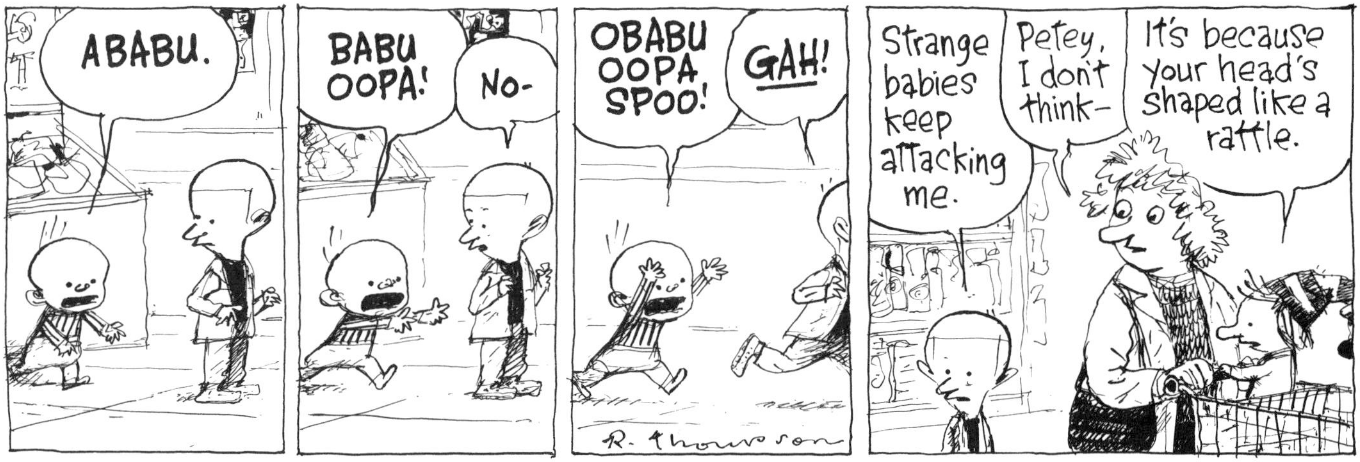
ABABU.
BABU OOPA!
No-
OBABU OOPA SPOO!
GAH!
Strange babies keep attacking me.
Petey, I don't think-
It's because your head's shaped like a rattle.

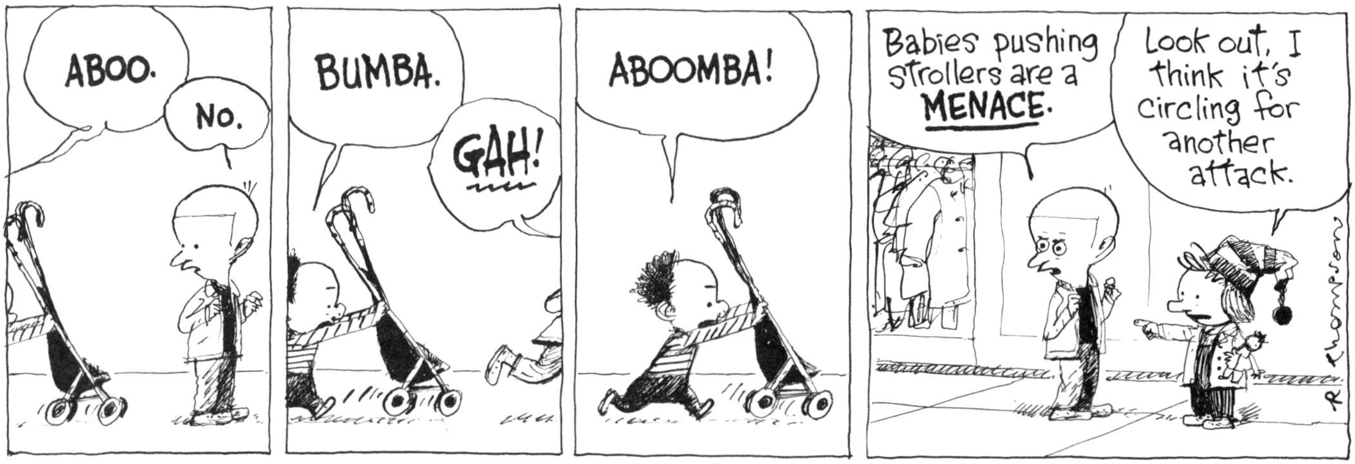
ABOO.
No.
BUMBA.
GAH!
ABOOMBA!
Babies pushing strollers are a MENACE.
Look out, I think it's circling for another attack.

Come here, Alice! Tell me about your day!
What? DADDY!! QUIT!
Tell me what you did at preschool!
DAAAAAD! DON'T! HEE HEE HEE HEE!
BOUNCE BOUNCE
Tell me the best thing that happened today.
DAAAAAAD! HEE HEE HEE HA HA!
BOUNCE BOUNCE
Tell me quick or you'll bounce through the ceiling!
HA HAHA HAHA!
BOUNCE BOUNCE
Whoops. Uh-oh.
CRASH
ALICE?!
OOOOOWHAAAAA
He did that to me when I was six and I didn't get a milk shake.
You're just trying to cheer me up.
R. Thompson

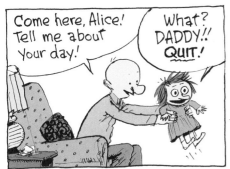

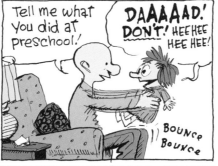

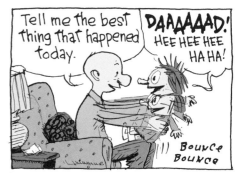

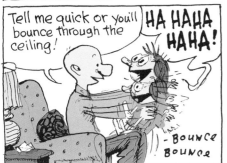

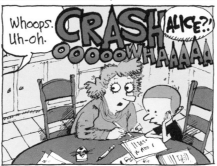

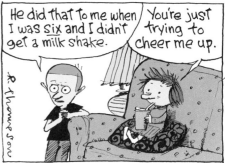

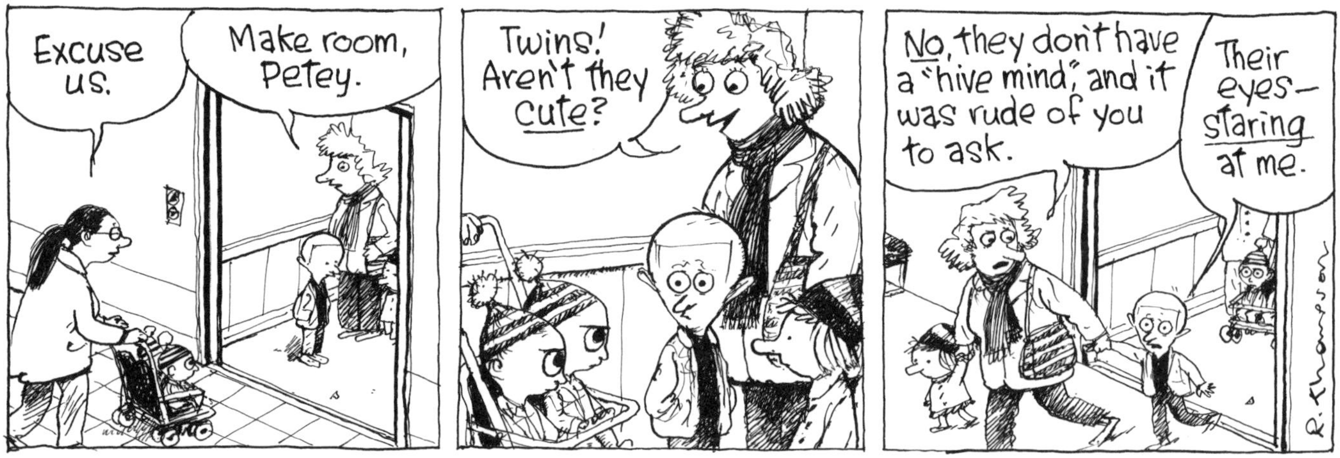
Excuse us.
Make room, Petey.
Twins! Aren't they cute?
No, they don't have a "hive mind," and it was rude of you to ask.
Their eyes— staring at me.

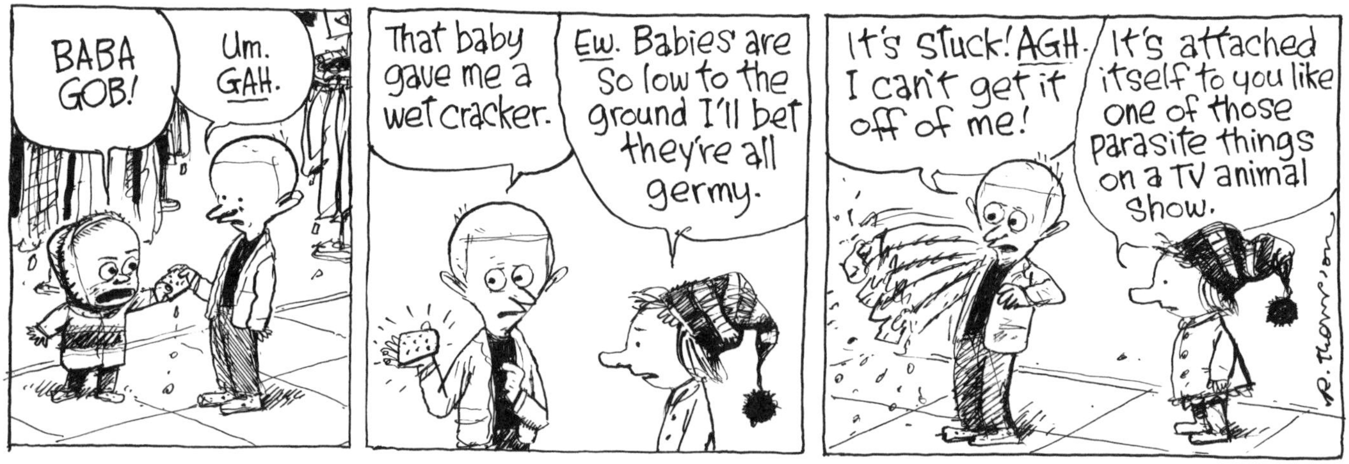
BABA GOB!
Um. GAH.
That baby gave me a wet cracker.
Ew. Babies are so low to the ground I'll bet they're all germy.
It's stuck! AGH. I can't get it off of me!
It's attached itself to you like one of those parasite things on a TV animal show.

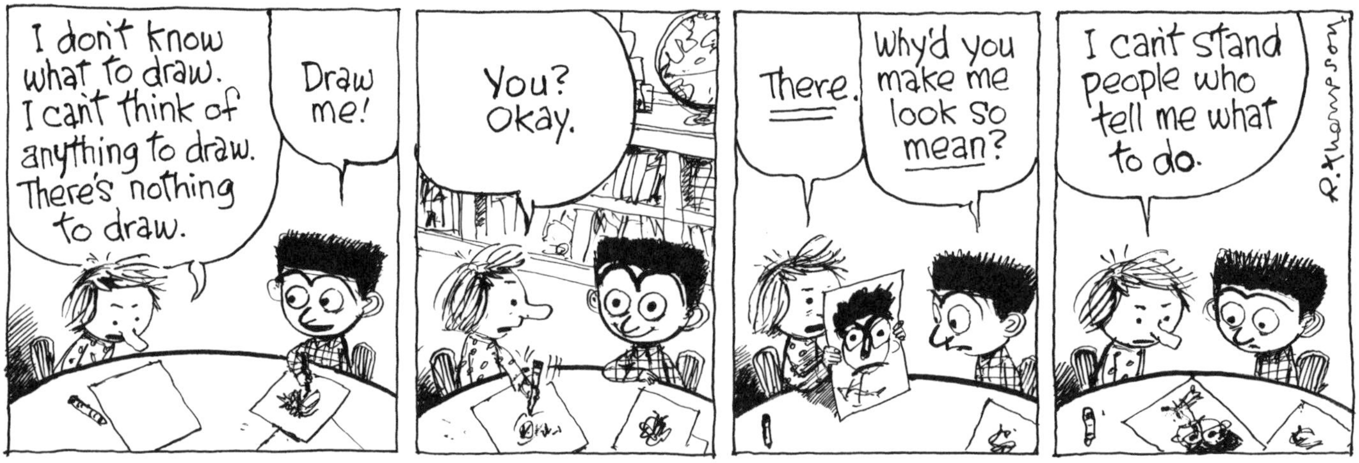
I don't know what to draw. I can't think of anything to draw. There's nothing to draw.
Draw me!
You? Okay.
There.
Why'd you make me look so mean?
I can't stand people who tell me what to do.

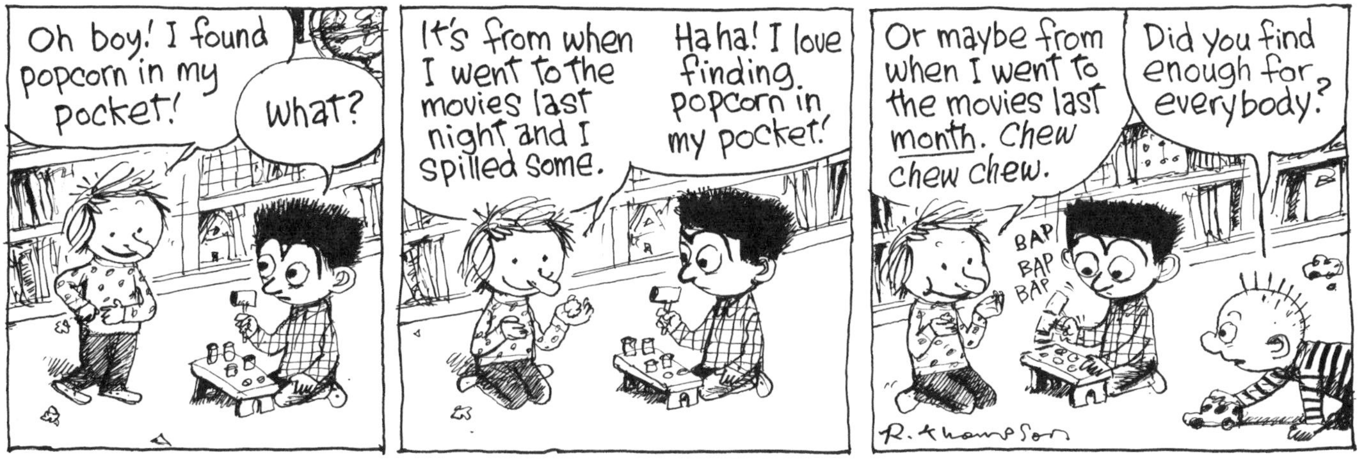
Oh boy! I found popcorn in my pocket!
What?
It's from when I went to the movies last night and I spilled some.
Ha ha! I love finding popcorn in my pocket!
Or maybe from when I went to the movies last month. Chew chew chew.
BAP BAP BAP
Did you find enough for everybody?
R. Thompson

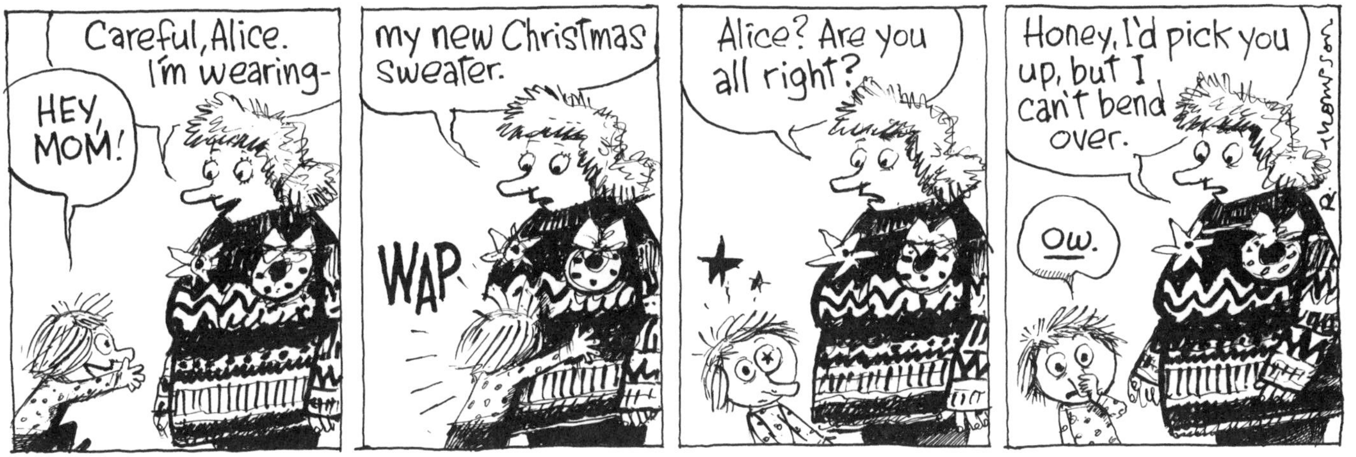
HEY, MOM!
Careful, Alice. I'm wearing-
my new Christmas sweater.
WAP
Alice? Are you all right?
Honey, I'd pick you up, but I can't bend over.
Ow.
R. Thompson

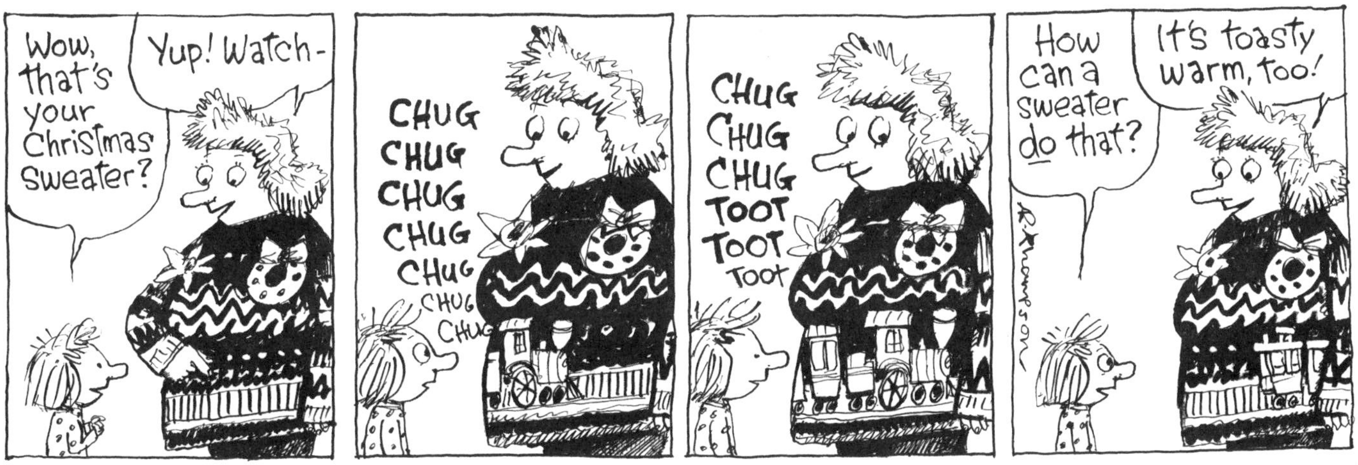
Wow, that's your Christmas sweater?
Yup! Watch-
CHUG CHUG CHUG CHUG CHUG CHUG CHUG
CHUG CHUG CHUG TOOT TOOT TOOT
R. Thompson
How can a sweater do that?
It's toasty warm, too!

Is this one of those dumb holiday comedies where the dad does stupid things?
I hope so.
Ssh.
I'll bet that Christmas tree falls over on him.
I hope so.
Ssh.
He's not going to climb the ladder.
YAY! Climb the ladder!
Oh NO! I lost a mitten in the tub of popcorn!
ALICE!
Don't worry, Alice. It'll be okay.
It's my favorite fuzzy mitten.
Ik.
We'll find it.
You were eating popcorn with your fuzzy mittens on?
YES.
Ssh.
Hey! If this was the movie, Daddy would accidentally eat the mitten!
SSH.
Eat the mitten, Daddy!
Who are you people?
R. Thompson

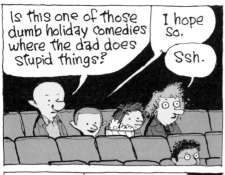

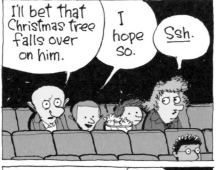

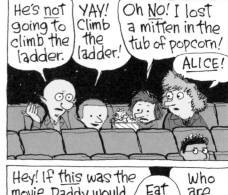

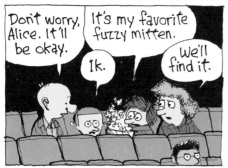

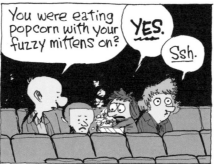

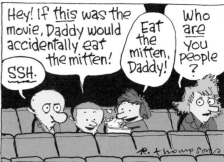

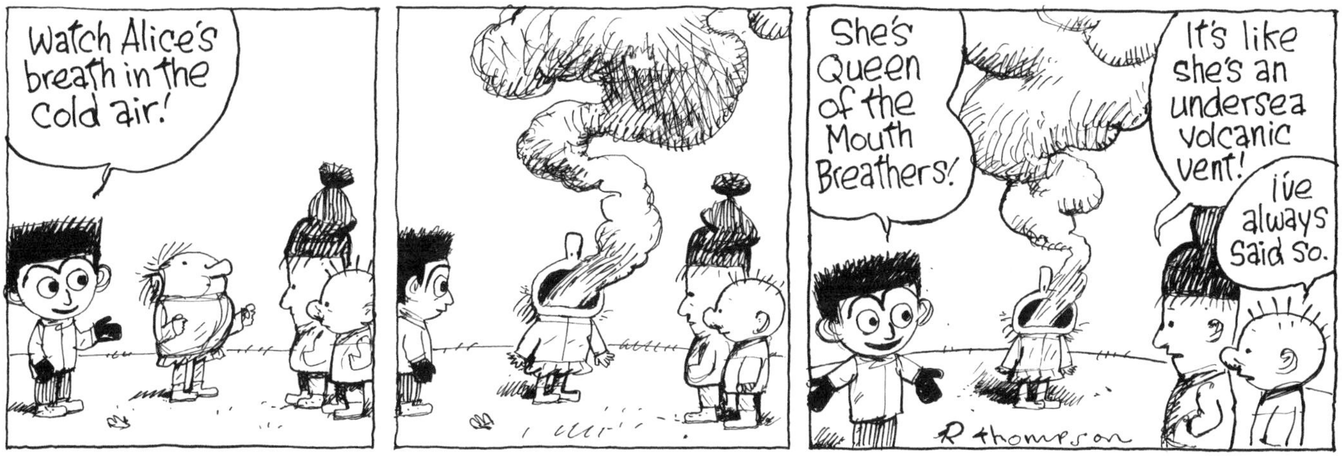
Watch Alice's breath in the cold air!
She's Queen of the Mouth Breathers!
It's like she's an undersea volcanic vent!
I've always said so.
R thompson

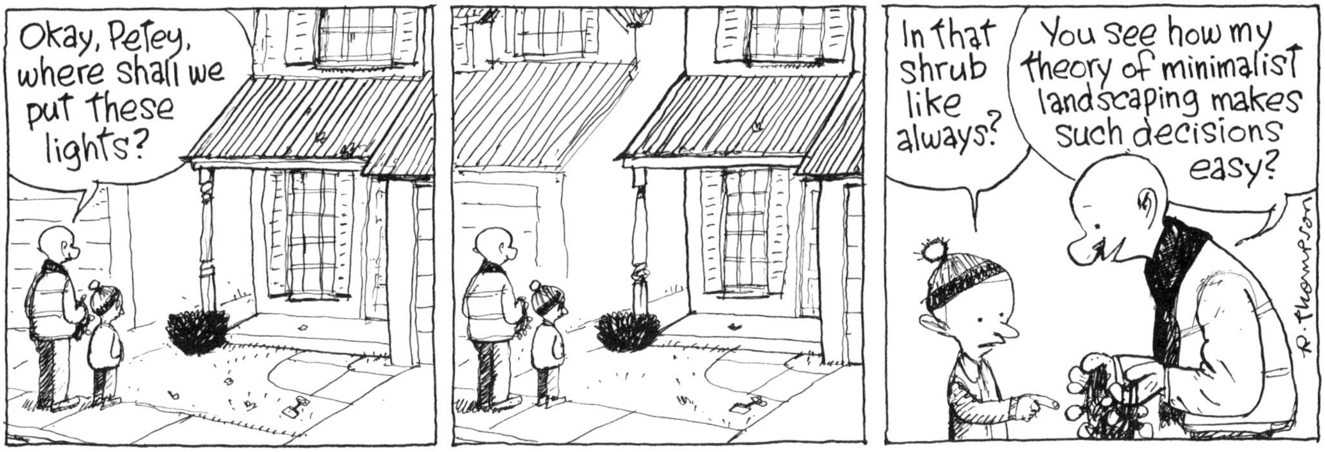
Okay, Petey, where shall we put these lights?
In that shrub like always?
You see how my theory of minimalist landscaping makes such decisions easy?
R. thompson

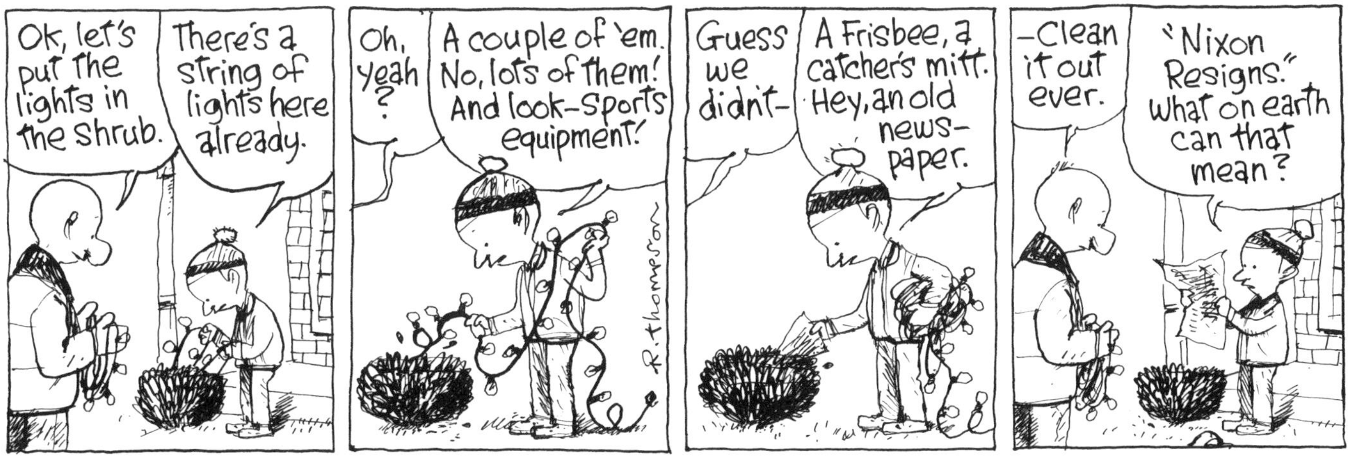
Ok, let's put the lights in the shrub.
There's a string of lights here already.
Oh, yeah?
A couple of 'em. No, lots of them! And look–Sports equipment!
R. thompson
Guess we didn't–
A Frisbee, a catcher's mitt. Hey, an old news-paper.
–Clean it out ever.
"Nixon Resigns." What on earth can that mean?

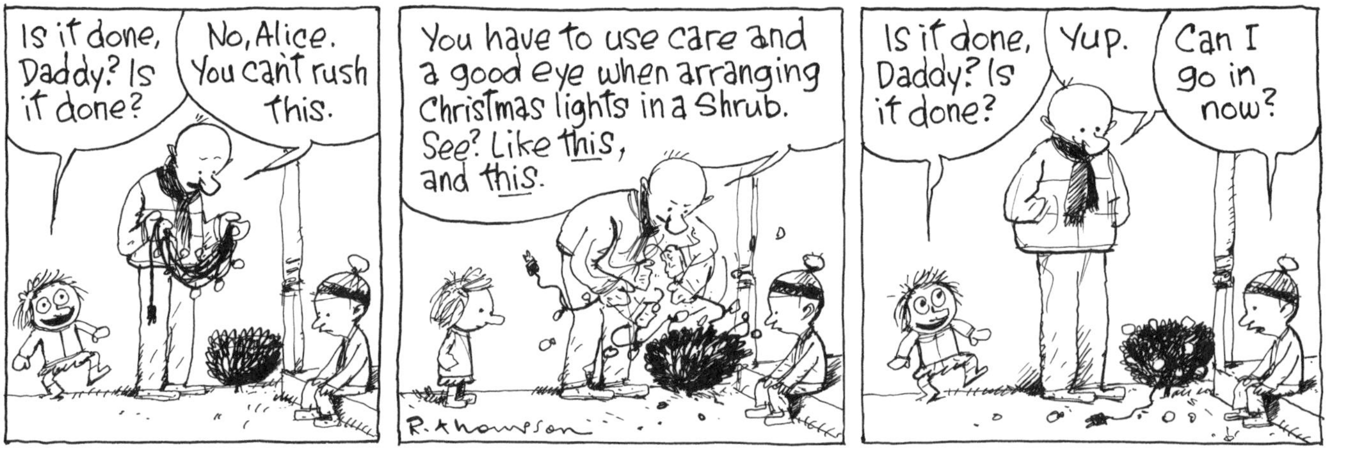

Is it done, Daddy? Is it done?
No, Alice. You can't rush this.
You have to use care and a good eye when arranging Christmas lights in a shrub. See? Like this, and this.
Is it done, Daddy? Is it done?
Yup.
Can I go in now?

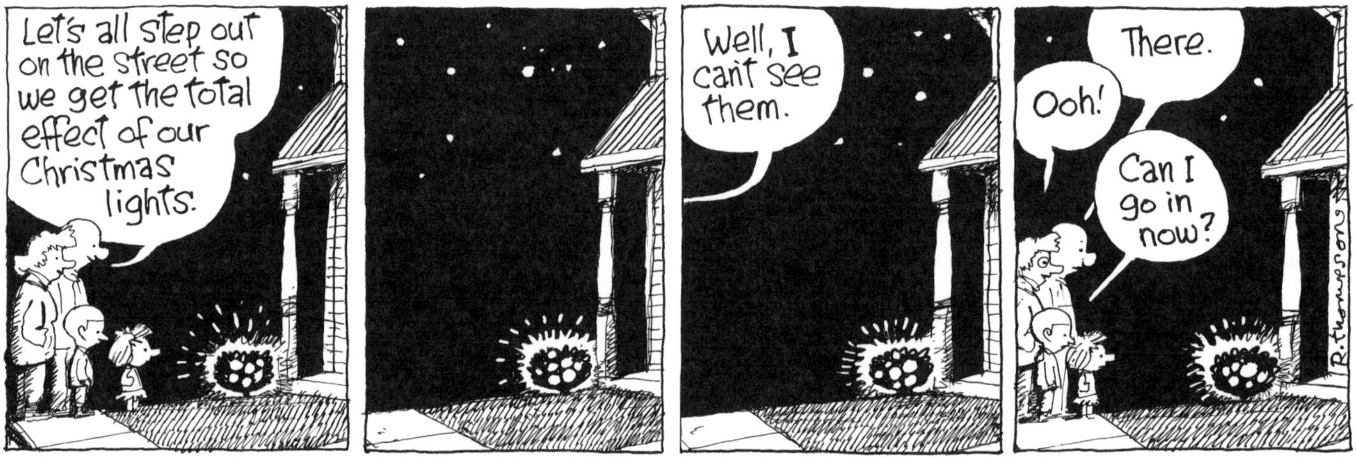

Let's all step out on the street so we get the total effect of our Christmas lights.
Well, I can't see them.
Ooh!
There.
Can I go in now?

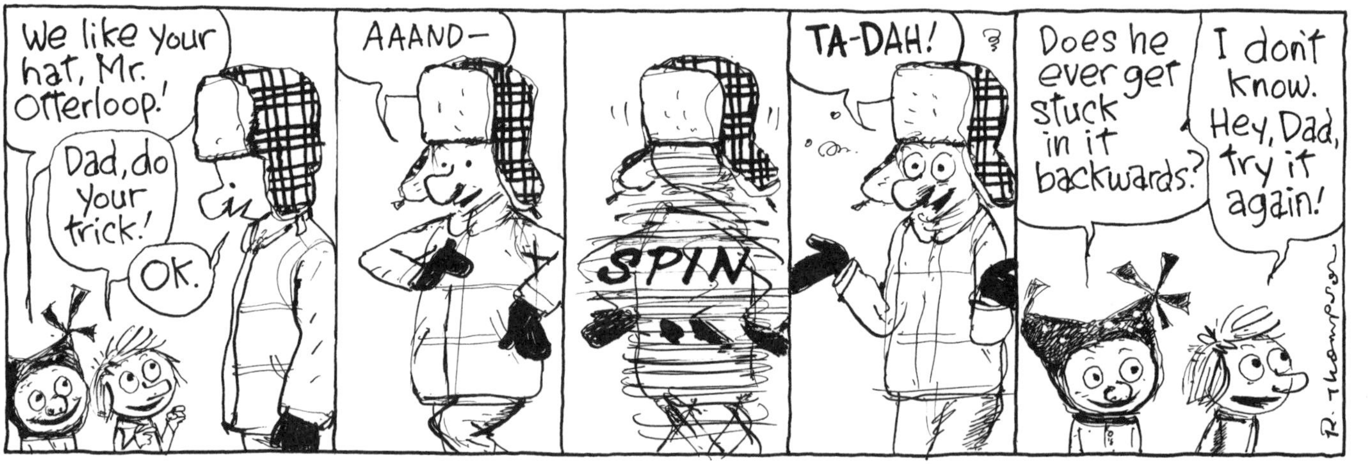

We like your hat, Mr. Otterloop!
Dad, do your trick!
OK.
AAAND—
SPIN
TA-DAH!
Does he ever get stuck in it backwards?
I don't know. Hey, Dad, try it again!

Should we get a photo of them on Santa's lap?
I guess.
Im not going to actually sit on his lap.
There's a Precious Memory Package with 25 photo cards, 20 8x10s...
Take off your hat, Alice.
I'll stand to one side with an air of quiet reserve.
NO.
A VISIT WITH SANTA
Six photo mugs, six photo magnets, five photo ornaments, four photo beer koozies, a photo mousepad...
Alice.
No. I like the hat on. Santa's wearing his hat.
All for $49.95.
Your turn, kids! Smile big!
HEY!
Aw, look! Grandma will love these!
Dibs on a beer koozie.
If you'd gotten the Precious Memory Deluxe Package, Grandma would get a tattoo.
HUMPH.
R. Thompson

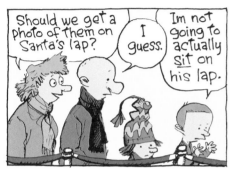

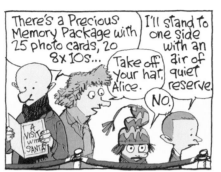

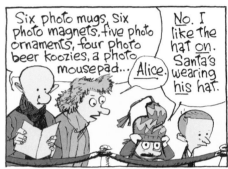

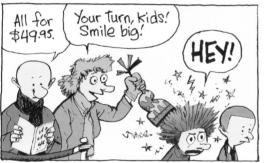

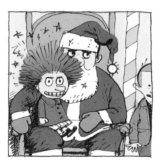

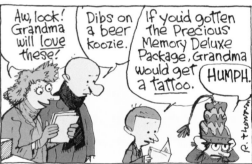

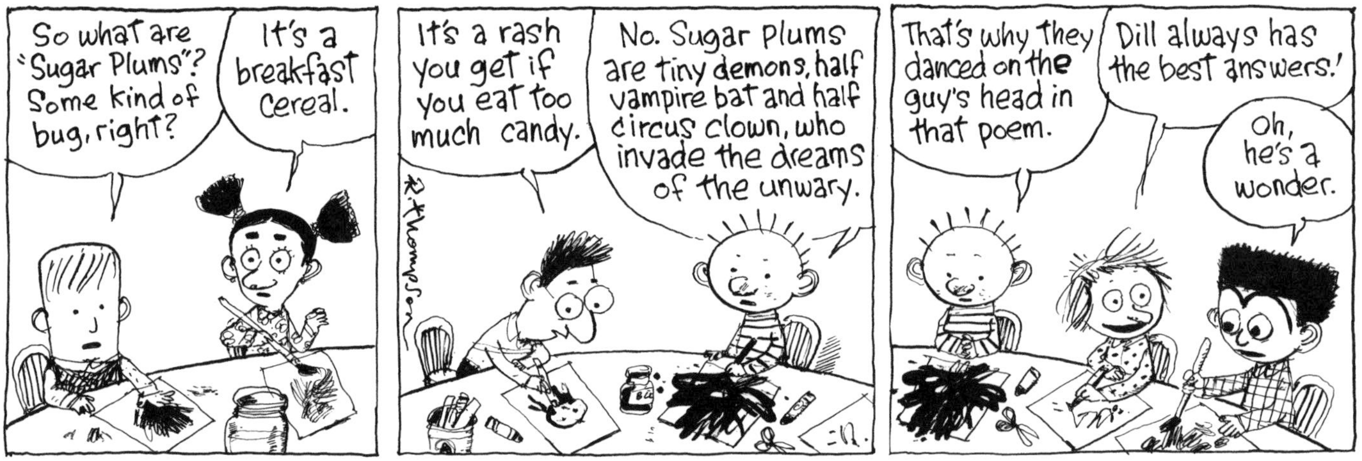
So what are "Sugar Plums"? Some kind of bug, right?
It's a breakfast cereal.
It's a rash you get if you eat too much candy.
No. Sugar Plums are tiny demons, half vampire bat and half circus clown, who invade the dreams of the unwary.
That's why they danced on the guy's head in that poem.
Dill always has the best answers!
Oh, he's a wonder.

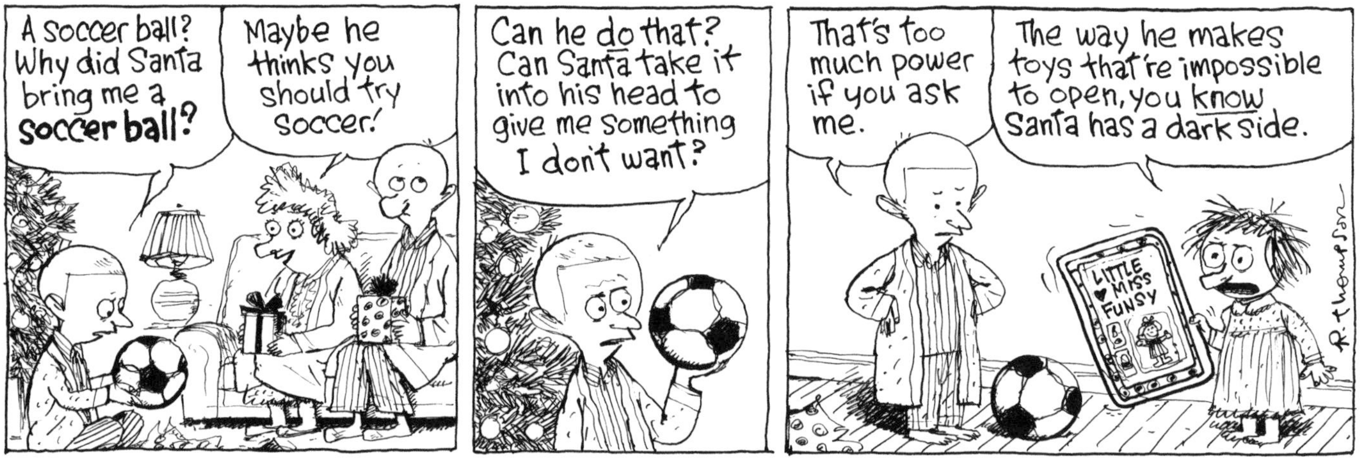
A soccer ball? Why did Santa bring me a **soccer ball**?
Maybe he thinks you should try soccer!
Can he do that? Can Santa take it into his head to give me something I don't want?
That's too much power if you ask me.
The way he makes toys that're impossible to open, you know Santa has a dark side.
LITTLE MISS FUNSY

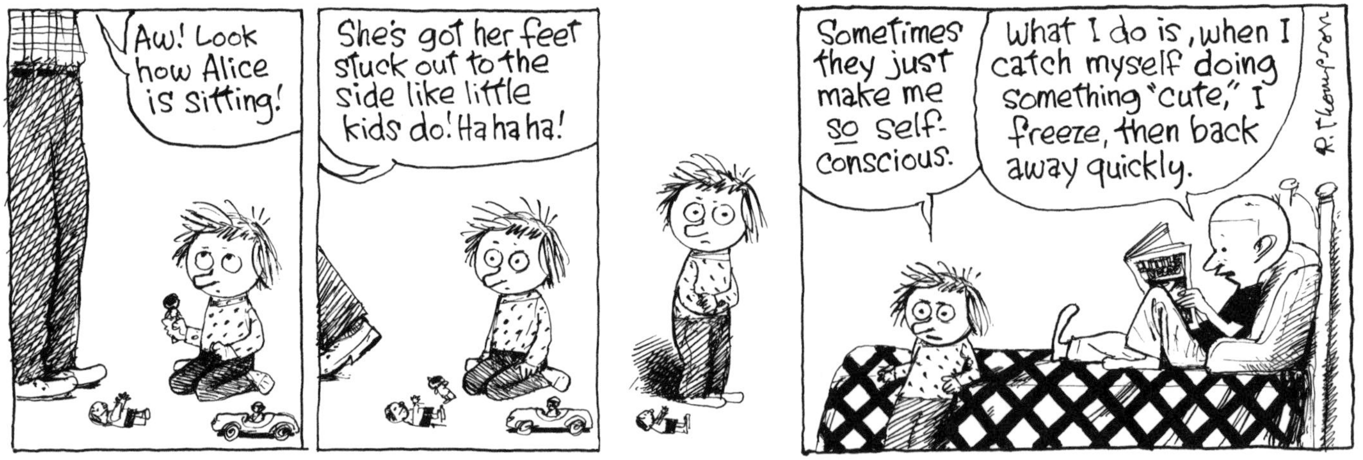
Aw! Look how Alice is sitting!
She's got her feet stuck out to the side like little kids do! Ha ha ha!
Sometimes they just make me so self-conscious.
What I do is, when I catch myself doing something "cute," I freeze, then back away quickly.

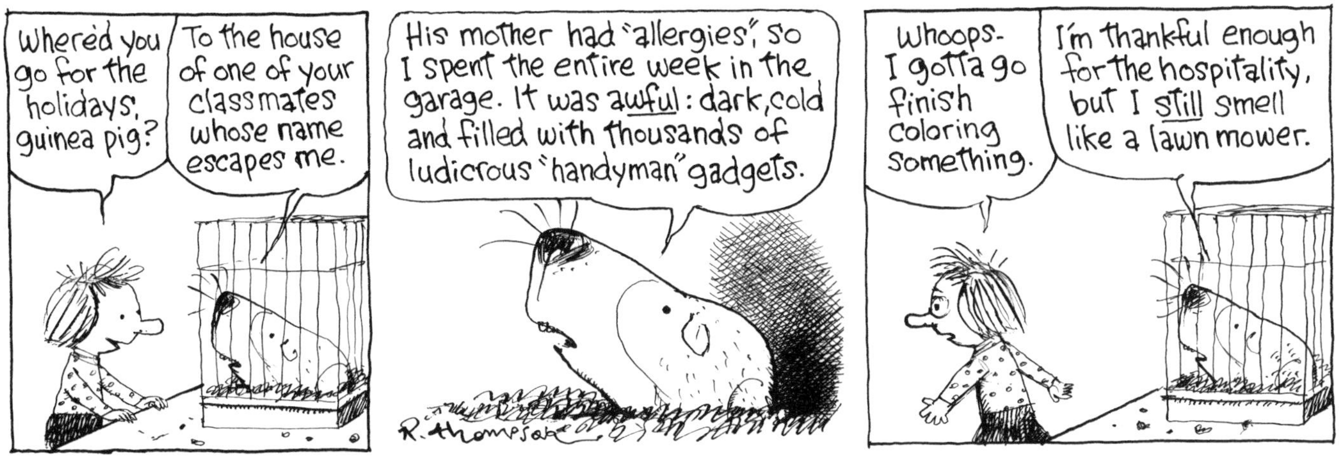
Where'd you go for the holidays, guinea pig?
To the house of one of your classmates whose name escapes me.
His mother had "allergies", so I spent the entire week in the garage. It was awful: dark, cold and filled with thousands of ludicrous "handyman" gadgets.
Whoops. I gotta go finish coloring something.
I'm thankful enough for the hospitality, but I still smell like a lawn mower.
R. Thompson

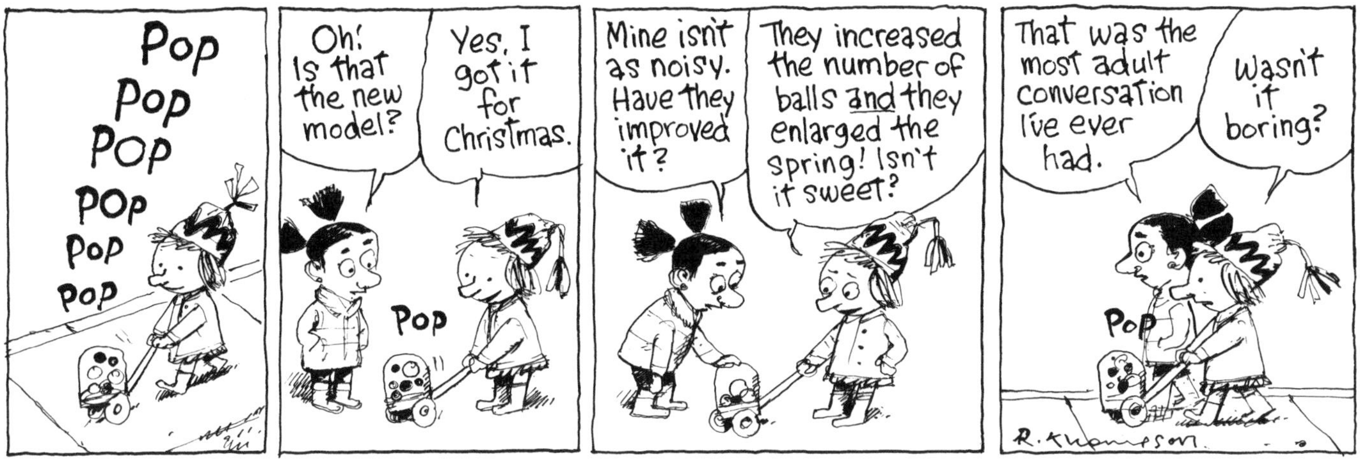
Pop
Pop
Pop
Pop
Pop
Pop
Oh! Is that the new model?
Yes, I got it for Christmas.
Pop
Mine isn't as noisy. Have they improved it?
They increased the number of balls and they enlarged the spring! Isn't it sweet?
That was the most adult conversation I've ever had.
Wasn't it boring?
Pop
R. Thompson

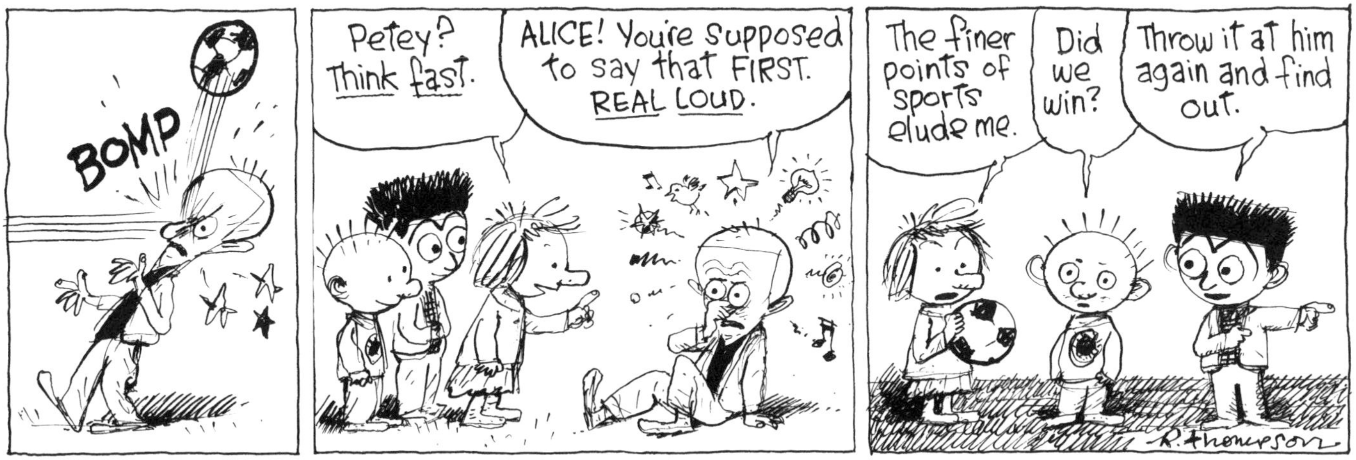
BOMP
Petey? Think fast.
ALICE! You're supposed to say that FIRST. REAL LOUD.
The finer points of sports elude me.
Did we win?
Throw it at him again and find out.
R. Thompson

Did you get that for Christmas?
Yes. Santa brought it.
What is it?
I don't know. I saw it in the store and I felt sorry for it.
It is pretty sad.
Nobody was buying it. It was pathetic. So I asked Santa for it.
I wish **I** had one.
That's the only one there is.

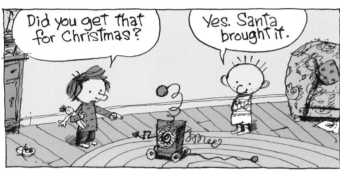

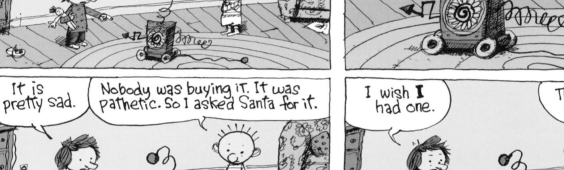

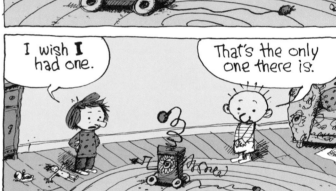

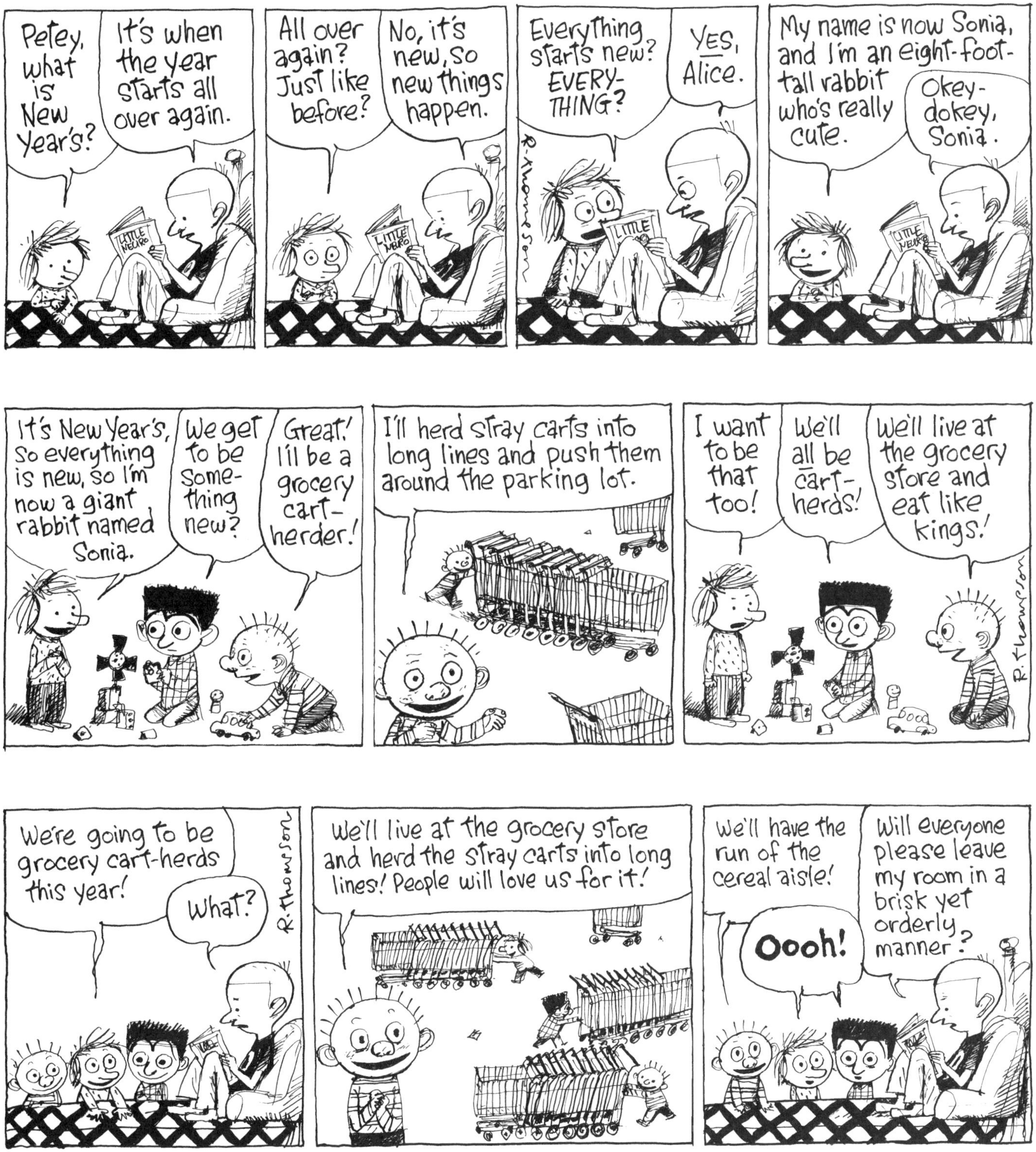
Petey, what is New Year's?
It's when the year starts all over again.
All over again? Just like before?
No, it's new, so new things happen.
Everything starts new? EVERY-THING?
YES, Alice.
My name is now Sonia, and I'm an eight-foot-tall rabbit who's really cute.
Okey-dokey, Sonia.
It's New Year's, so everything is new, so I'm now a giant rabbit named Sonia.
We get to be some-thing new?
Great! I'll be a grocery cart-herder!
I'll herd stray carts into long lines and push them around the parking lot.
I want to be that too!
We'll all be cart-herds!
We'll live at the grocery store and eat like kings!
We're going to be grocery cart-herds this year!
What?
We'll live at the grocery store and herd the stray carts into long lines! People will love us for it!
We'll have the run of the cereal aisle!
Oooh!
Will everyone please leave my room in a brisk yet orderly manner?

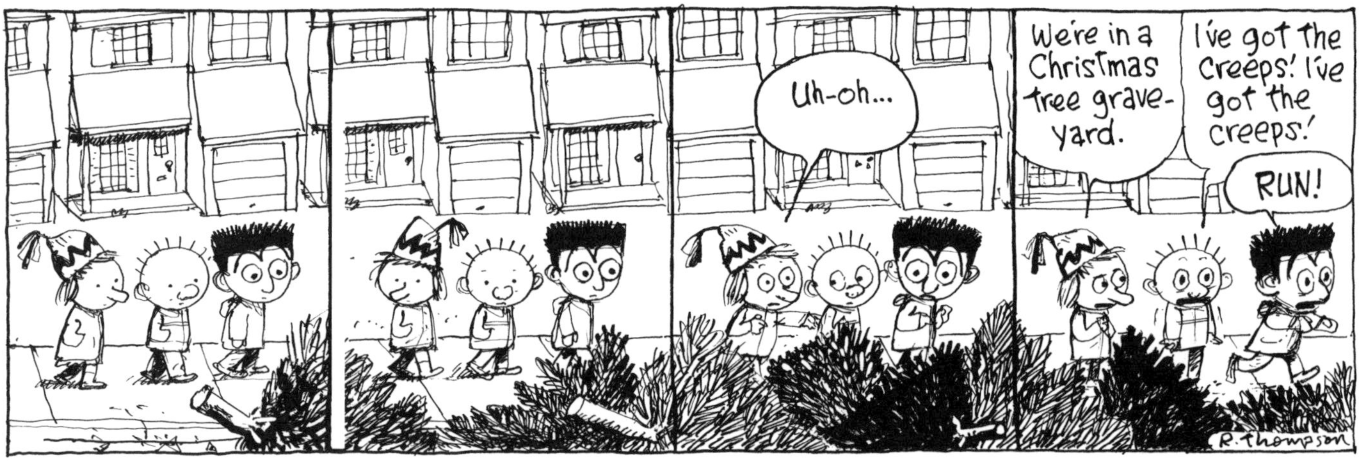
Uh-oh...
We're in a Christmas tree grave-yard.
I've got the creeps! I've got the creeps!
RUN!
R. Thompson

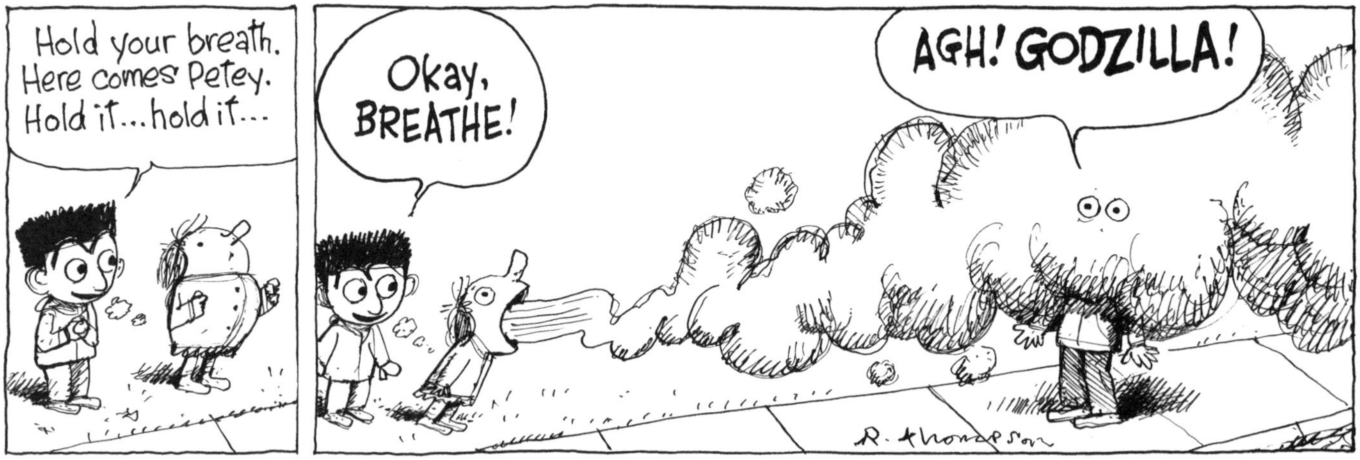
Hold your breath. Here comes Petey. Hold it... hold it...
Okay, BREATHE!
AGH! GODZILLA!
R. Thompson

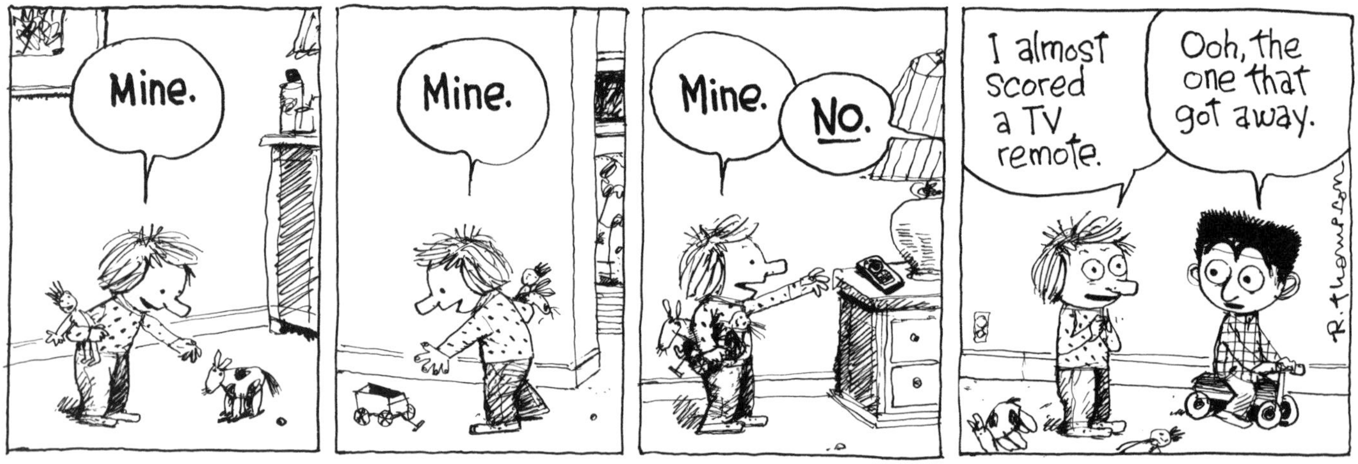
Mine.
Mine.
Mine.
NO.
I almost scored a TV remote.
Ooh, the one that got away.
R. Thompson

My life intersects with Alice's just enough to be surreal.

Hmm?

Daddy's getting on my nerves. He's always right there.

It's 'cause our house is so small. If he'd get a better job, we could move someplace bigger.

30 PIECE PUZZLE

R. THOMPSON

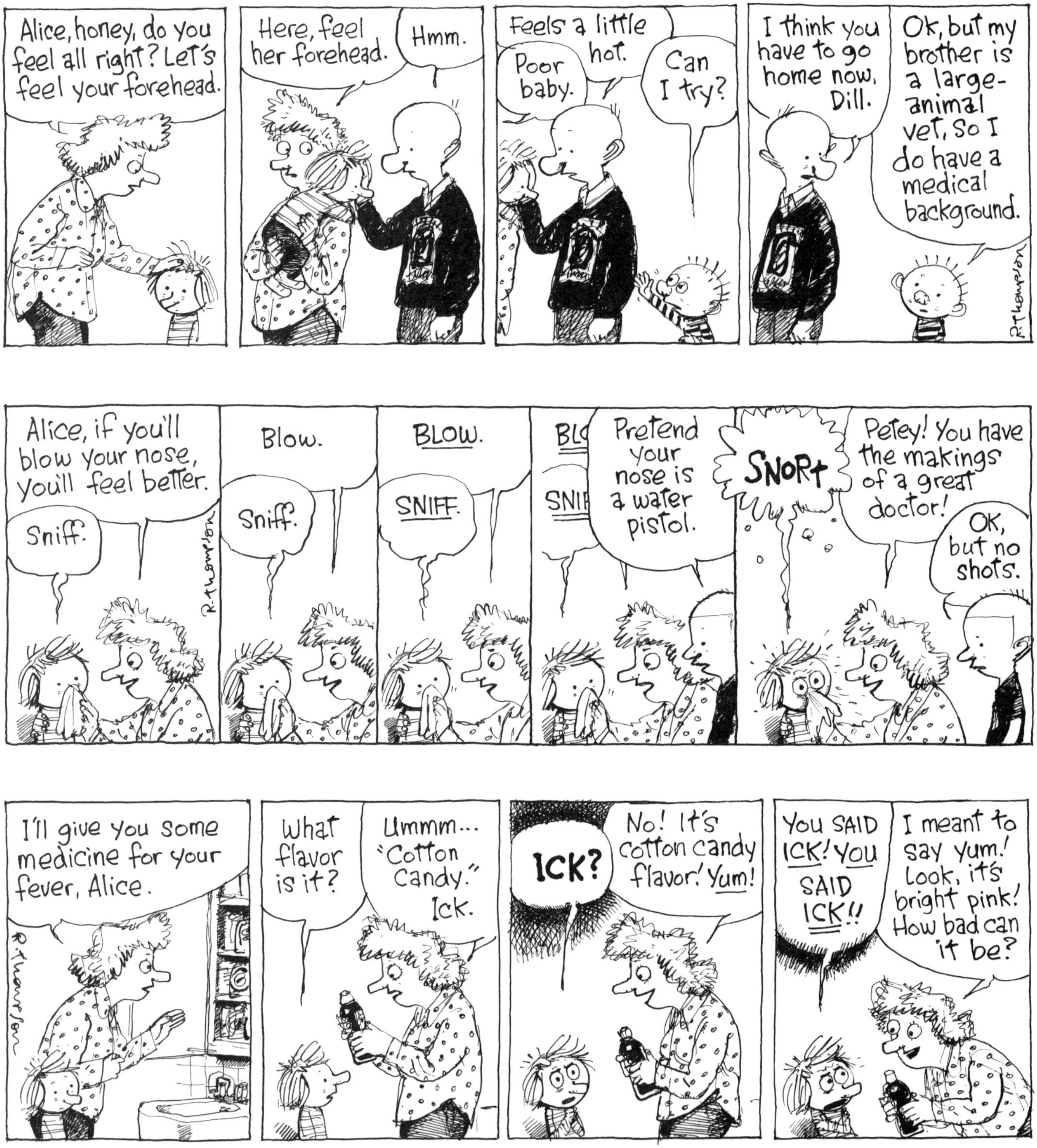
Alice, honey, do you feel all right? Let's feel your forehead.
Here, feel her forehead.
Hmm.
Feels a little hot.
Poor baby.
Can I try?
I think you have to go home now, Dill.
Ok, but my brother is a large-animal vet, so I do have a medical background.
R. Thompson
Alice, if you'll blow your nose, you'll feel better.
Sniff.
R. Thompson
Blow.
Sniff.
BLOW.
SNIFF.
Pretend your nose is a water pistol.
SNORt
Petey! You have the makings of a great doctor!
OK, but no shots.
I'll give you some medicine for your fever, Alice.
R. Thompson
What flavor is it?
Ummm... "Cotton Candy." Ick.
ICK?
No! It's cotton candy flavor! Yum!
You SAID ICK! YOU SAID ICK!!
I meant to say yum! Look, it's bright pink! How bad can it be?

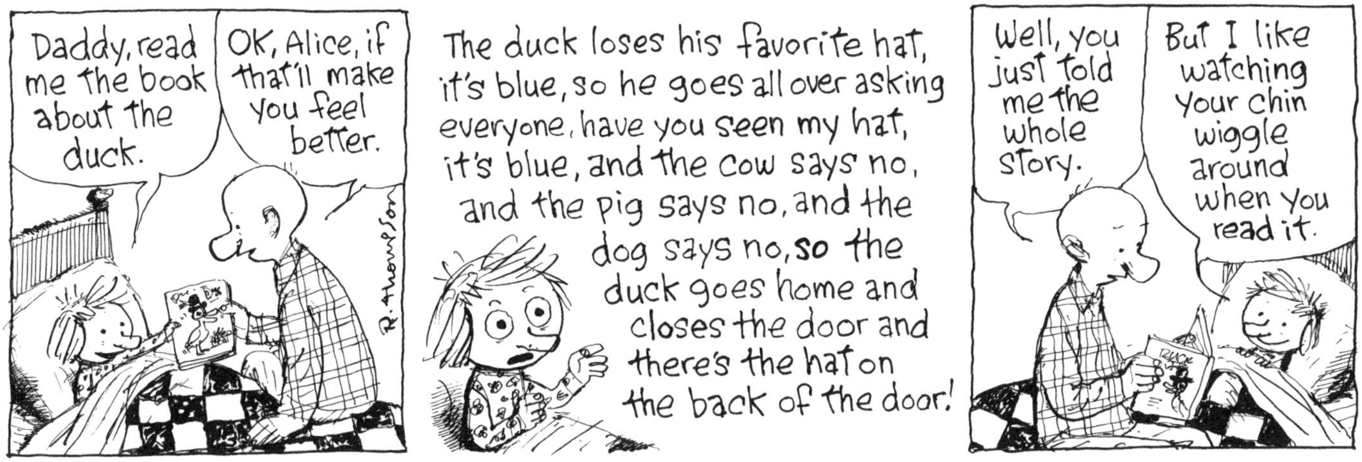
Daddy, read me the book about the duck.
OK, Alice, if that'll make you feel better.
The duck loses his favorite hat, it's blue, so he goes all over asking everyone, have you seen my hat, it's blue, and the cow says no, and the pig says no, and the dog says no, so the duck goes home and closes the door and there's the hat on the back of the door!
Well, you just told me the whole story.
But I like watching your chin wiggle around when you read it.
R. Thompson

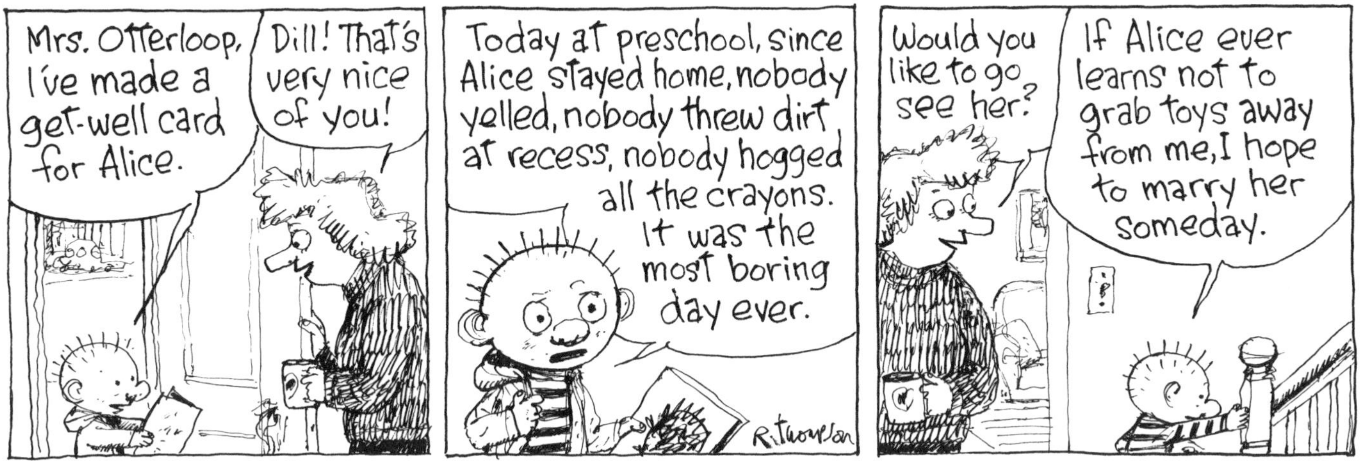
Mrs. Otterloop, I've made a get-well card for Alice.
Dill! That's very nice of you!
Today at preschool, since Alice stayed home, nobody yelled, nobody threw dirt at recess, nobody hogged all the crayons. It was the most boring day ever.
Would you like to go see her?
If Alice ever learns not to grab toys away from me, I hope to marry her someday.
R. Thompson

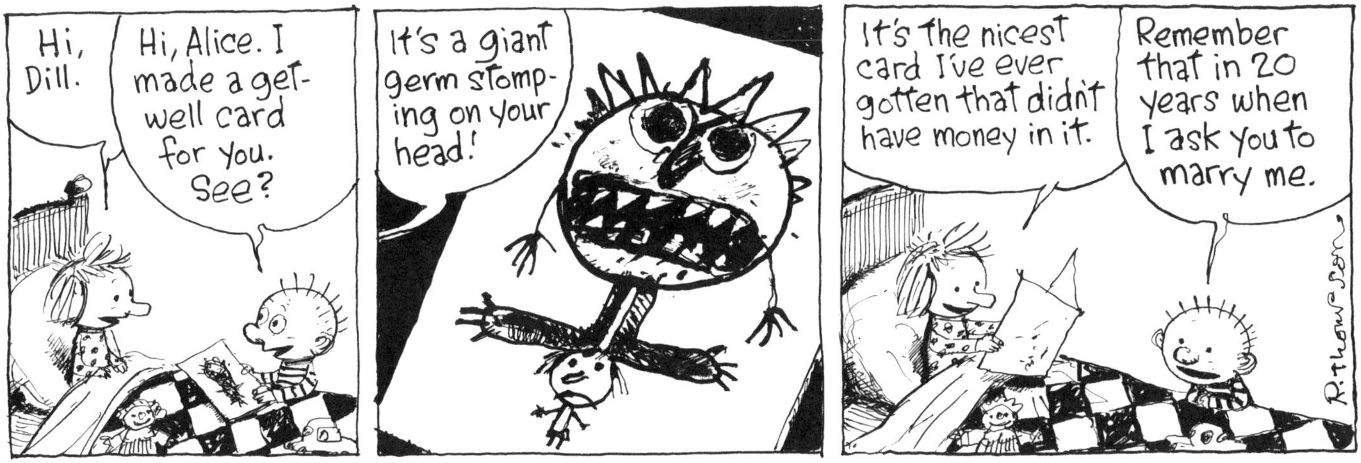
Hi, Dill.
Hi, Alice. I made a get-well card for you. See?
It's a giant germ stomping on your head!
It's the nicest card I've ever gotten that didn't have money in it.
Remember that in 20 years when I ask you to marry me.
R. Thompson

Our class guinea pig is so cute! What's your name, guinea pig?

Danders. Mr. Danders, though it might well be Dr. Danders.

If ever anyone earned an honorary doctorate, it would be me.

For I've spent my life here, in the groves of academe, breathing the tangy scent of Play-Doh, the humid reek of the coat cubbies.

Attending to the soft scratch of crayon on paper, the lulling drone of story time.

With the knowledge I've gleaned, I could've excelled in many fields.

DANDERS
POET,
JURIST,
S'URGEON,
BANJO
VIRTUOSO

But no! My duties lie here! Generations of Blisshaven Preschool students have looked to me, faithful Danders, for a hearty "GWEEP" of encouragement when learning palls and their weary heads nod!

GWEEP!

That GWEEPing noise was you? I thought it was Miss Bliss' stomach.

Alas! Do all my efforts go unrecognized?

R. Thompson

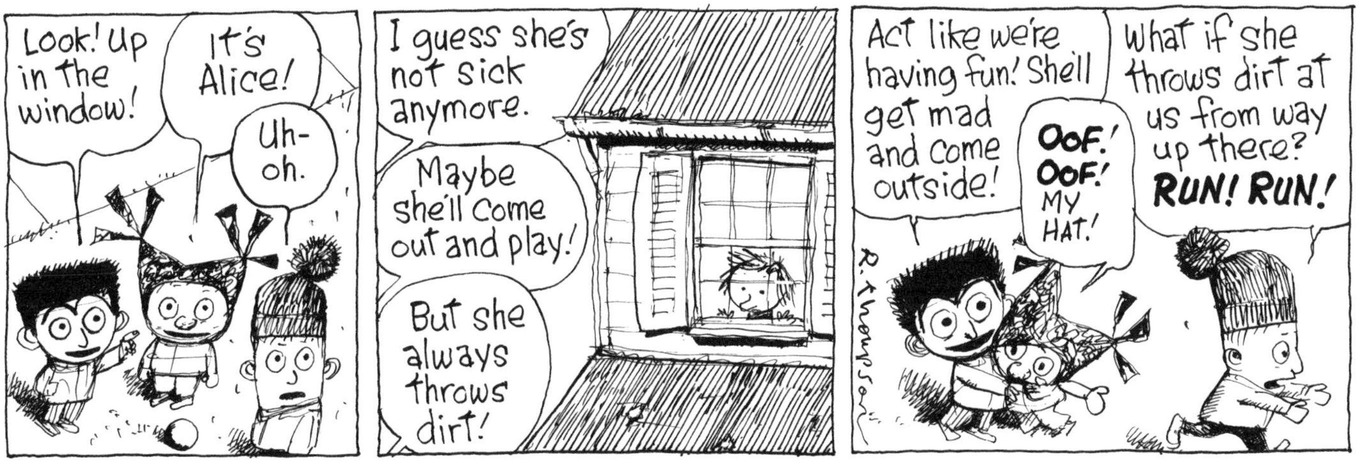
Look! Up in the window!
It's Alice!
Uh-oh.
I guess she's not sick anymore.
Maybe she'll come out and play!
But she always throws dirt!
Act like we're having fun! She'll get mad and come outside!
OOF! OOF! MY HAT!
What if she throws dirt at us from way up there? RUN! RUN!
R. Thompson

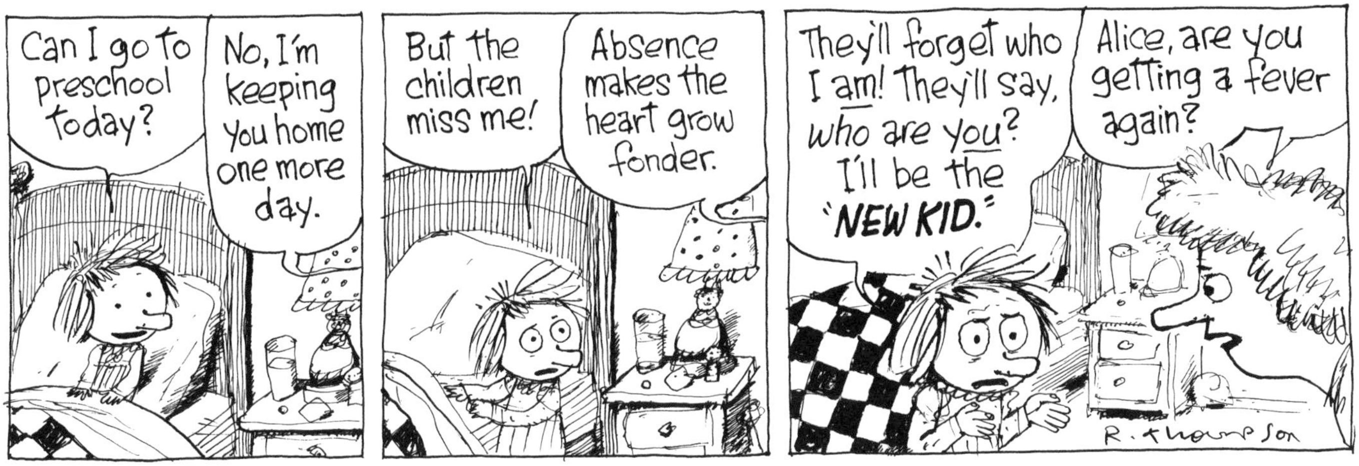
Can I go to preschool today?
No, I'm keeping you home one more day.
But the children miss me!
Absence makes the heart grow fonder.
They'll forget who I am! They'll say, who are you? I'll be the "NEW KID."
Alice, are you getting a fever again?
R. Thompson

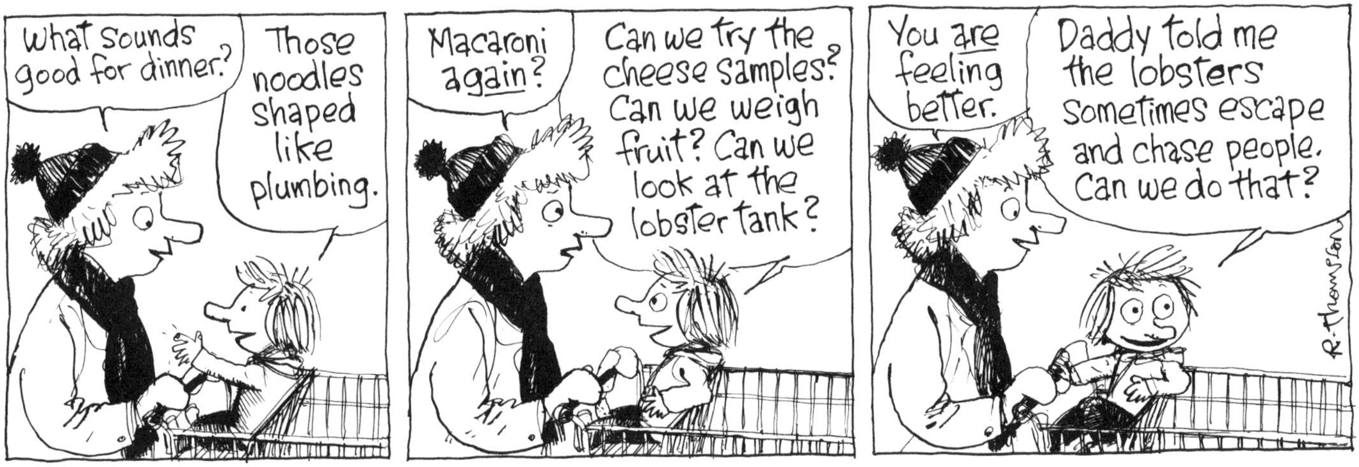
What sounds good for dinner?
Those noodles shaped like plumbing.
Macaroni again?
Can we try the cheese samples? Can we weigh fruit? Can we look at the lobster tank?
You are feeling better.
Daddy told me the lobsters sometimes escape and chase people. Can we do that?
R. Thompson

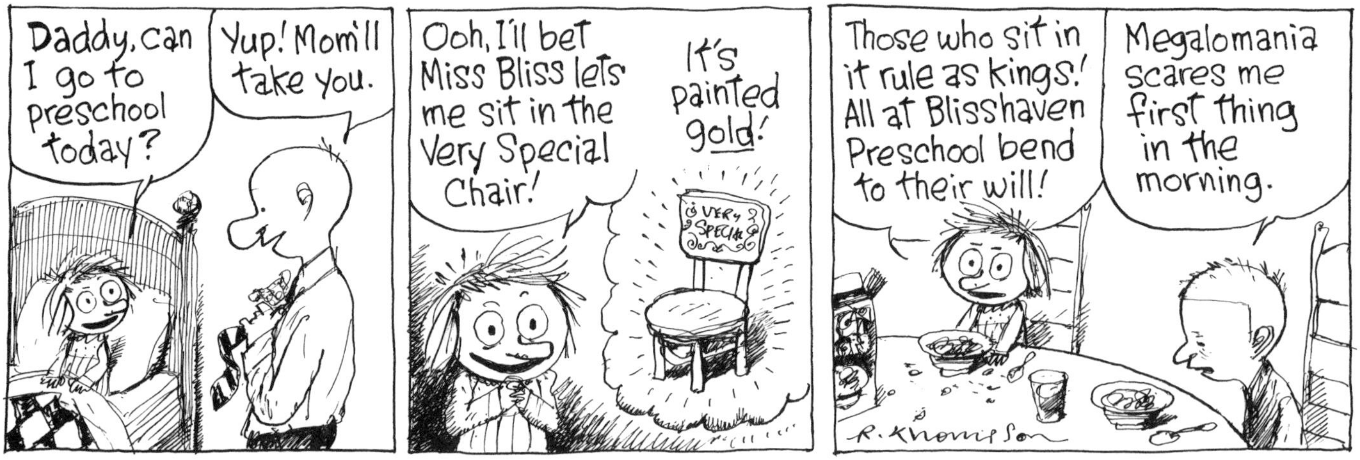
Daddy, can I go to preschool today?
Yup! Mom'll take you.
Ooh, I'll bet Miss Bliss lets me sit in the Very Special Chair!
It's painted gold!
Those who sit in it rule as kings! All at Blisshaven Preschool bend to their will!
Megalomania scares me first thing in the morning.

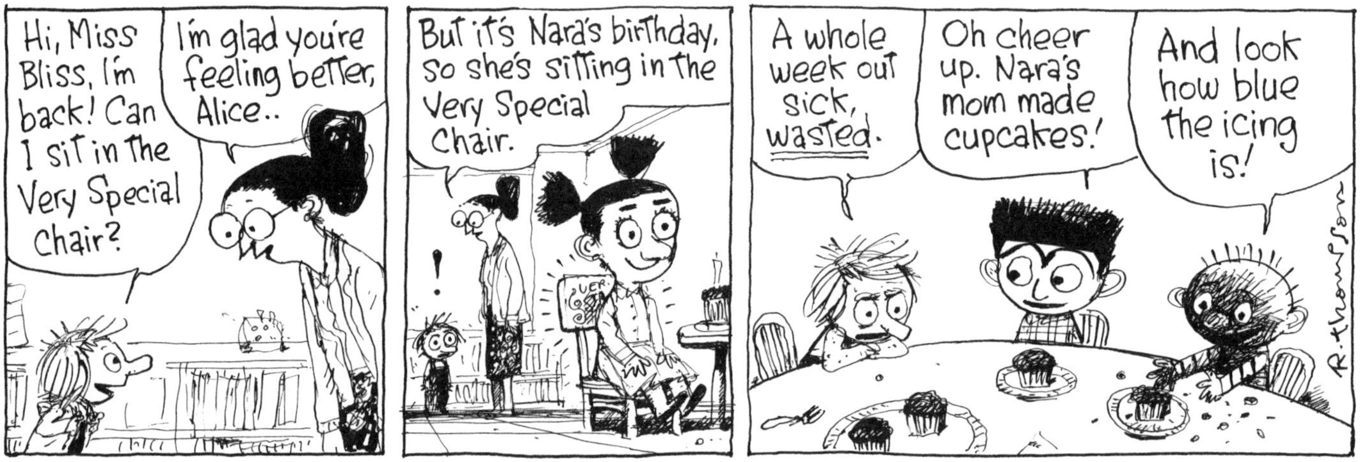
Hi, Miss Bliss, I'm back! Can I sit in the Very Special Chair?
I'm glad you're feeling better, Alice..
But it's Nara's birthday, so she's sitting in the Very Special Chair.
!
A whole week out sick, wasted.
Oh cheer up. Nara's mom made cupcakes!
And look how blue the icing is!

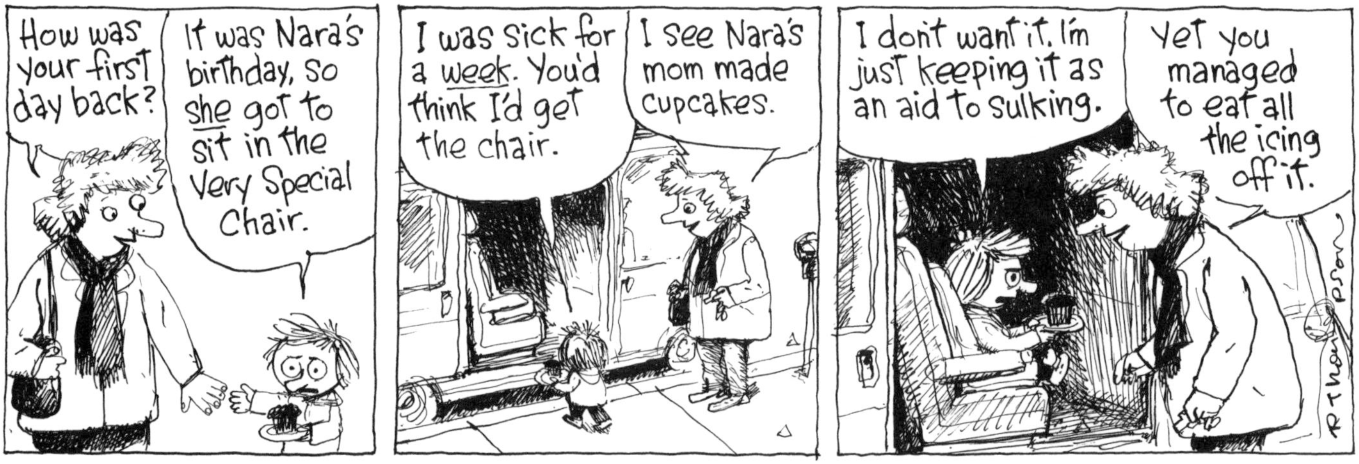
How was your first day back?
It was Nara's birthday, so she got to sit in the Very Special Chair.
I was sick for a week. You'd think I'd get the chair.
I see Nara's mom made cupcakes.
I don't want it. I'm just keeping it as an aid to sulking.
Yet you managed to eat all the icing off it.

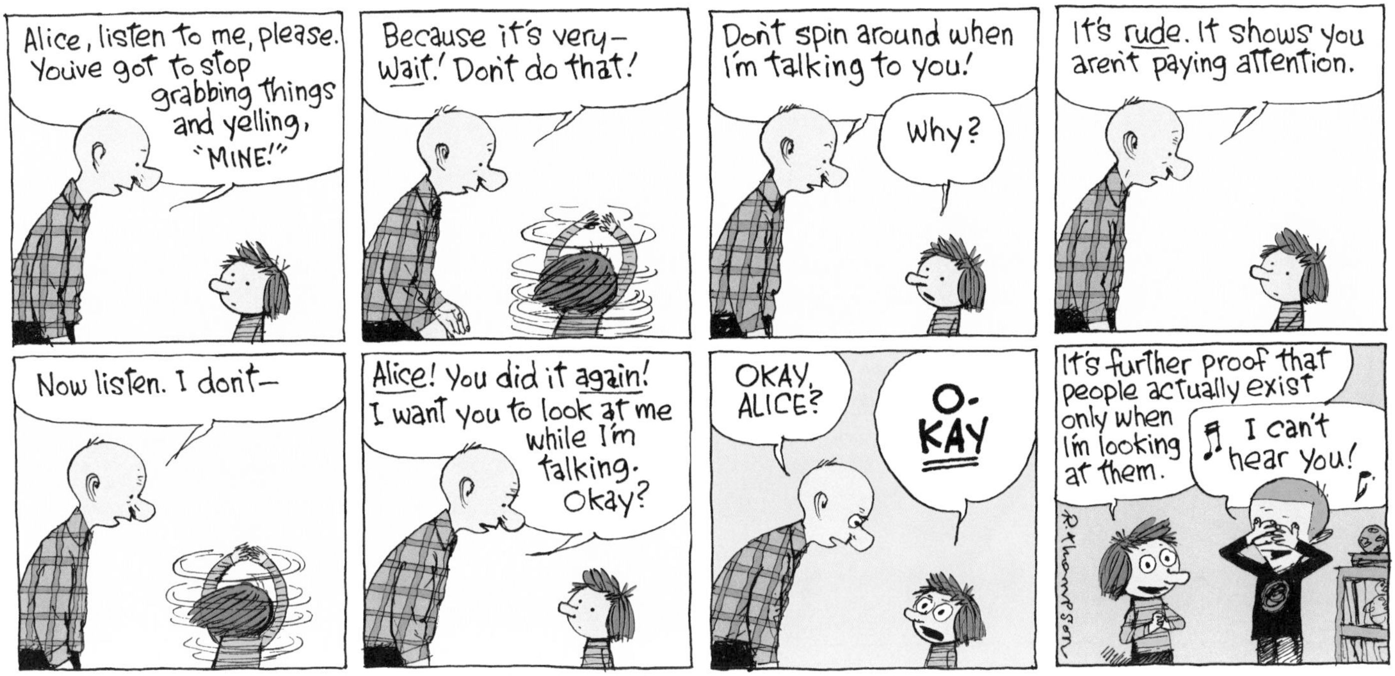
Alice, listen to me, please. You've got to stop grabbing things and yelling, "MINE!"
Because it's very— Wait! Don't do that!
Don't spin around when I'm talking to you!
Why?
It's rude. It shows you aren't paying attention.
Now listen. I don't—
Alice! You did it again! I want you to look at me while I'm talking. Okay?
OKAY, ALICE?
O-KAY
It's further proof that people actually exist only when I'm looking at them.
I can't hear you!
R.Thompson

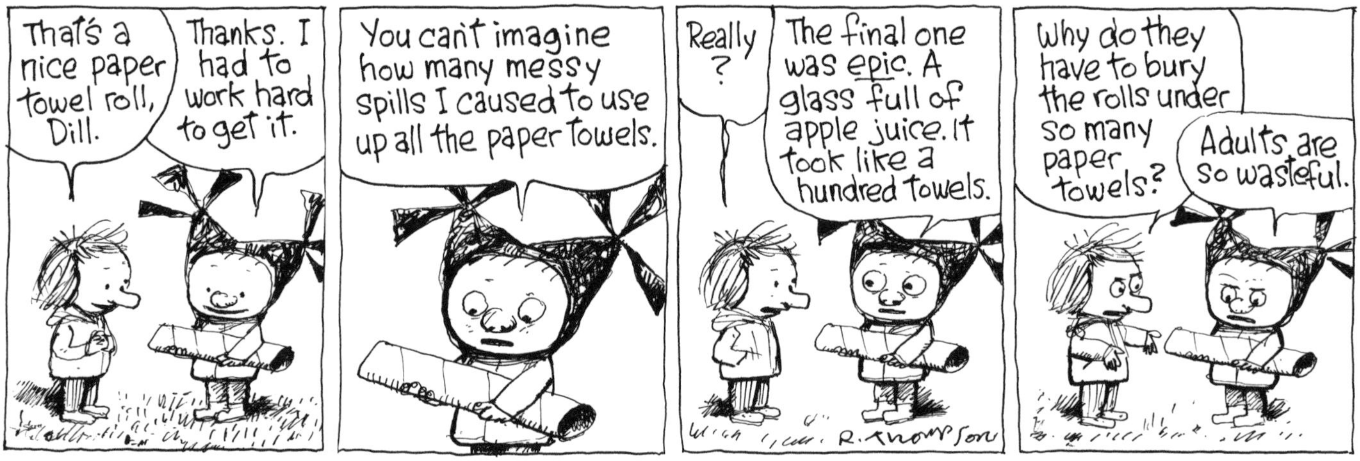
That's a nice paper towel roll, Dill.
Thanks. I had to work hard to get it.
You can't imagine how many messy spills I caused to use up all the paper towels.
Really?
The final one was epic. A glass full of apple juice. It took like a hundred towels.
Why do they have to bury the rolls under so many paper towels?
Adults are so wasteful.
R. Thompson

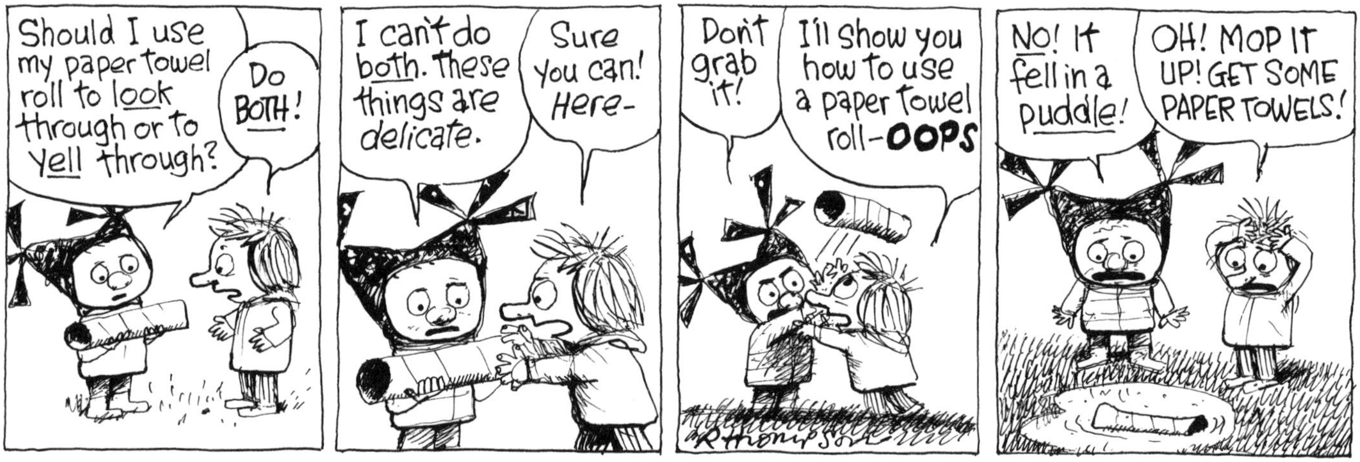
Should I use my paper towel roll to look through or to yell through?
Do BOTH!
I can't do both. These things are delicate.
Sure you can! Here-
Don't grab it!
I'll show you how to use a paper towel roll-**OOPS**
No! It fell in a puddle!
OH! MOP IT UP! GET SOME PAPER TOWELS!
R. Thompson

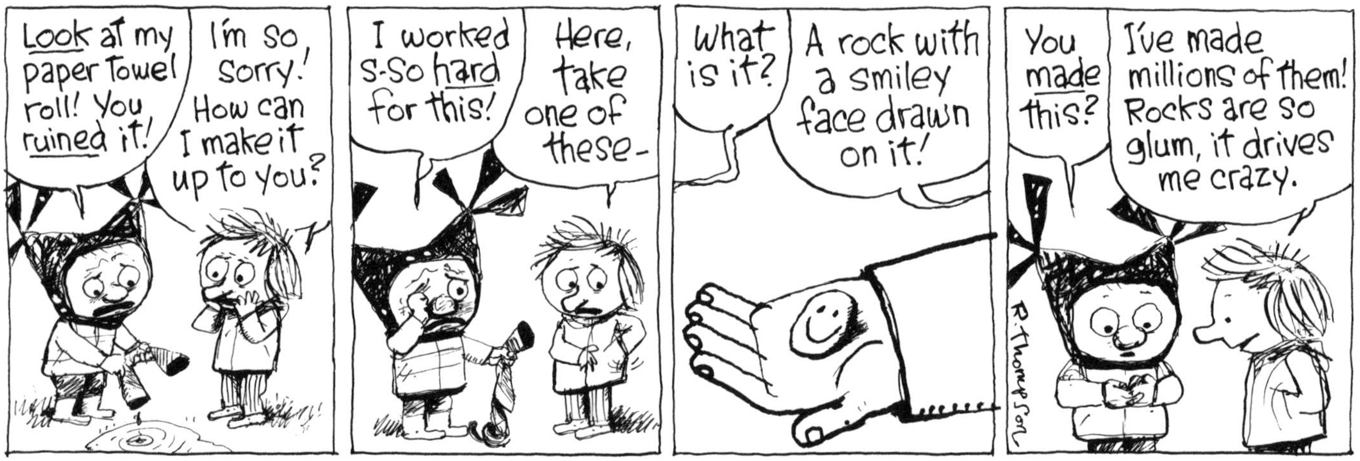
Look at my paper towel roll! You ruined it!
I'm so sorry! How can I make it up to you?
I worked s-so hard for this!
Here, take one of these-
What is it?
A rock with a smiley face drawn on it!
You made this?
I've made millions of them! Rocks are so glum, it drives me crazy.
R. Thompson

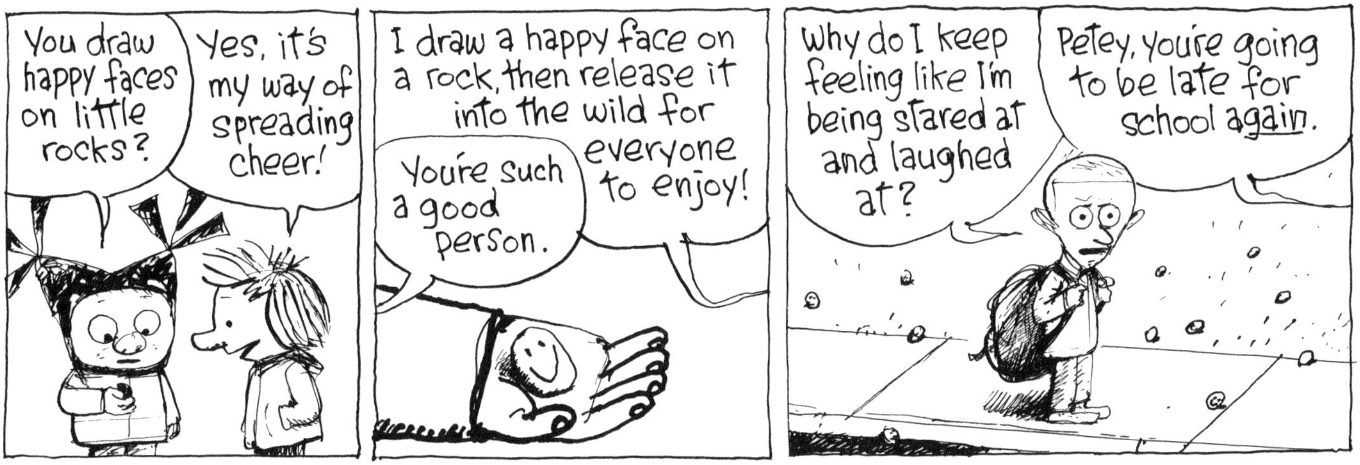
You draw happy faces on little rocks?
Yes, it's my way of spreading cheer!
I draw a happy face on a rock, then release it into the wild for everyone to enjoy!
You're such a good person.
Why do I keep feeling like I'm being stared at and laughed at?
Petey, you're going to be late for school again.

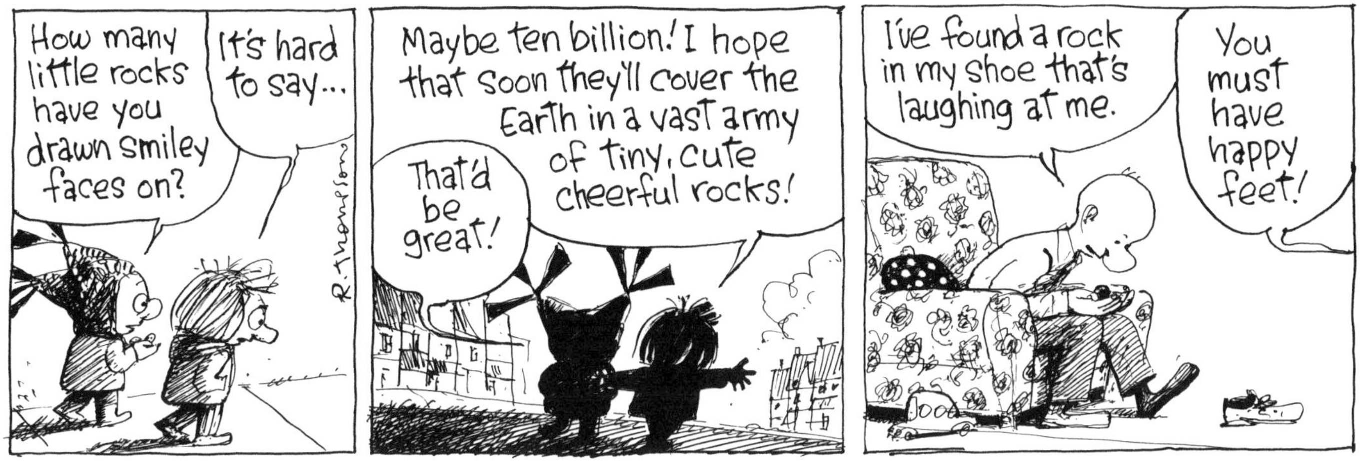
How many little rocks have you drawn smiley faces on?
It's hard to say...
R. Thompson
Maybe ten billion! I hope that soon they'll cover the Earth in a vast army of tiny, cute cheerful rocks!
That'd be great!
I've found a rock in my shoe that's laughing at me.
You must have happy feet!

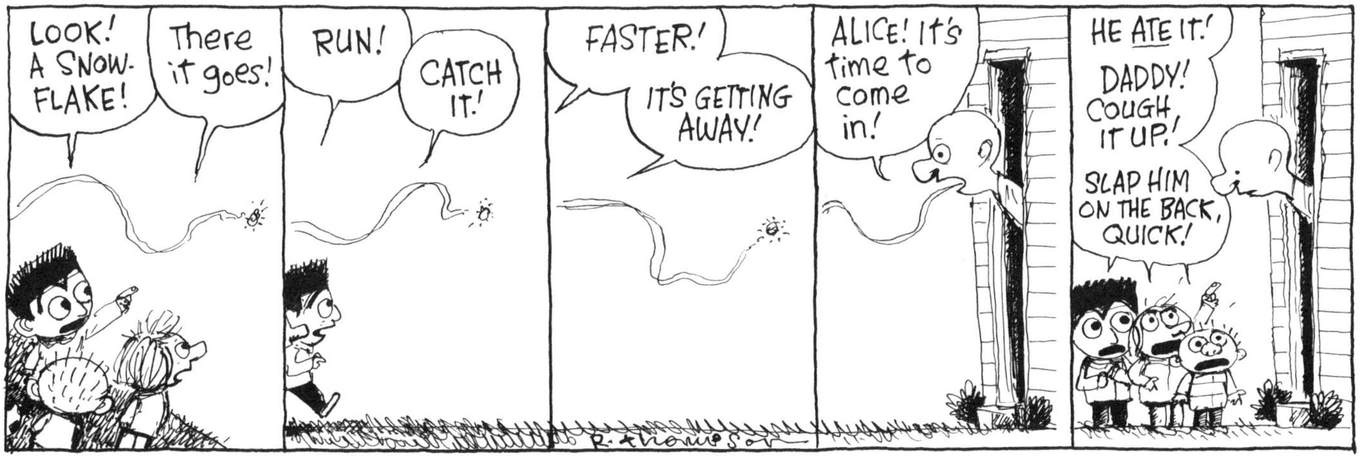
LOOK! A SNOW-FLAKE!
There it goes!
RUN!
CATCH IT!
FASTER!
IT'S GETTING AWAY!
ALICE! It's time to come in!
HE ATE IT!
DADDY! COUGH IT UP!
SLAP HIM ON THE BACK, QUICK!
R. Thompson

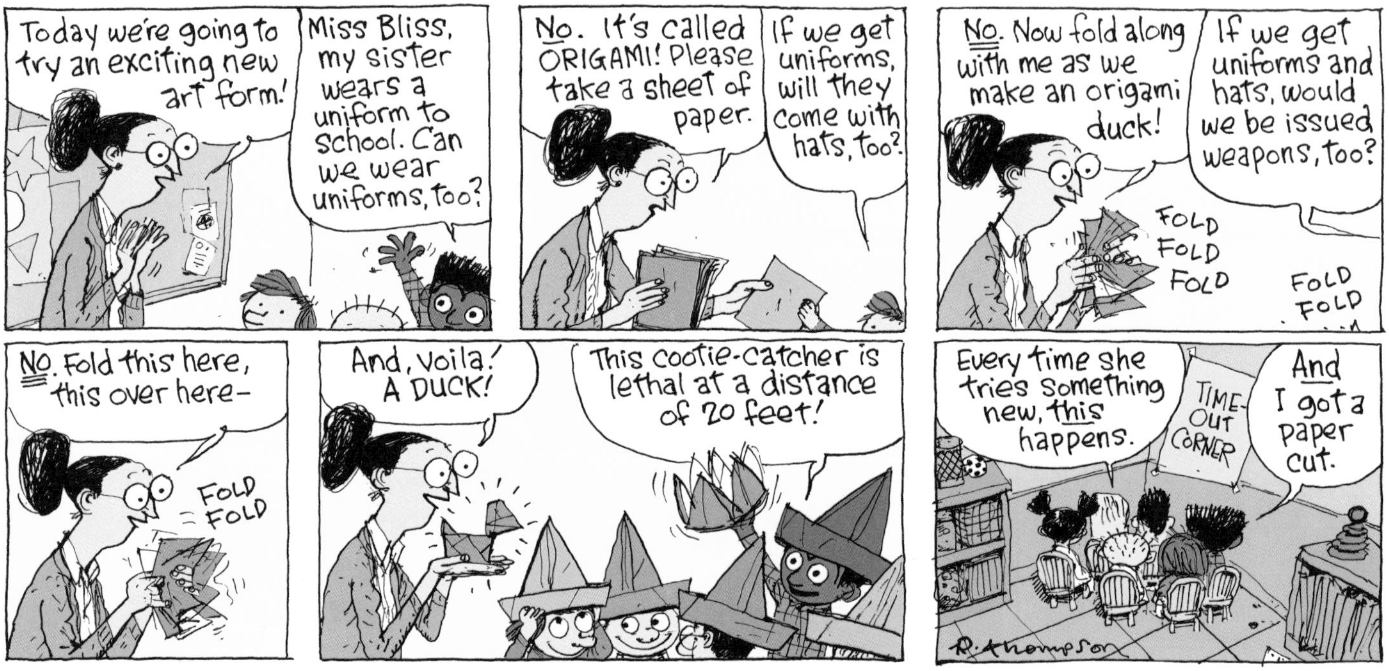
Today we're going to try an exciting new art form!
Miss Bliss, my sister wears a uniform to school. Can we wear uniforms, too?
No. It's called ORIGAMI! Please take a sheet of paper.
If we get uniforms, will they come with hats, too?
No. Now fold along with me as we make an origami duck!
If we get uniforms and hats, would we be issued weapons, too?
FOLD FOLD FOLD
FOLD FOLD
No. Fold this here, this over here-
FOLD FOLD
And, voila! A DUCK!
This cootie-catcher is lethal at a distance of 20 feet!
Every time she tries something new, this happens.
TIME-OUT CORNER
And I got a paper cut.
R. Thompson

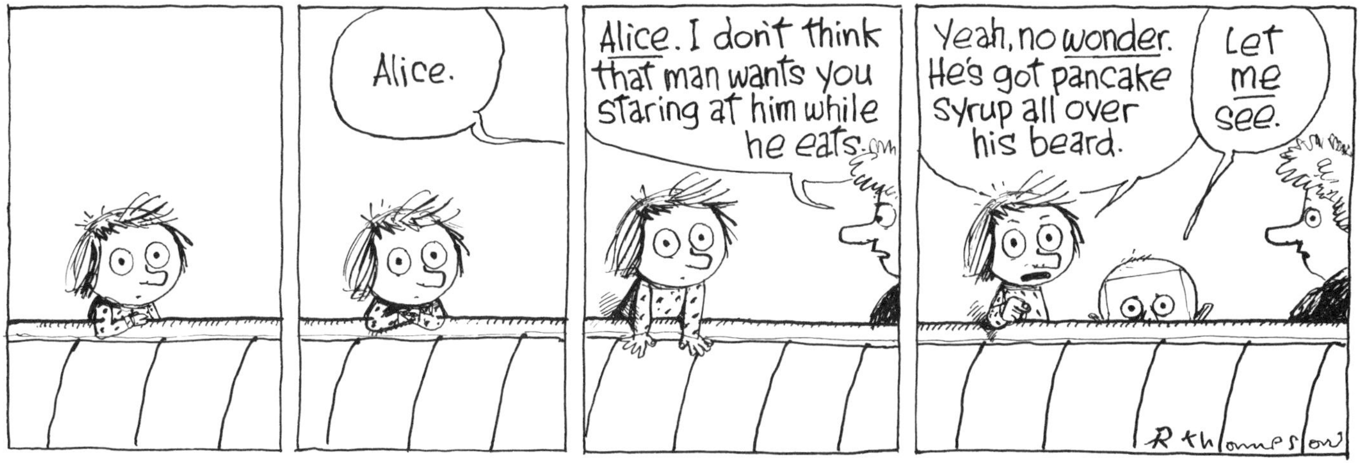
Alice.
Alice. I don't think that man wants you staring at him while he eats.
Yeah, no wonder. He's got pancake syrup all over his beard.
Let me see.
R. Thompson

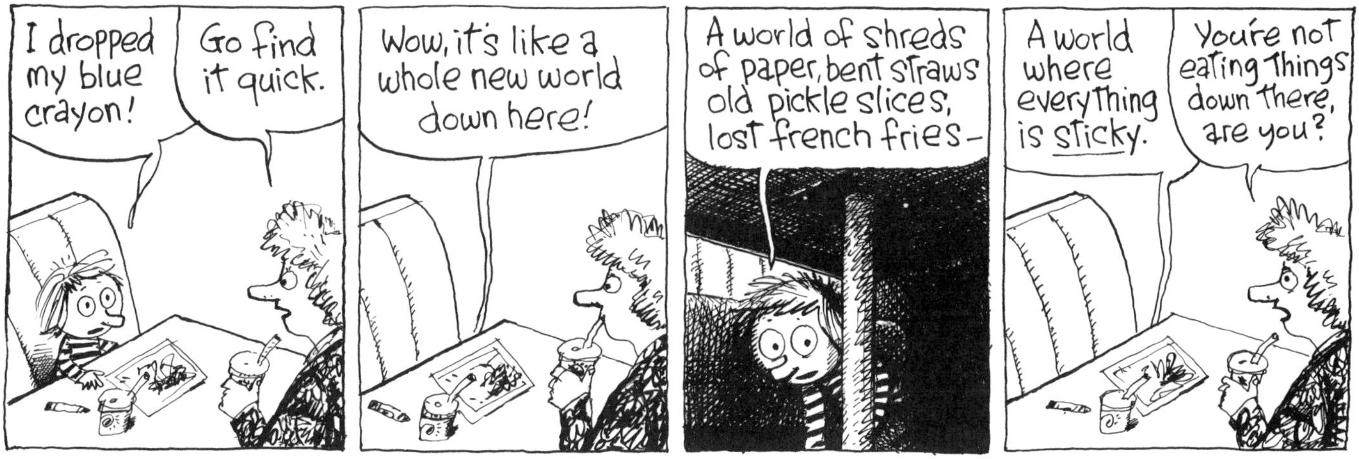
I dropped my blue crayon!
Go find it quick.
Wow, it's like a whole new world down here!
A world of shreds of paper, bent straws old pickle slices, lost french fries-
A world where everything is sticky.
You're not eating things down there, are you?

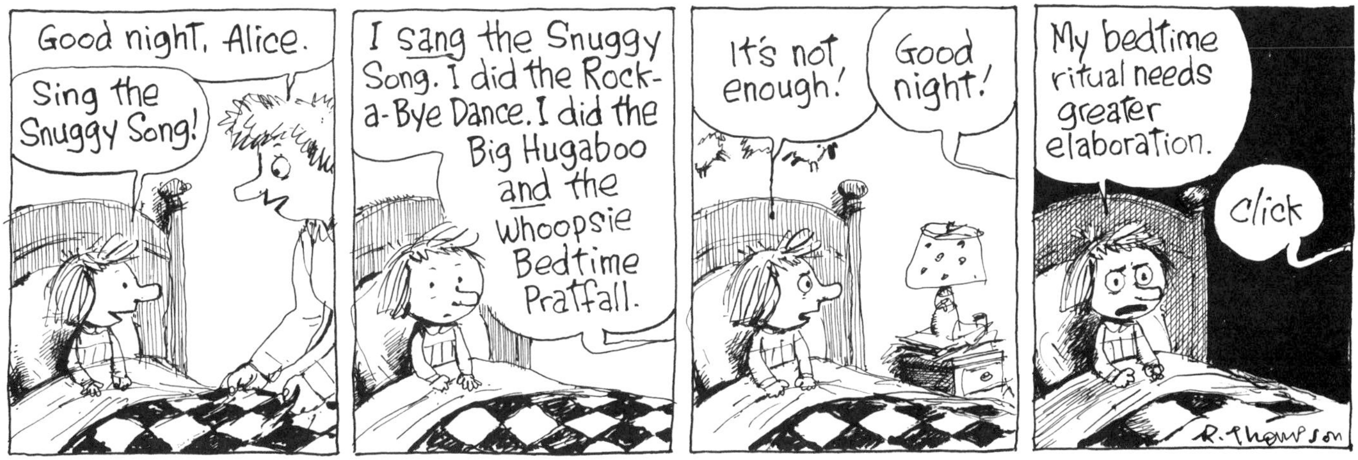
Good night, Alice.
Sing the Snuggy Song!
I sang the Snuggy Song. I did the Rock-a-Bye Dance. I did the Big Hugaboo and the Whoopsie Bedtime Pratfall.
It's not enough!
Good night!
My bedtime ritual needs greater elaboration.
Click
R. Thompson

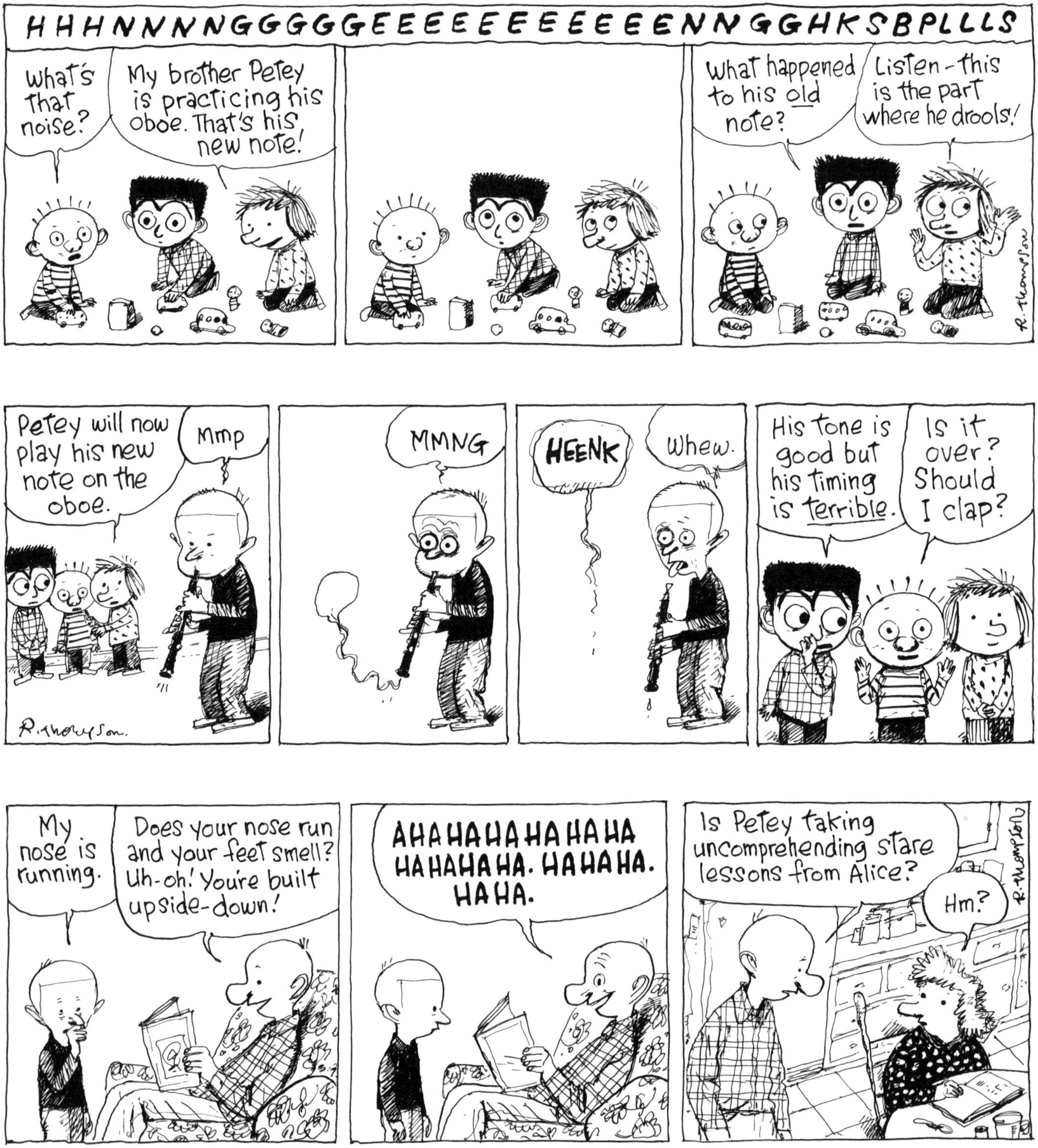

HHHNNNNGGGGGEEEEEEEEEEEENNGGHKSBPLLLS
What's that noise?
My brother Petey is practicing his oboe. That's his new note!
What happened to his old note?
Listen - this is the part where he drools!
R. Thompson
Petey will now play his new note on the oboe.
Mmp
R. Thompson
MMNG
HEENK
Whew.
His tone is good but his timing is terrible.
Is it over? Should I clap?
My nose is running.
Does your nose run and your feet smell? Uh-oh! You're built upside-down!
AHAHAHAHAHAHAHA HAHAHAHA. HAHAHA. HAHA.
Is Petey taking uncomprehending stare lessons from Alice?
Hm?
R. Thompson

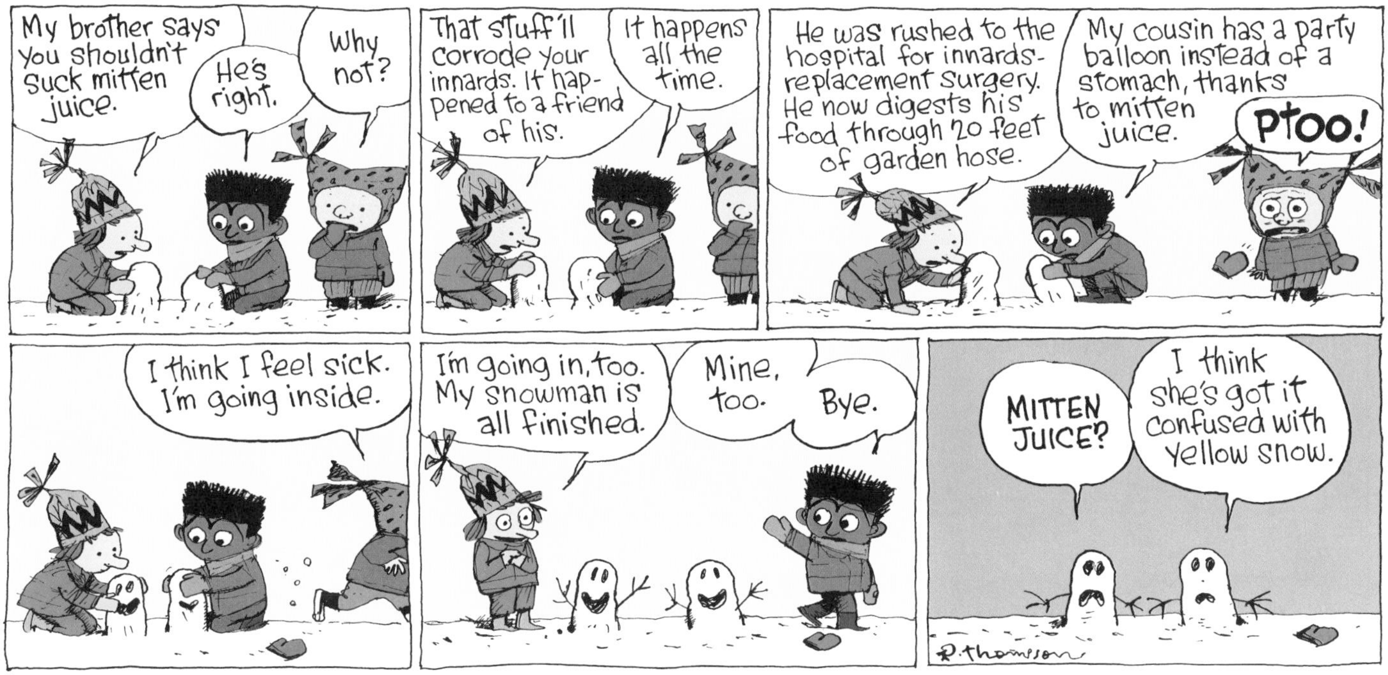
My brother says you shouldn't suck mitten juice.
He's right.
Why not?
That stuff'll corrode your innards. It happened to a friend of his.
It happens all the time.
He was rushed to the hospital for innards-replacement surgery. He now digests his food through 20 feet of garden hose.
My cousin has a party balloon instead of a stomach, thanks to mitten juice.
PTOO!
I think I feel sick. I'm going inside.
I'm going in, too. My snowman is all finished.
Mine, too.
Bye.
MITTEN JUICE?
I think she's got it confused with yellow snow.
R. Thompson

Panel 1:

Dill, what's that thing in your yard?

My brothers are building a trebuchet.

Panel 2:

It's like a catapult. It can throw things real far.

Panel 3:

They've promised me a ride in it when it's finished!

LUCKY. Can I come, too?

Panel 4:

Dill's brothers are building a trebuchet. Why doesn't Petey build stuff?

Petey made a very nice horsehead bookend for me once.

Panel 5:

I keep it up high on the shelf with all my favorite fragile things.

Panel 6:

I pinched my finger doing it, too. See the scar?

Big deal! How many horsehead books do we have anyway?

Alice.

Panel 7:

Alice, where are you taking that ice cube tray?

Up to the bathroom.

Panel 8:

If you flush an ice cube down the potty before you go to bed, it'll snow that night for sure! I'm going to dump the whole tray in!

Panel 9:

Or you could go to the store and get some bags of party ice—

You may flush one ice cube, Alice.

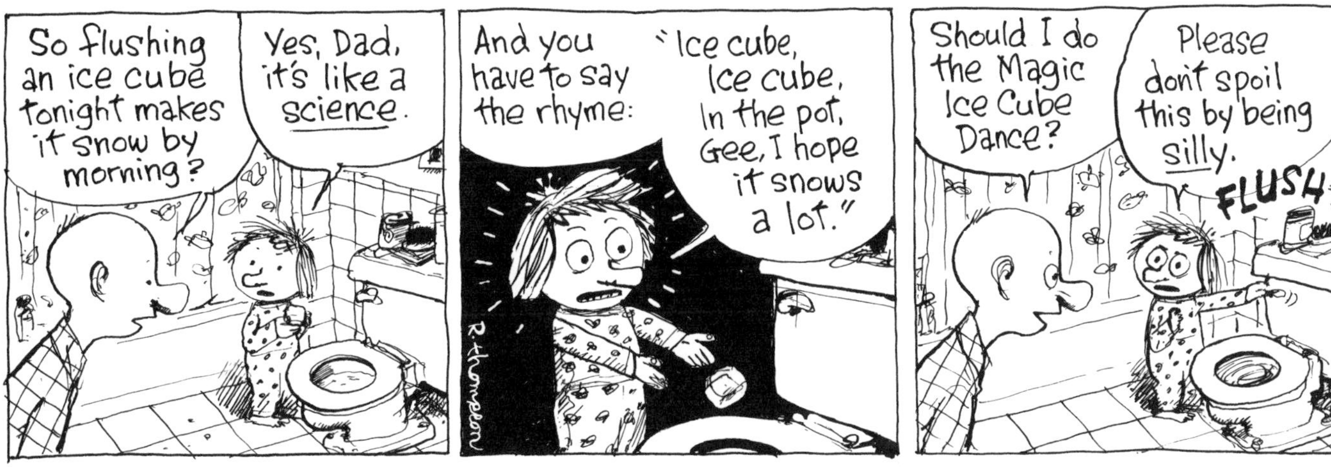
So flushing an ice cube tonight makes it snow by morning?
Yes, Dad, it's like a science.
And you have to say the rhyme:
"Ice cube, Ice cube, In the pot, Gee, I hope it snows a lot."
Should I do the Magic Ice Cube Dance?
Please don't spoil this by being silly.
FLUSH

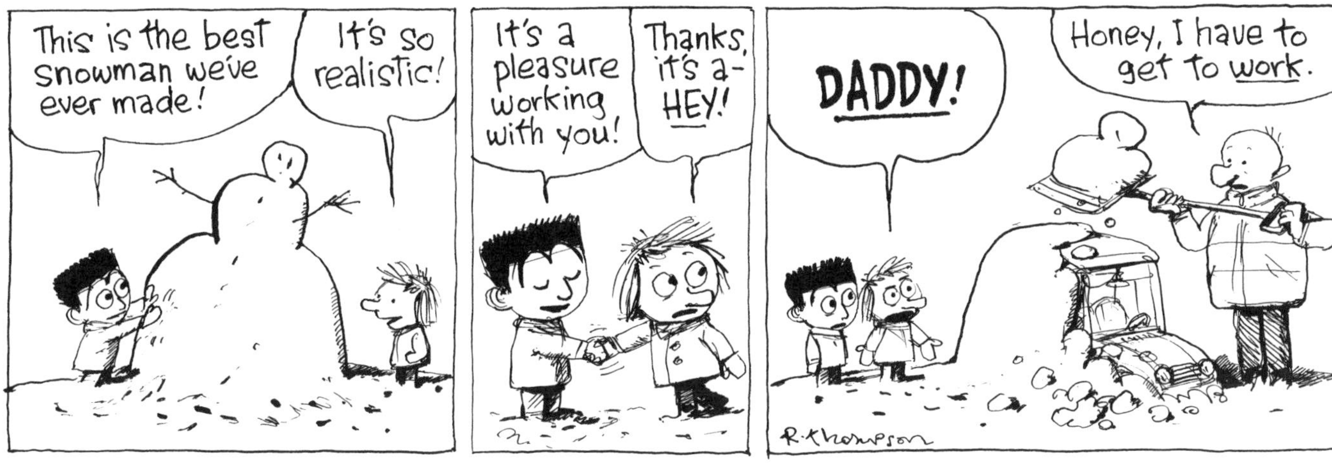
This is the best snowman we've ever made!
It's so realistic!
It's a pleasure working with you!
Thanks, it's a- HEY!
DADDY!
Honey, I have to get to work.

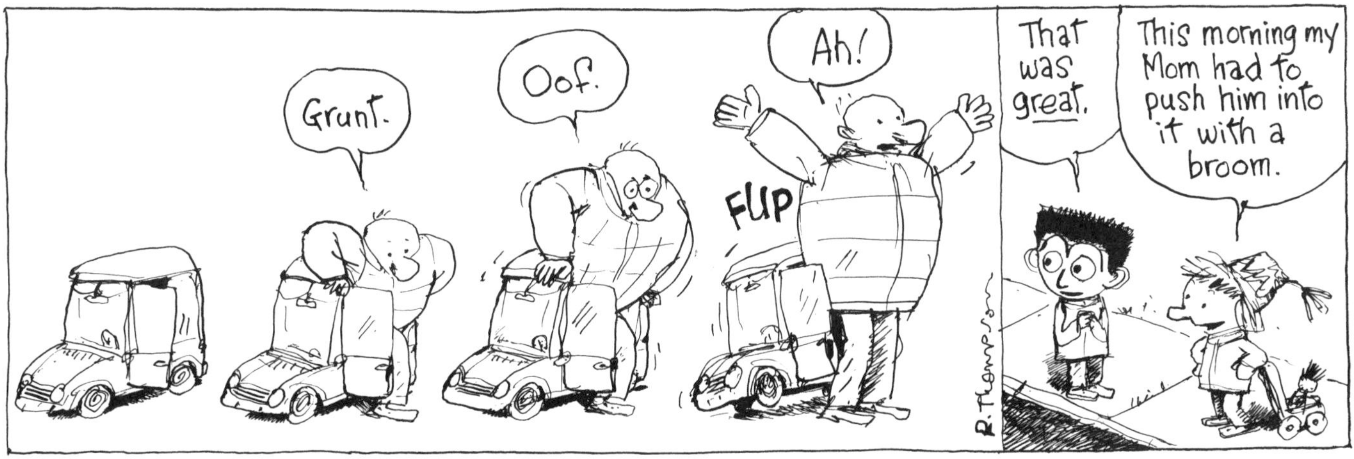
Grunt.
Oof.
FLIP
Ah!
That was great.
This morning my Mom had to push him into it with a broom.

Today we'll be making beautiful Valentines to share with our parents!

Ooh!

We'll use construction paper, glitter, glue and cotton balls. And remember, Creativity plus Neatness equals Art!

Beni, please be careful using the glue. Kevin, don't wave the scissors.

Alice, not so much glitter. Dillon, keep your shoes on. Marcus, stop that. COUGH.

Nara, not in your hair. COUGH. Not in Alice's hair either. COUGH COUGH.

COUGH. All right, we should be COUGH finished COUGH. Please put your COUGH on the COUGH COUGH COUGH.

Then Miss Bliss kept on coughing and had to go to the doctor to be treated for acute glitterlung.

Aw, the poor woman! You should make her a card.

R. Thompson

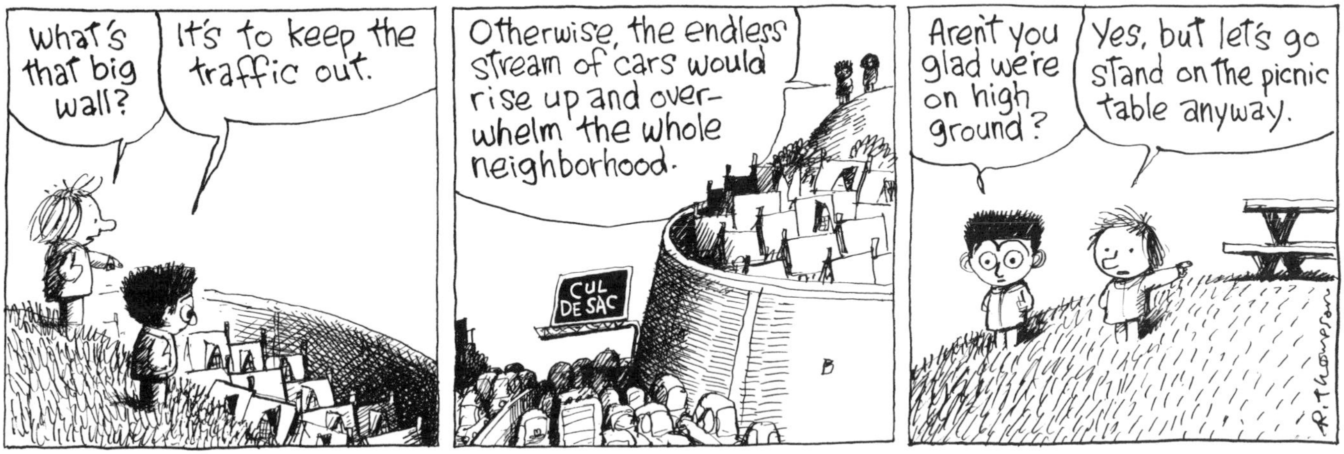
What's that big wall?
It's to keep the traffic out.
Otherwise, the endless stream of cars would rise up and overwhelm the whole neighborhood.
CUL DE SAC
Aren't you glad we're on high ground?
Yes, but let's go stand on the picnic table anyway.
R. Thompson

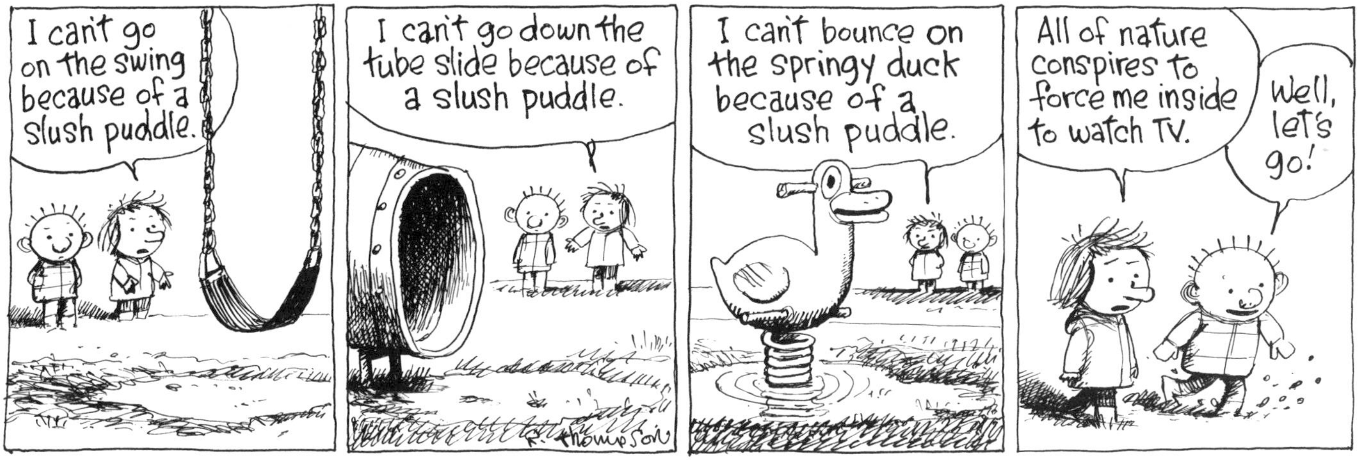
I can't go on the swing because of a slush puddle.
I can't go down the tube slide because of a slush puddle.
R. Thompson
I can't bounce on the springy duck because of a slush puddle.
All of nature conspires to force me inside to watch TV.
Well, let's go!

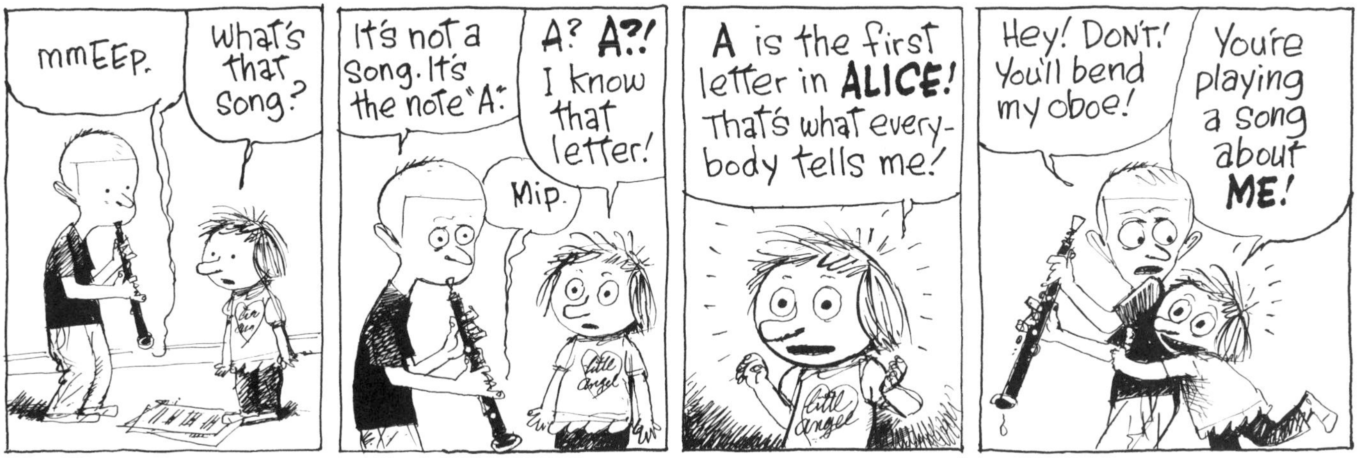
mmEEP.
What's that song?
It's not a song. It's the note "A."
A? A?! I know that letter!
Mip.
A is the first letter in ALICE! That's what everybody tells me!
Little Angel
Hey! DON'T! You'll bend my oboe!
You're playing a song about ME!

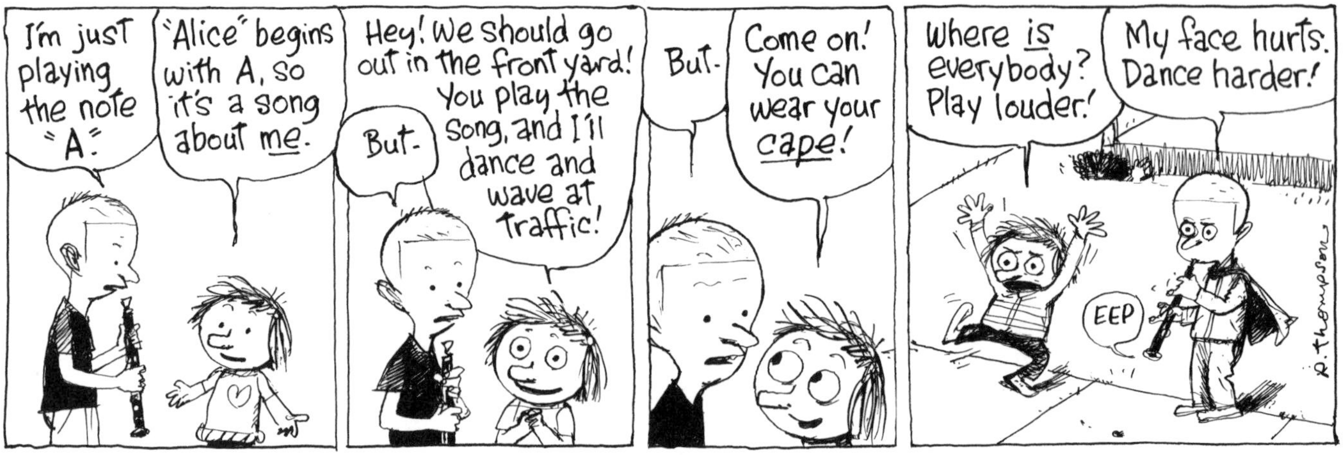
I'm just playing the note "A."
"Alice" begins with A, so it's a song about me.
Hey! We should go out in the front yard! You play the song, and I'll dance and wave at traffic!
But-
But-
Come on! You can wear your cape!
Where is everybody? Play louder!
EEP
My face hurts. Dance harder!

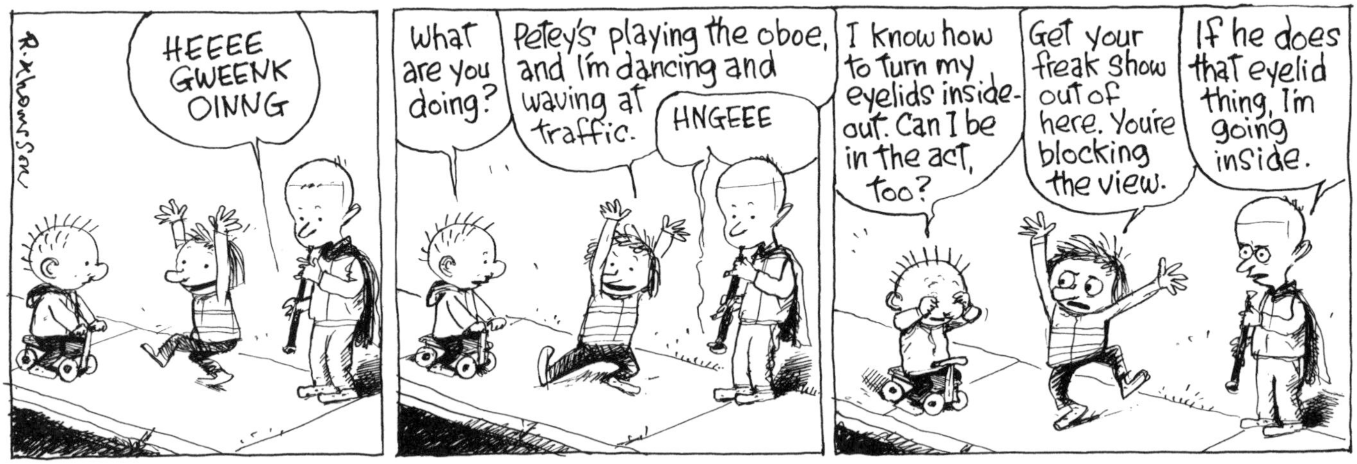
HEEEE GWEENK OINNG
What are you doing?
Petey's playing the oboe, and I'm dancing and waving at traffic.
HNGEEE
I know how to turn my eyelids inside-out. Can I be in the act, too?
Get your freak show out of here. You're blocking the view.
If he does that eyelid thing, I'm going inside.

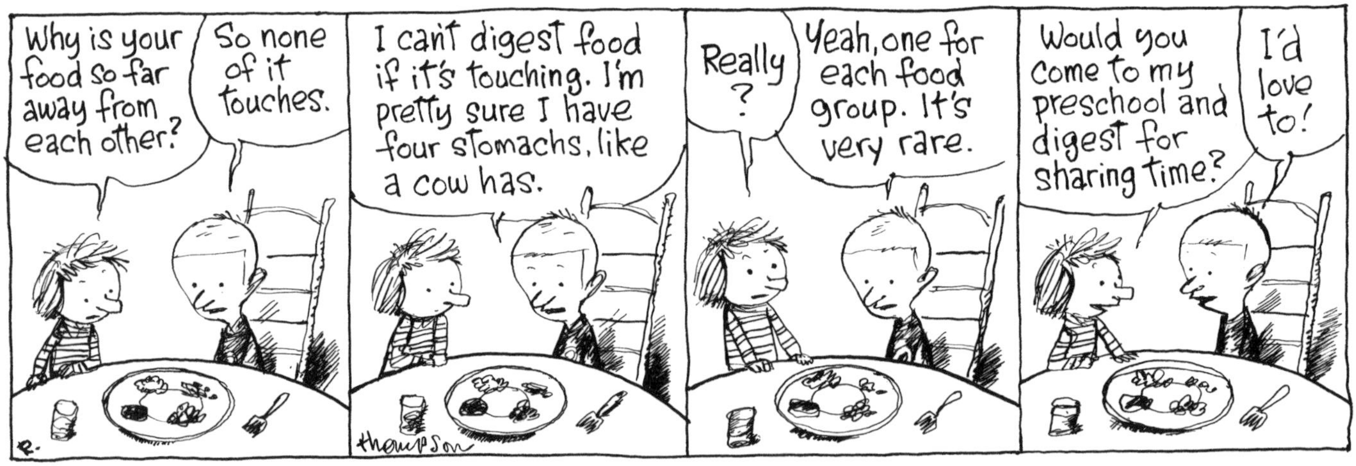
Why is your food so far away from each other?
So none of it touches.
I can't digest food if it's touching. I'm pretty sure I have four stomachs, like a cow has.
Really?
Yeah, one for each food group. It's very rare.
Would you come to my preschool and digest for sharing time?
I'd love to!

Look! What's that?
What?
Oh, it's just a pile of snow.
It's so big.
VAL-U-LESS
They call it Old Mount Soot. It forms in the parking lot every year whether it snows or not.
Mom, can I climb on it?
No, it's dirty.
On its icy, begrimed slopes dwell tiny, dirty trolls called the Sooti. They sneak down and carry off unwary bargain-hunting shoppers to their doom.
Really?
That's why you find abandoned shopping carts everywhere.
Wow. Nature is so cool.
Look! Here's a cart, and somebody's left all their coupons in it!

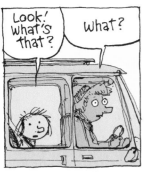

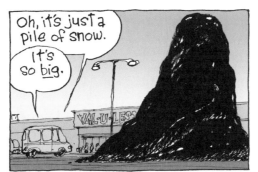

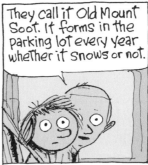

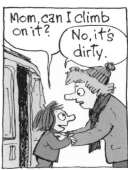

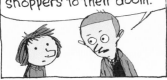

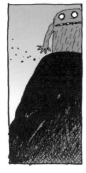

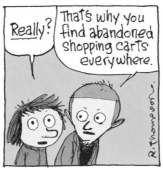

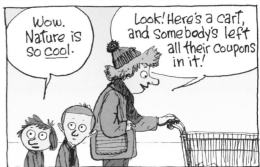

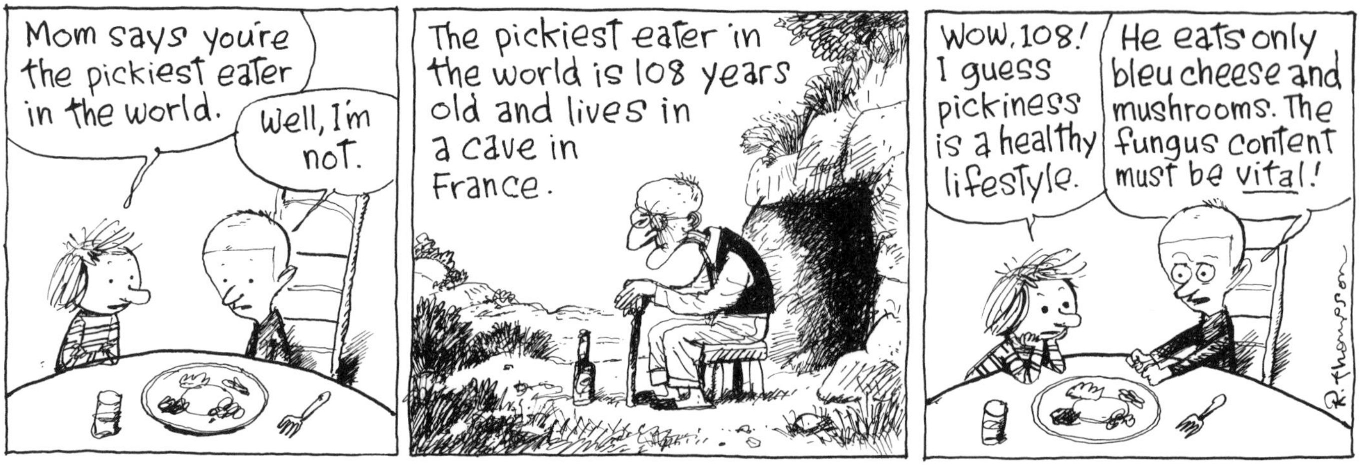
Mom says you're the pickiest eater in the world.
Well, I'm not.
The pickiest eater in the world is 108 years old and lives in a cave in France.
WOW, 108! I guess pickiness is a healthy lifestyle.
He eats only bleu cheese and mushrooms. The fungus content must be vital!

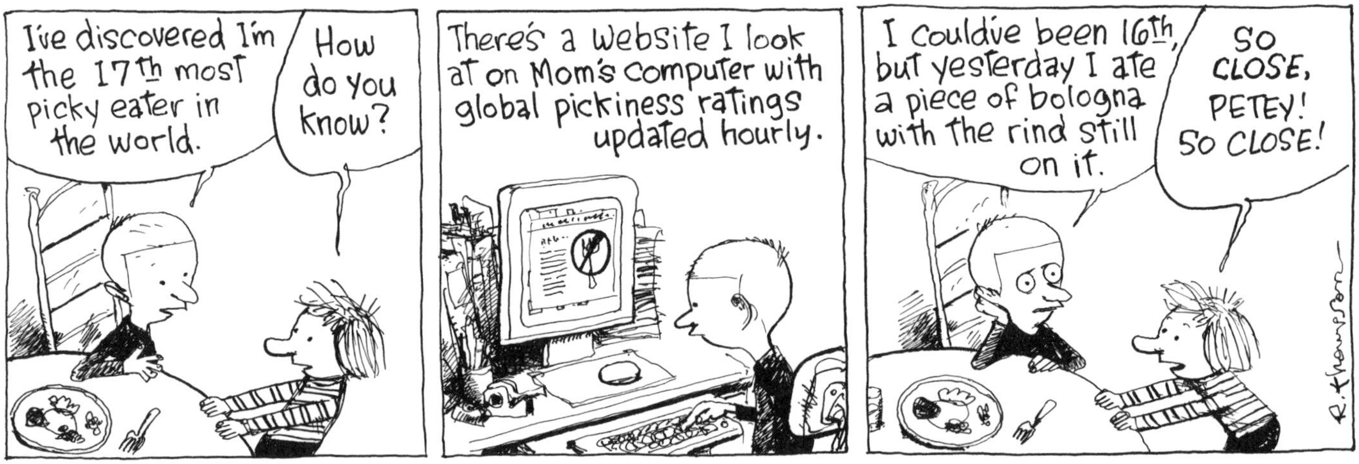
I've discovered I'm the 17th most picky eater in the world.
How do you know?
There's a website I look at on Mom's computer with global pickiness ratings updated hourly.
I could've been 16th, but yesterday I ate a piece of bologna with the rind still on it.
SO CLOSE, PETEY! SO CLOSE!

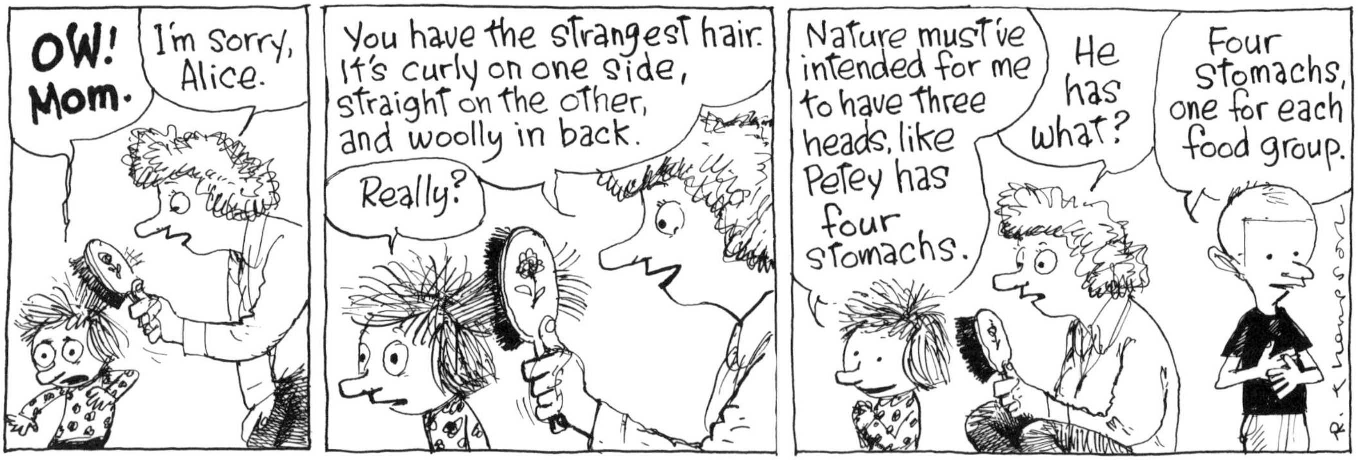
OW! Mom.
I'm sorry, Alice.
You have the strangest hair. It's curly on one side, straight on the other, and woolly in back.
Really?
Nature must've intended for me to have three heads, like Petey has four stomachs.
He has what?
Four stomachs, one for each food group.

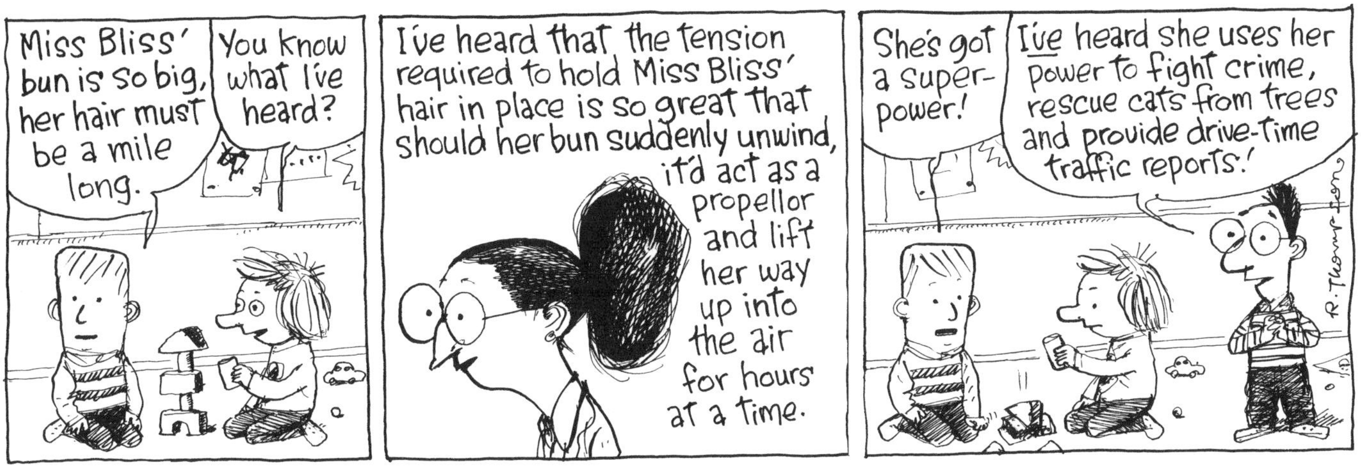
Miss Bliss' bun is so big, her hair must be a mile long.
You know what I've heard?
I've heard that the tension required to hold Miss Bliss' hair in place is so great that should her bun suddenly unwind, it'd act as a propellor and lift her way up into the air for hours at a time.
She's got a super-power!
I've heard she uses her power to fight crime, rescue cats from trees and provide drive-time traffic reports!
R. Thompson

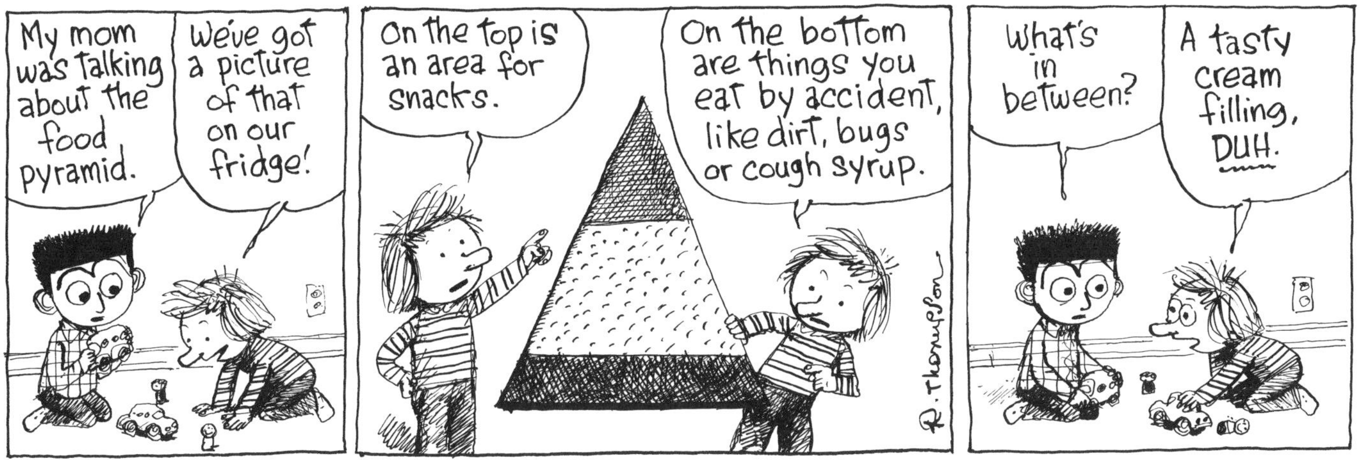
My mom was talking about the food pyramid.
We've got a picture of that on our fridge!
On the top is an area for snacks.
On the bottom are things you eat by accident, like dirt, bugs or cough syrup.
R. Thompson
What's in between?
A tasty cream filling, DUH.

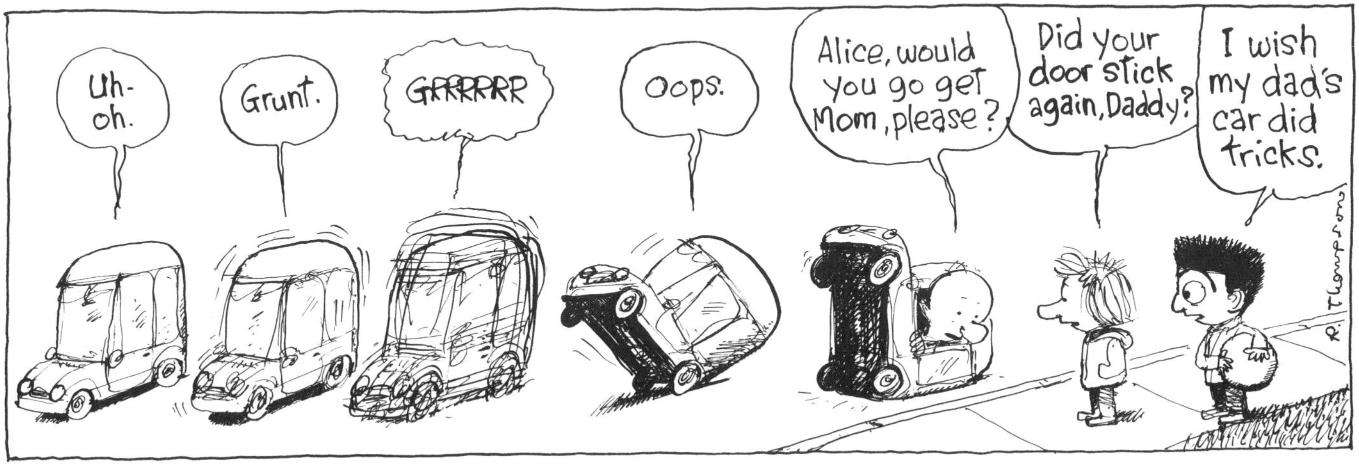
Uh-oh.
Grunt.
GRRRRRR
Oops.
Alice, would you go get Mom, please?
Did your door stick again, Daddy?
I wish my dad's car did tricks.
R. Thompson

C'mon, Petey! You can do it!
Mom, I don't know–
GO, PETEY, GO!
NO, WAIT, I CAAAAAAA
Omigosh– Petey?
MUSH
PETEY? CAN YOU STAND UP?
I–I don't know–
Yeah, I guess so.
YAY! WHO'S MOM'S BIG BOY? LET'S DO IT AGAIN!
ARE YOU CRAZY? ARE YOU TRYING TO KILL ME?
Is your brother in another awkward stage?
I call it "Keeping Mom's Expectations Low" and I'm all for it.
R. Thompson

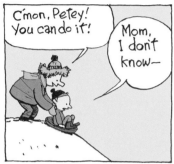

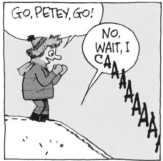

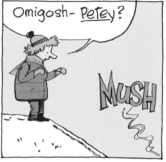

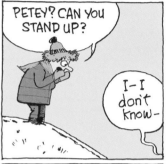

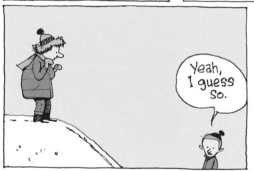

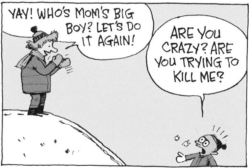

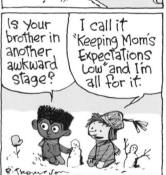

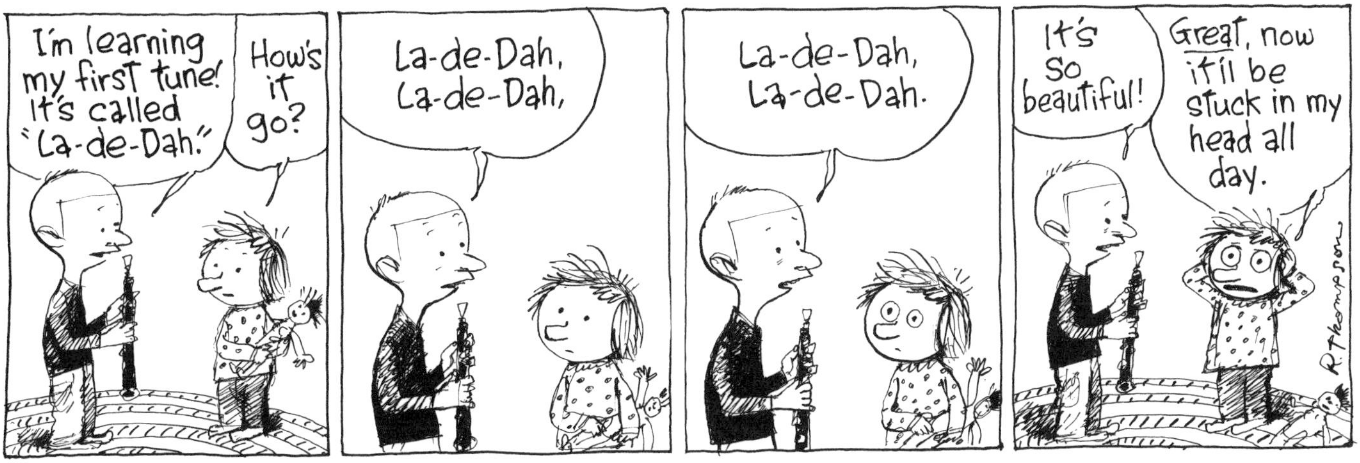
I'm learning my first tune! It's called "La-de-Dah."
How's it go?
La-de-Dah, La-de-Dah,
La-de-Dah, La-de-Dah.
It's so beautiful!
Great, now it'll be stuck in my head all day.
R. Thompson

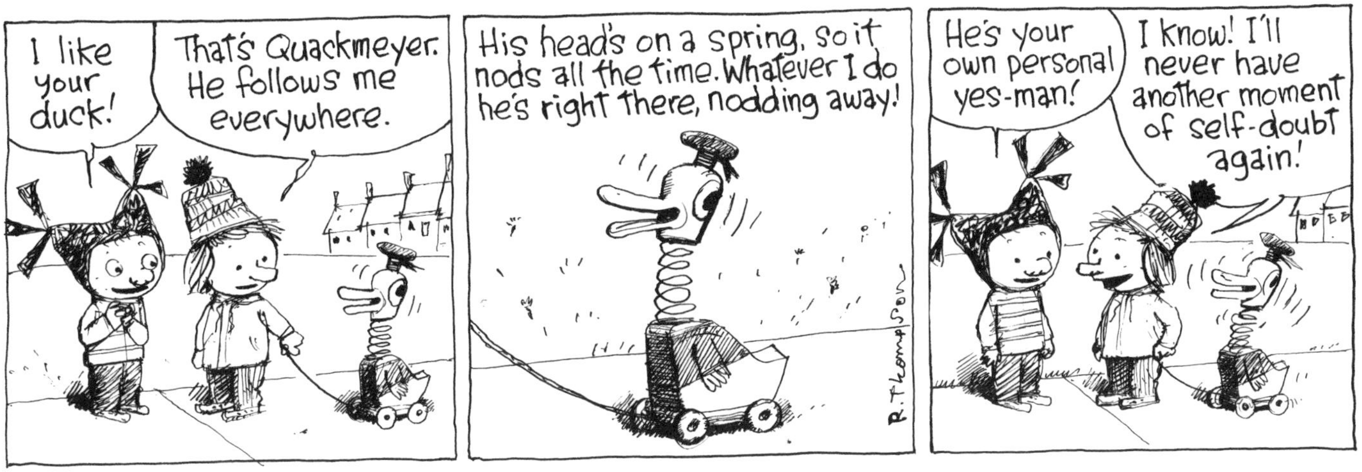
I like your duck!
That's Quackmeyer. He follows me everywhere.
His head's on a spring, so it nods all the time. Whatever I do he's right there, nodding away!
R. Thompson
He's your own personal yes-man!
I know! I'll never have another moment of self-doubt again!

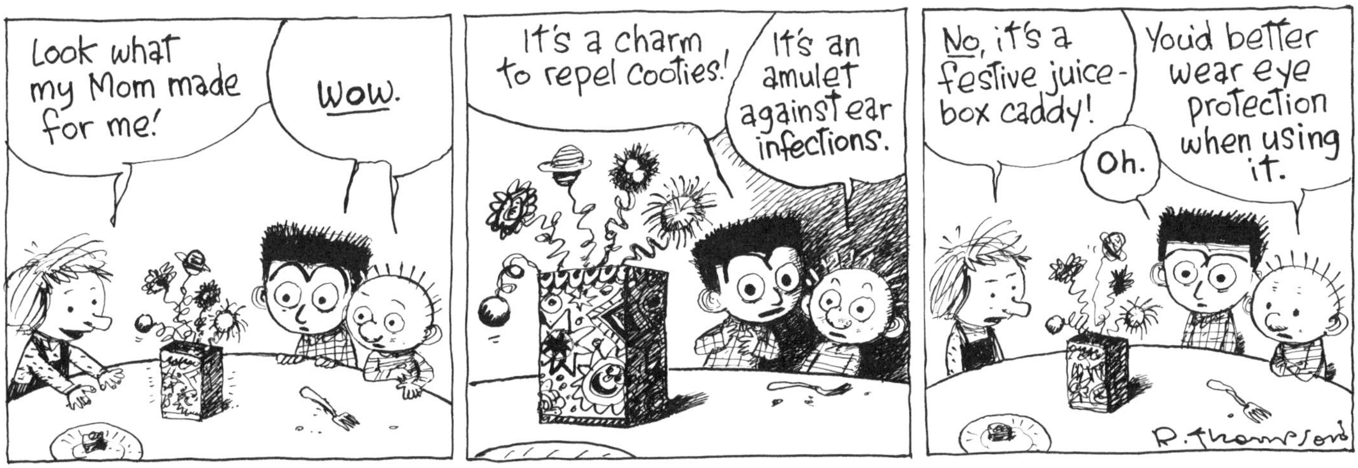
Look what my Mom made for me!
Wow.
It's a charm to repel cooties!
It's an amulet against ear infections.
No, it's a festive juice-box caddy!
Oh.
You'd better wear eye protection when using it.
R. Thompson

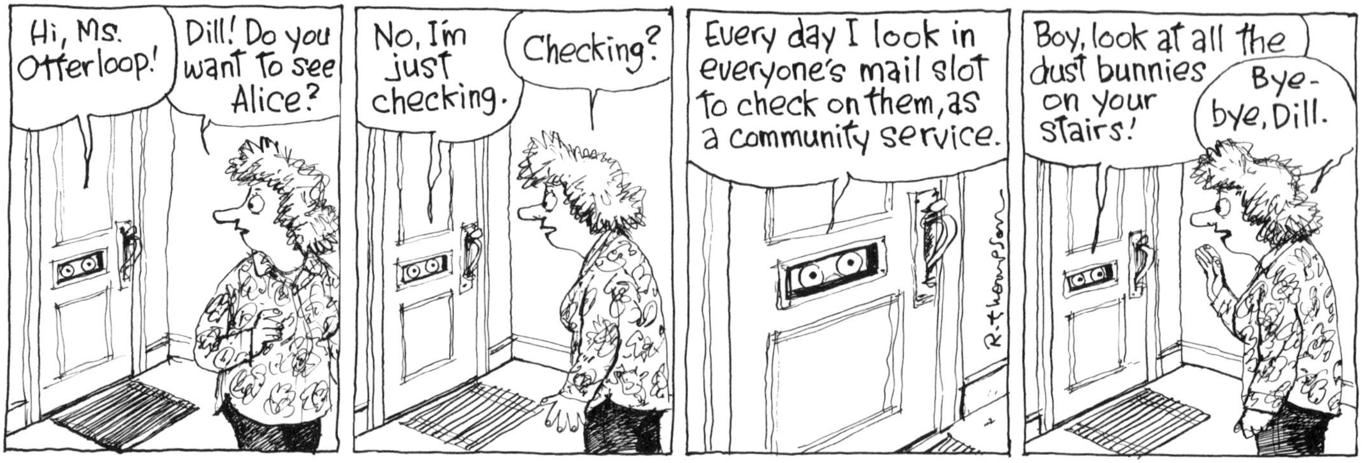
Hi, Ms. Otterloop!
Dill! Do you want to see Alice?
No, I'm just checking.
Checking?
Every day I look in everyone's mail slot to check on them, as a community service.
Boy, look at all the dust bunnies on your stairs!
Bye-bye, Dill.
R. thompson

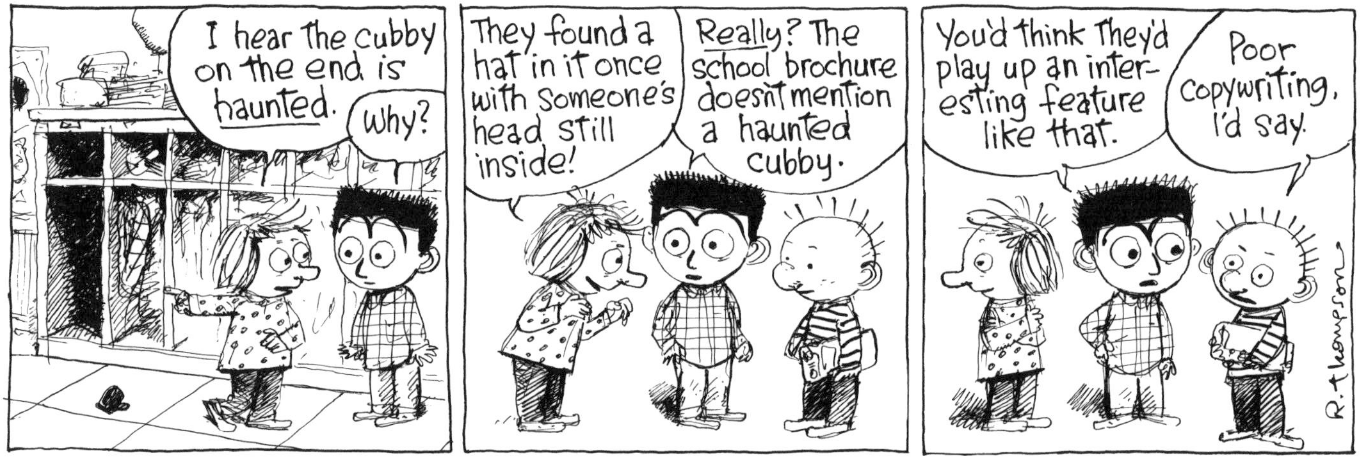
I hear the cubby on the end is haunted.
Why?
They found a hat in it once with someone's head still inside!
Really? The school brochure doesn't mention a haunted cubby.
You'd think they'd play up an interesting feature like that.
Poor copywriting, I'd say.
R. thompson

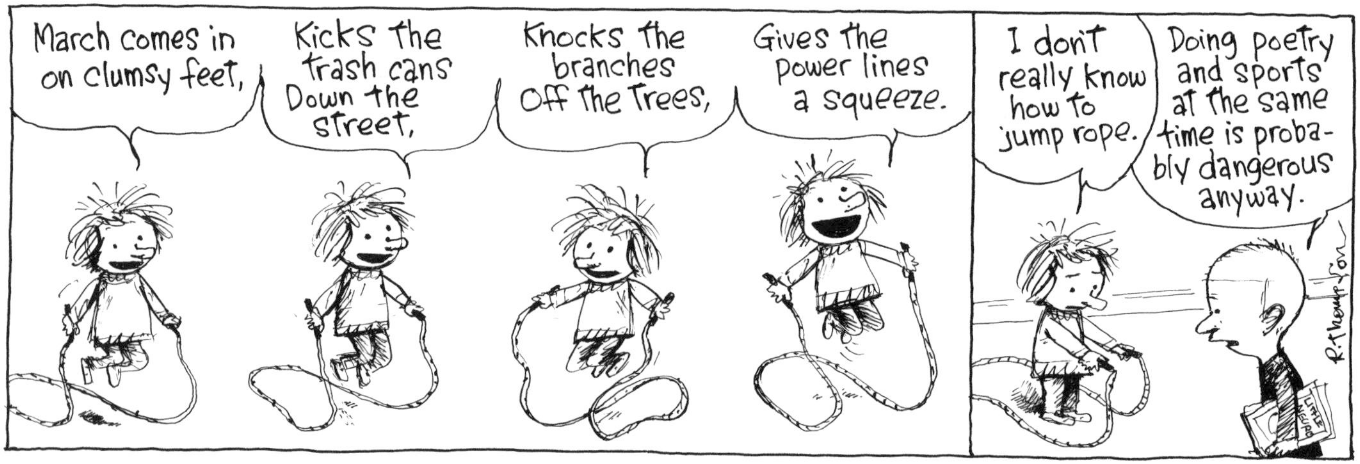
March comes in on clumsy feet,
Kicks the trash cans Down the street,
Knocks the branches Off the Trees,
Gives the power lines a squeeze.
I don't really know how to jump rope.
Doing poetry and sports at the same time is probably dangerous anyway.
R. thompson

Can we go to the toy store?
In a little while.
Daddy, carry me.
Let's walk for now, Alice.
But I'm really, tired. Carry me.
We haven't walked very far.
DADDY, PLEASE? Carry me!
OK, come here. Don't jump.
JUMP
SMACK
GAH-
Oops.
Can we go to the toy store when Daddy's nose stops bleeding?
Ask him when he comes out of the men's room.
I wish he'd hurry. I'm tired of sitting.
R. Thompson

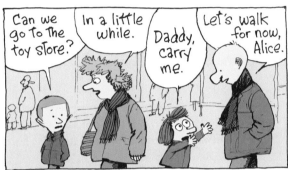

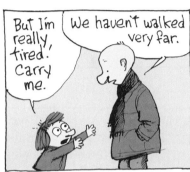

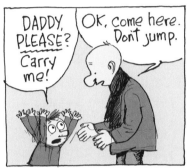

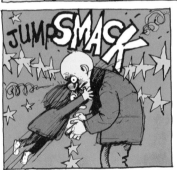

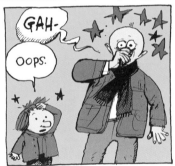

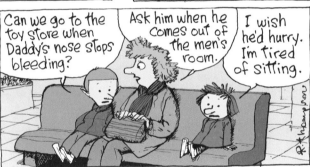

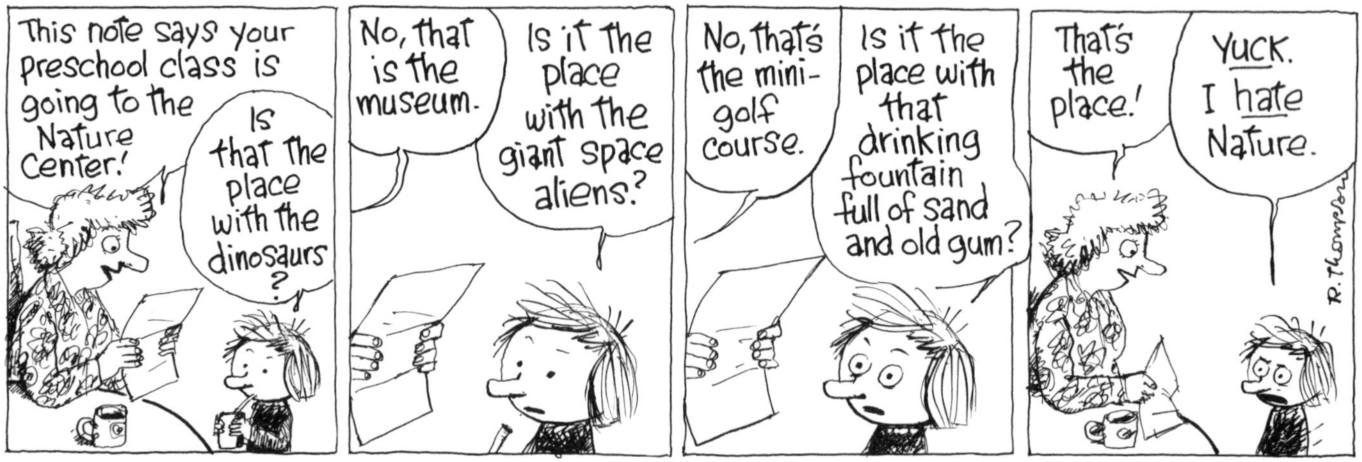
This note says your preschool class is going to the Nature Center!
Is that the place with the dinosaurs?
No, that is the museum.
Is it the place with the giant space aliens?
No, that's the mini-golf course.
Is it the place with that drinking fountain full of sand and old gum?
That's the place!
YUCK. I hate Nature.
R. Thompson

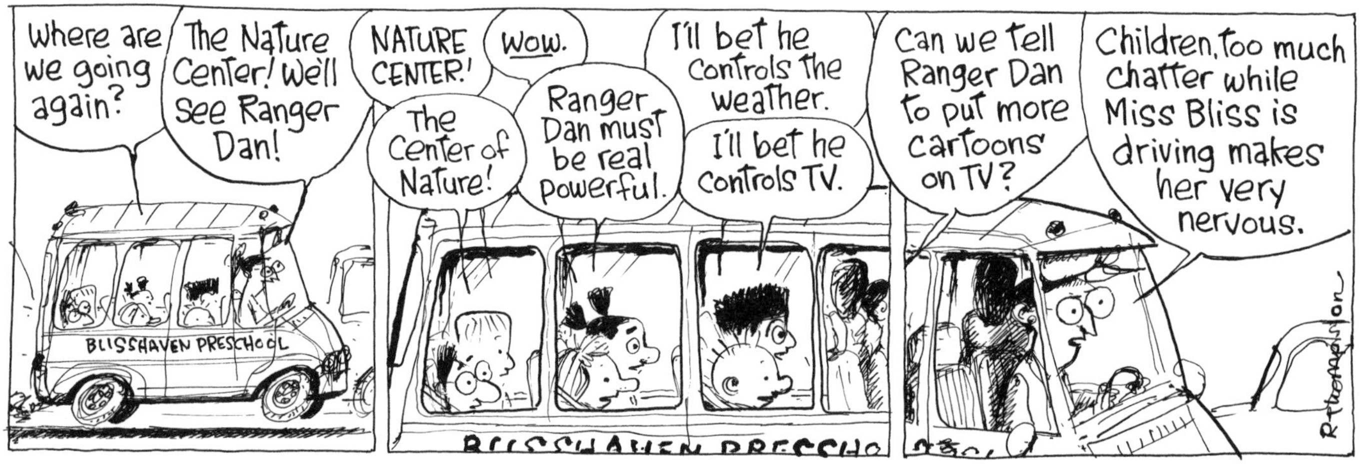
Where are we going again?
The Nature Center! We'll see Ranger Dan!
BLISSHAVEN PRESCHOOL
NATURE CENTER!
WOW.
The Center of Nature!
Ranger Dan must be real powerful.
I'll bet he controls the weather.
I'll bet he controls TV.
Can we tell Ranger Dan to put more cartoons on TV?
Children, too much chatter while Miss Bliss is driving makes her very nervous.
R. Thompson

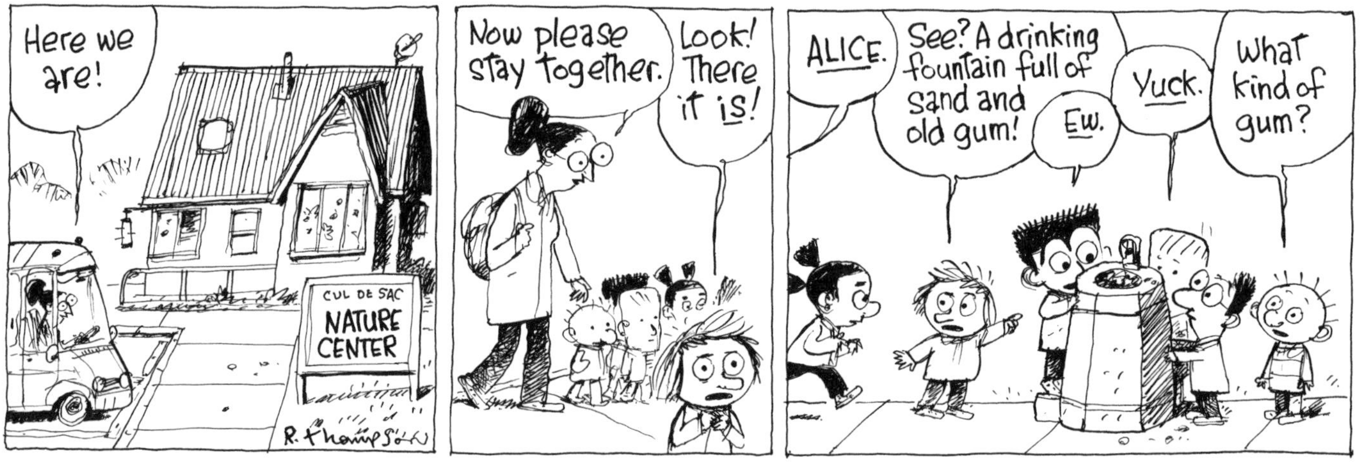
Here we are!
CUL DE SAC
NATURE CENTER
R. Thompson
Now please stay together.
Look! There it is!
ALICE.
See? A drinking fountain full of sand and old gum!
Ew.
Yuck.
What kind of gum?

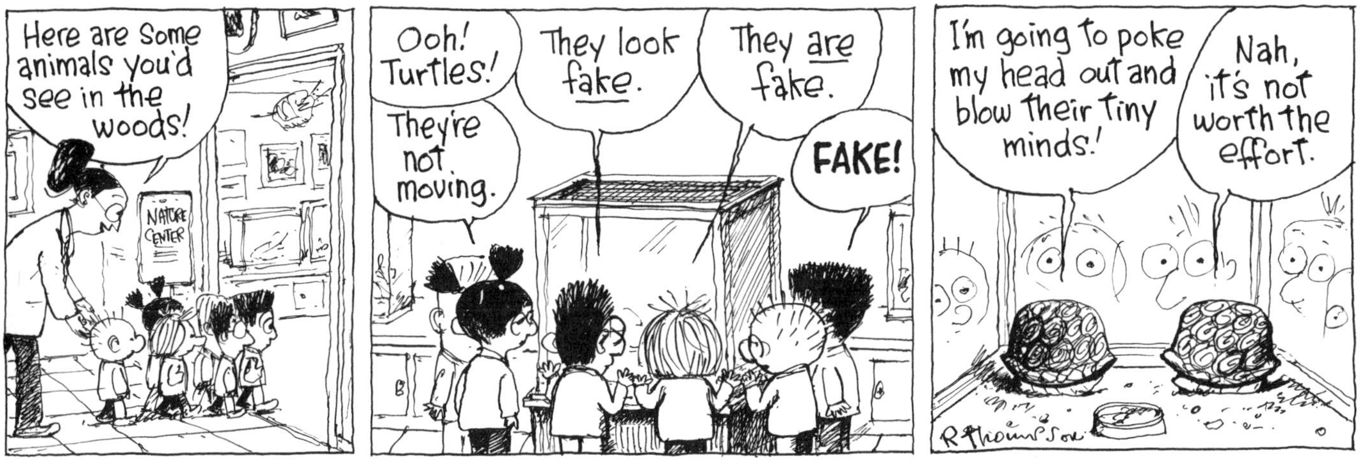
Here are some animals you'd see in the woods!
NATURE CENTER
Ooh! Turtles!
They're not moving.
They look fake.
They are fake.
FAKE!
I'm going to poke my head out and blow their tiny minds!
Nah, it's not worth the effort.

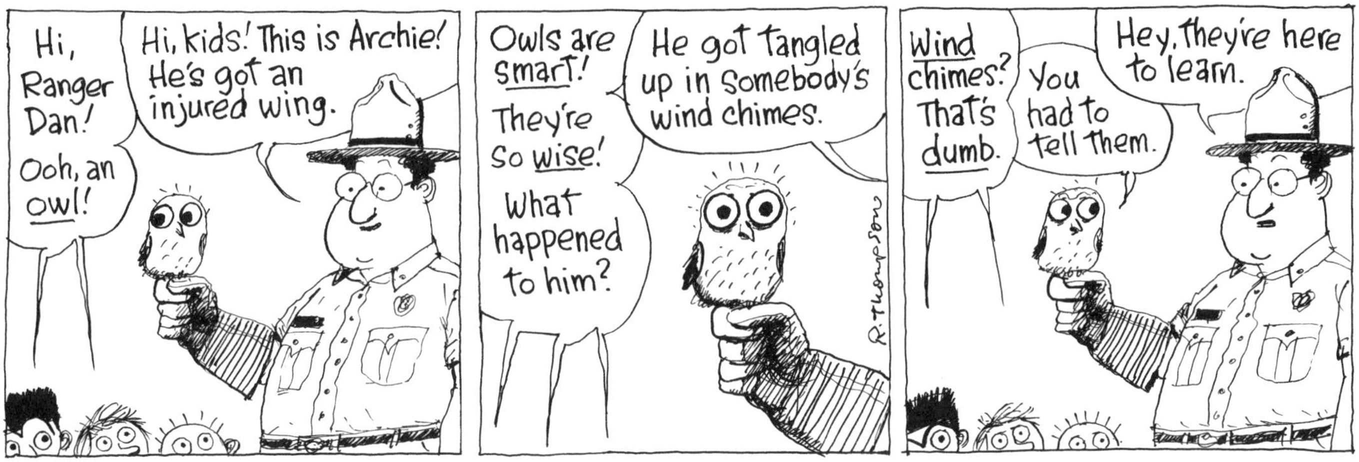
Hi, Ranger Dan!
Ooh, an owl!
Hi, kids! This is Archie! He's got an injured wing.
Owls are smart!
They're so wise!
What happened to him?
He got tangled up in somebody's wind chimes.
Wind chimes? That's dumb.
You had to tell them.
Hey, they're here to learn.

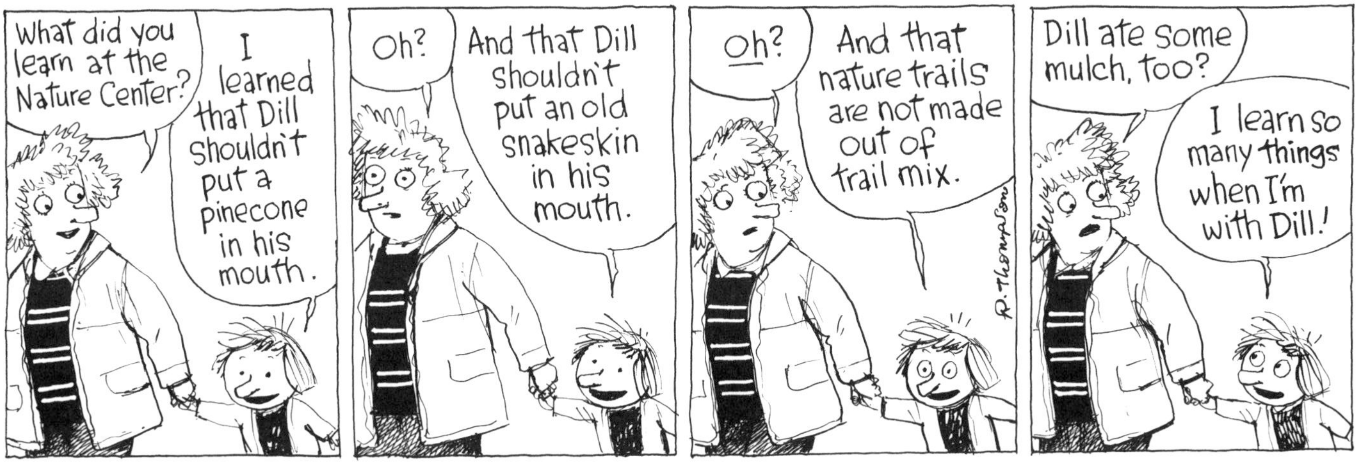
What did you learn at the Nature Center?
I learned that Dill shouldn't put a pinecone in his mouth.
Oh?
And that Dill shouldn't put an old snakeskin in his mouth.
Oh?
And that nature trails are not made out of trail mix.
Dill ate some mulch, too?
I learn so many things when I'm with Dill!

HEY LOOK! THE MOON IS OUT!

IT'S DAYTIME! THE MOON SHOULDN'T BE OUT!

Something is wrong! The moon snuck into the sky during the day!

No, wait. See, it's because the moo-

What if it's really nighttime?

You mean...?

Yes! It's nighttime and the sun snuck into the sky!

No!

No wonder I'm tired and cranky! I'm going inside!

Me too!

But, no, see, the moon goes around the earth... and... um...

I hate being the voice of reason.

Huh?

Alice? Why are you taking a nap?

R. Thompson